T0305140

The Economics of Keynes

NEW DIRECTIONS IN MODERN ECONOMICS
Series Editor: Malcolm C. Sawyer,
Professor of Economics, University of Leeds, UK

New Directions in Modern Economics presents a challenge to orthodox economic thinking. It focuses on new ideas emanating from radical traditions including post-Keynesian, Kaleckian, neo-Ricardian and Marxian. The books in the series do not adhere rigidly to any single school of thought but attempt to present a positive alternative to the conventional wisdom.

A list of published titles in this series is printed at the end of this volume.

The Economics of Keynes

A New Guide to *The General Theory*

Mark Hayes

Senior Research Fellow,
Homerton College, University of Cambridge, UK
Visiting Fellow,
Durham Business School, University of Durham, UK
Newcastle Business School, Northumbria University, UK

NEW DIRECTIONS IN MODERN ECONOMICS

Edward Elgar
Cheltenham, UK • Northampton, MA, USA

Published by
Edward Elgar Publishing Limited
Glensanda House
Montpellier Parade
Cheltenham
Glos GL50 1UA
UK

Edward Elgar Publishing, Inc.
William Pratt House
9 Dewey Court
Northampton
Massachusetts 01060
USA

A catalogue record for this book
is available from the British Library

Library of Congress Control Number: 2006934132

ISBN-13: 978 1 84720 082 2 (cased)
ISBN-10: 1 84720 082 6 (cased)

Printed and bound in Great Britain by MPG Books Ltd, Bodmin, Cornwall

Contents

Contents of Appendices   vii
Foreword   ix
Preface   xi

FIVE PROPOSITIONS OF *THE GENERAL THEORY*   1

PROLOGUE   2

    P.1   Equilibrium   3
    P.2   Competition   9
    P.3   Money   14
    P.4   Expectation   16
    P.5   Liquidity   20
    APPENDIX TO THE PROLOGUE   24

1.   TWO THEORIES OF EMPLOYMENT   46

    1.1   General Theory or Special Case?   48
    1.2   The Classical Theory of Employment   50
    1.3   The Point Of Effective Demand as the Position of System
          Equilibrium   54
    1.4   Summary   59
    APPENDIX TO CHAPTER 1   62

2.   DEFINITIONS AND IDEAS   69

    2.1   Defining Price and Quantity   70
    2.2   Expectation as Determining Output and Employment   73
    2.3   The Investment-Saving Identity   78
    2.4   Summary   83
    APPENDIX TO CHAPTER 2   86

3.   THE PROPENSITY TO CONSUME   119

     3.1   Average and Marginal   120
     3.2   Consumption and Employment   124
     3.3   Income, Effective Demand and the Multiplier   125
     3.4   Summary   127
     APPENDIX TO CHAPTER 3   129

4.   THE INDUCEMENT TO INVEST   138

     4.1   A Hierarchy Of Liquidity   139
     4.2   Stocks and Flows   144
     4.3   The State of Long-Term Expectation   147
     4.4   The Nature of Liquidity   151
     4.5   Summary   154
     APPENDIX TO CHAPTER 4   156

5.   EMPLOYMENT, MONEY AND THE PRICE-LEVEL   174

     5.1   The Equilibrium Sub-System of *The General Theory*   175
     5.2   The Influence of Money-Wages on Employment   177
     5.3   The Influence of Employment on Money-Wages and Prices   179
     5.4   Money and the Price-Level   181
     APPENDIX TO CHAPTER 5   184

6.   POLICY IMPLICATIONS   197

     6.1   Notes on the Trade Cycle   198
     6.2   Other Remedies for Chronic Under-Employment   200
     6.3   Political Implications   203
     6.4   Conclusion   205

EPILOGUE   206

     E.1   Stagflation   208
     E.2   Full Employment   213
     E.3   Growth and Innovation   219
     E.4   Conclusion   221
     APPENDIX TO THE EPILOGUE   223

References   238
Index   247

Contents of Appendices

PROLOGUE

AP.1.1	Keynes and Marshall	24
AP.2.1	Perfect competition	25
AP.2.2	Keynes's agents	28
AP.2.3	Capital-goods and capital markets	30
AP.2.4	The independence of supply and demand	33
AP.2.5	The degree of competition	34
AP.3.1	Unit of account, store of value and means of payment	36
AP.3.2	Endogenous money	37
AP.4.1	Expectation and expectations	39
AP.4.2	Expectation and probability	39
AP.5.1	Fundamental uncertainty	43

1. TWO THEORIES OF EMPLOYMENT

A1.2.1	Involuntary unemployment	62
A1.3.1	The relative prices of the principle of effective demand	63
A1.3.2	Keynes and Walras	67

2. DEFINITIONS AND IDEAS

A2.1.1	Homogeneous labour	86
A2.1.2	Keynes and Sraffa	86
A2.1.3	More on user cost	88
A2.1.4	The linear Z function	91
A2.2.1	Long-period employment	94
A2.2.2	Production time and convergence to long-period equilibrium	96
A2.2.3	Expectations and realised results	101
A2.3.1	The Keynesian cross	106
A2.3.2	Keynes's income vs. Gross National Product	108
A2.3.3	Saving and finance	108
A2.3.4	Equilibrium income vs. income as an equilibrium value	113

3.   THE PROPENSITY TO CONSUME

A3.1.1   *Patinkin and the proportional multiplier*   *129*
A3.2.1   *Factor income and effective demand*   *130*
A3.3.1   *The multiplier as a condition of market-period equilibrium*   *132*
A3.3.2   *Hansen's versions of the multiplier*   *135*

4.   THE INDUCEMENT TO INVEST

A4.2.1   *The marginal efficiency of capital and user cost*   *156*
A4.3.1   *Fundamental value and conventional value*   *159*
A4.4.1   *Liquidity and the 'liquidity' of organised investment markets* *164*
A4.4.2   *The meaning of the stability of value*   *166*
A4.4.3   *Actuarial vs. liquidity risk*   *169*

5.   EMPLOYMENT, MONEY AND THE PRICE-LEVEL

A5.1.1   *Hicks's IS-LM diagram*   *184*
A5.1.2   *The AD/AS diagram*   *185*
A5.2.1   *The money-wage in an open economy*   *187*
A5.3.1   *Measuring changes in the price-level*   *188*
A5.3.2   *The long period, the short term and the period of production*   *190*
A5.3.3   *'True' inflation at full employment*   *191*
A5.3.4   *The employment function*   *192*
A5.4.1   *A mathematical slip*   *195*

EPILOGUE

AE.1.1   *Real wages and money-wages*   *223*
AE.2.1   *Liquidity risk and corporate finance*   *224*
AE.2.2   *The reform of company law*   *230*
AE.3.1   *Involuntary unemployment and global poverty*   *233*
AE.4.1   *Keynes and Pigou*   *236*

Foreword

It is both a privilege and a pleasure to write a Foreword to Mark Hayes's splendid monograph on the approach and method of *The General Theory* and, especially, on what they both owe to Keynes's upbringing as a Marshallian. There are (at least) two ways of doing serious works of interpretation. The first is to develop on the basis of past training and reading the thesis to be exposited. The 'scholarship' can then be put in afterwards, both as good manners and also, perhaps, to give an appearance of having built on what has gone before. The second is to concentrate on primary sources – in Hayes's case his deep understanding of the writings of Marshall and Keynes – in order to explain the development of original ideas in landmark texts, here, of course, *The General Theory*.

Hayes's monograph is almost entirely an example of the second approach and this is one of its strengths. He understands thoroughly Marshall's value theory and monetary theory. He resurrects the almost forgotten market period in Marshall's analysis of value and price setting and shows the absolutely central, vital role it plays in the development of Keynes's analysis in *The General Theory*. That is not to say that the short period and Keynes's own concept of the long period are not important. They are. But the decision-makers in Keynes's narrative must base their short-period expectations on the information contained in market periods and thereby set in motion processes that converge to a position of long-period equilibrium only if a given state of expectation persists.

Hayes also resurrects the significance of the distinction between the two concepts of aggregate demand in *The General Theory* for a proper understanding of Keynes's procedures and results. This is more than welcome, for the first concept – what business people expect about prices and sales before making production, employment, and accumulation decisions – has virtually disappeared from text-book expositions of Keynesian economics. Yet without it, it is not possible logically to show how the second concept – the planned expenditures on investment and consumption goods *as seen by the onlooking macroeconomist* – plays its part in the determination of the point of effective demand.

Hayes's subsequent explanations of the analysis and contributions of *The General Theory* are built on these basic, central, core foundations. Not only does this allow us to understand more deeply *The General Theory* itself, it also allows us to see why Keynes's contributions and approach are still so relevant today for our understanding of the workings of modern economies and our suggestions for realistic, humane and practical policies.

Hayes's volume is a work of exemplary scholarship, the outcome of prolonged and deep thought. Alas, all the incentives in modern academia pull against work such as this being done. It is to the author's great credit that he has resisted them in order to give us this volume of lasting significance.

G.C. Harcourt
Jesus College
Cambridge

Preface

This book is an essay in the explanation of *The General Theory of Employment, Interest and Money* (Keynes, *C.W.* VII, hereafter *The General Theory*, or *G.T.* in chapter and page references). It is not a concordance (such as Glahe's very useful book, 1991) nor a commentary in the biblical sense, nor a study in the history of economic thought, nor a full survey of the derivative literature. It is in the nature of a travel guide, which describes and explains the significance of the main features of a town or country, rather than a street map or architectural history. A travel guide is no substitute for a visit, but it can make the visit more fruitful. In this case, the features described are the six Books of *The General Theory* to which the central chapters of this book correspond. The Prologue addresses the tacit assumptions or axioms on which *The General Theory* is based, which travellers must appreciate if they are not to lose their way. The Epilogue considers the progress and direction of the continuing research programme and policy agenda based on *The General Theory,* and the extent to which they require modification of Keynes's axioms.

The book is addressed mainly to the advanced student of orthodox ('Classical') economics, for whom these days *The General Theory* is almost certainly foreign territory. Under the 'Classical' rubric defined by Keynes (*G.T.* 3) I must include, not only the modern 'neo-classical' school, but also, somewhat ironically, the 'New Keynesian'. This book is also addressed to the student sympathetic to 'Post Keynesian' ideas, since it highlights the differences between Keynes and the Post Keynesians, and raises questions about the direction and flavour of future research. I have no doubt that this book will draw some fire, although I trust also some support, from both schools.

The thesis of this book is that *The General Theory* is a difficult, but not an incoherent or tendentious text. A problem for the reader of Keynes's book is the breadth and depth of its scope, which makes the text very dense, despite its length of some 400 pages, with some major theoretical innovations described in only a few words. Yet the main difficulty is in the 'mind-set' of the reader, a point of which Keynes himself was acutely aware, and reflects the fact that the reader of *The General Theory* is usually a professional economist, trained (or being trained) in particular techniques of analysis, and to look at the economy from a perspective derived ultimately from the Ricardian theory of rent. The methodological hypothesis of this book is that Keynes meant exactly what he wrote, and that except in a very few cases of manifest drafting error, affecting one or two individual words or symbols, he made no complete statement that he did not consider consistent with the work as a whole. The implication of this hypothesis is that many of the puzzles expressed in the derivative literature are, in principle, open to resolution without damaging the integrity of the work as a whole. This book is by no means the first attempt along these lines, and is unlikely to be the last, if only because it is addressed to readers within the particular context and common understanding of economics in the first decade of the 21st century: a context and understanding which will surely change.

Such an enterprise must be undertaken with circumspection by the author, and viewed with at least some scepticism by the reader. Is there really anything new or fruitful to be said about a work which has been subject to intense scrutiny for 70 years, and 'settled' on more than one occasion? I draw confidence from the point just made, that our understanding of *The General Theory* must alter as our understanding of the nature of economics as a whole changes. There is scope for a fresh look at a major work like *The General Theory* every decade or so. This interpretation could not have been reached other than by reflection on the work of a long line of distinguished authors, both sympathetic and hostile to *The General Theory*. The philosophy of science suggests that a major set of truly original ideas, such as Keynes's, cannot be received by the academic community and incorporated into the body of established knowledge without running the gauntlet of a barrage of constructive criticism. The existence of unresolved puzzles and apparent paradox is the major spur to scientific progress. The most hostile critics of Keynes have sometimes done him good service in enabling their readers, including those sympathetic to Keynes, to isolate the points of departure.

The title and structure of this book invite comparison with Alvin Hansen's *Guide to Keynes* (1953) and the title, with Axel Leijonhufvud's *Keynesian Economics and the Economics of Keynes* (1968), although there the resemblance ends. The latter has proved, I think, a false trail for reasons that will emerge in this book. For a long time, Hansen's book was considered a definitive text of the Old Keynesian neo-classical synthesis. By the time Paul Davidson and Victoria Chick, among others, had emerged to challenge the Hicks-Hansen interpretation, they had followed Joan Robinson, Nicholas Kaldor and Piero Sraffa in putting some distance between their own economics and those of both Keynes and the 'Keynesians', preferring to be known as Post Keynesians. So there are several guides to Post Keynesian economics, including Eichner (1979), Sawyer (1988), Holt and Pressman (2001), and King's historical survey (2002). Both Davidson (1972) and Chick (1983) went considerably beyond *The General Theory* in seeking to apply Keynes's insights to contemporary problems, including for example the emphasis on corporate securities in Davidson and on inflation in Chick, and so too does the collaborative *Second Edition* (Harcourt and Riach, 1997). So this book is, in one sense, a less ambitious enterprise than any of these, with its terms of reference limited to those of *The General Theory* itself. However, if the interpretation put forward here is correct, it has important implications for the direction of the research programme initiated by Keynes.

The core propositions of this book are set out in highly compressed form on page 1, and the reader is warned that, taken as a whole, they represent a significant departure from previous interpretations of *The General Theory*. I urge the reader to consider what I have written, not what you may think I have written at first glance! For the reader already familiar with *The General Theory,* the novel features of this interpretation include: the emphasis on its Marshallian heritage and on the importance of equilibrium and competition; Keynes's treatment of time and equilibrium periods, and the significance of Keynes's long period; the importance of user cost; the distinction between income, aggregate and effective demand; the nature of the multiplier; the understanding of the state of expectation, both short-term and long-term; and the meaning of liquidity.

Colleagues have made it clear to me that I cannot emphasise enough the centrality of Keynes's concept of income as the money-value of output, not expenditure, as well as my view that the point of effective demand does not correspond to the fulfilment of short-term expectations but is nevertheless a position of short-period competitive equilibrium. On this point I am departing from a consensus about Keynes's use of expectations that stretches back to the 1930s. The methodological root of my difference from Hicks (1939), Kregel (1976) and Chick (1983, 1998) appears to be my claim that Keynes's 'day' is a unit of calendar time that is linked also to both Marshall's short and market equilibrium periods. Put another way, my thesis largely hangs upon the definition of the technical short period that I attribute to Keynes, as involving a single day rather than Marshall's several months or a year, and with more emphasis, following Joan Robinson, on the adjective 'short-period' than on the substantive 'short period' (Harcourt, 1995). The (under-)employment equilibrium of *The General Theory* is static (in the technical sense, not implying a lack of change over time) and instantaneous (within the quantum limit given by the day), yet always based on forward-looking expectation and capable of shifting discontinuously from day to day; I hold that Keynes treats short-period equilibrium as established in a single very short interval of calendar time, for practical purposes at a point in time, rather than through a process over time. By contrast, Keynes's unique and hitherto problematic definition of long-period equilibrium is indeed reached, in theory, by a dynamic process of convergence over time. Furthermore, my interpretation of liquidity as independence of value from changes in the state of long-term expectation goes well beyond the definition in terms of marketability or convertibility set out by Davidson (1972, 2002), and is associated with a quite different meaning of the degree of competition; although the importance of the unknown future is thereby enhanced, and Keynes's hierarchy of liquidity becomes comprehensible.

Examples of consequential theoretical claims that may come as a surprise are that, in *The General Theory*, employment is treated as in continuous equilibrium; that there is no income-expenditure identity or 'sequence' multiplier; and that there is no assumption of a closed economy. The principal policy implications of *The General Theory* itself, namely the ineffectiveness of wage-cuts and monetary policy for the attainment of full employment, emerge directly from its theoretical analysis: in similar fashion, my tentative conclusions in the Epilogue, about the remedy for stagflation and the reform of corporate ownership, follow directly from the identification of user cost as a link between money and the price-level, and from the extension of liquidity-preference to corporate finance.

In these pages, I make no more use of advanced mathematical proofs than did Keynes, but I have found the use of symbols, and even the odd diagram, can help in understanding the complex verbal arguments of *The General Theory*. I have heeded Marshall's and Keynes's warnings against inappropriate mathematical abstraction, and taken care to distinguish what can, and what cannot, be expressed about economics in the form of mathematical theorems and simplified functional graphs. Nevertheless, verbal expression, too, has its limitations, and indeed the case of *The General Theory* is a classic example of the difficulty of conveying meaning through even the most carefully chosen words. In particular, the mathematical distinction between vector and scalar quantities sheds a great deal of light on Keynes's argument, and captures a great deal of its subtlety.

To understand both this book and *The General Theory* itself does require a firm grounding in traditional Marshallian value theory, which fortunately, for this purpose, remains the core of undergraduate text-books on microeconomics. The macroeconomic theory of current text-books is mainly a new form of the Classical theory that Keynes sought to refute, and a hasty comparison with this book will certainly lead to confusion. In an effort to clarify the main differences, I have used Mankiw's popular *Macroeconomics* (2003) as a benchmark, and referred in the Notes to the major points of departure and indeed contradiction. It is well worth reading Marshall's *Principles*, especially Book V, before turning to *The General Theory*. An understanding of the principles of Walrasian general equilibrium theory is also assumed.

The book is written at three levels. The main text of each chapter presents the main argument, without detailed explanation or any more use of mathematics than can be found in *The General Theory* itself. The main text is self-contained and can be read straight through on a first reading to give the reader an overall perspective. Secondly, all but one of the chapters have an explanatory appendix, which together represent nearly half the book. These explore in greater detail some major points made in the main text and cross-reference between the chapters as appropriate. References to sections in the appendices are written in the form A5.3.4, where this means the fourth note on Section 3 of Chapter 5 (the Prologue and Epilogue are referred to by letters, in order to allow the chapter numbers to correspond to the Books of *The General Theory* itself). Separate contents pages list the sections of the appendices with their page numbers. Thirdly, the Notes to each chapter and appendix make some detailed technical points and references to the literature. I have tried not to labour the obvious, and have written only what appears to me to contribute something new, or if familiar, to be necessary as a step in the exposition. Half this book (and nearly all the Notes) are devoted to *G.T.* Books I and II (only 20 per cent of Keynes's), since most of the puzzles have arisen from Keynes's elusive conceptual framework, mainly set out fairly tersely in those Books, which this book aims to clarify.

What this book does not offer is a tour of the vast literature derived from *The General Theory*, partly because the book would have to be at least twice its present length, but mainly because any attempt by me to compare and contrast my own interpretation with those of others will inevitably lead to unnecessary controversy: it is better left to other, independent, judges. I have thought it more important to set out my case as clearly as I can, unencumbered by skirmishes on the flanks or a detailed genealogy. In my bibliography, I have referred only either to seminal or other strictly relevant pieces, or to the most recent work of which I am aware, as an up-to-date entry point to a particular topic: I do not pretend to have referred to all major work on the topics addressed by Keynes. For similar reasons, I have also decided against offering a synopsis of *The General Theory*, even though this would no doubt be welcomed by many students, in order not to 'block the view'.

Nearly all will have a pre-conceived idea of what it says, which this book almost certainly challenges, and I do not wish to compound confusion by simplification, leading to arguments over whether a synopsis adequately reflects the work itself. A travel guide is not usually terribly helpful unless you are on the spot, and there is no substitute for reading Keynes's book itself, ideally in parallel with this one.

The origins of this book date back to the mid 1970s, when I witnessed at first hand, as a bemused undergraduate, the battle for the soul of Cambridge economics between Joan Robinson (seconded by John Eatwell) and Frank Hahn. The reader will note that I learned much from both sides. Among those who influenced me most closely was Brian Reddaway, then the holder of Marshall's chair, who taught me the importance of facing awkward facts, rather than trying to explain them away. I had no idea at the time how greatly this reflected the influence of Keynes himself on Reddaway. I started to read *The General Theory* again in 1988, and when I returned to academic study in 2000, rather like Rip van Winkle, I found the landscape of economics almost unrecognisable. Over the last six years, and mainly in the last two, I have slowly put together this book, which turns out to shed light, not only on *The General Theory*, but on what has happened to economics.

I am deeply grateful to Victoria Chick, Geoff Harcourt, and Malcolm Sawyer for their generosity in giving time to make detailed comments on the manuscript, which greatly helped me to improve and clarify my presentation, for which I remain solely responsible, including any errors and omissions. I am also grateful to the publishers of the *Journal of Post Keynesian Economics* and the *Review of Political Economy* for permission to reproduce sections from published articles (Hayes, 2006b, 2007) and to Palgrave Macmillan on behalf of the Royal Economic Society for permission to quote extensively from *The General Theory*.

Mark Hayes
21 September 2006

Five Propositions of *The General Theory*

EQUILIBRIUM

Employment is in continuous 'daily' equilibrium corresponding to the point of effective demand, although equilibrium does not mean that all available labour and capital-goods are employed and factor markets clear, nor that expectations are fulfilled.

COMPETITION

Competition in supply and demand is the motive force which holds the system in equilibrium. Agents take prices in each market to be independent of their own actions. The degree of competition is not the same as the degree of monopoly.

MONEY

Equilibrium reflects decisions to incur money-expense by employers, investors and consumers, and not the optimal allocation of factors of production. Money is an integral part of the theory of value and employment, and not a veil. The factor cost-unit is not an equilibrium value.

EXPECTATION

Decisions to produce, consume and invest are based on expectation. Effective demand corresponds to the state of expectation at any time. The long and short term are not the same as the long and short equilibrium periods. The future is unknown, and long-term expectations are fundamentally uncertain.

LIQUIDITY

Liquidity means more than convertibility and includes invariance of value to changes in the state of expectation. Assets possess this property in different degrees, so that money is more liquid than bonds, and both are more liquid than capital-goods.

Prologue

Much of the discussion of *The General Theory* has been at cross-purposes. The purpose of this preliminary chapter is to set out a view of the tacit assumptions, definitions and axioms of *The General Theory*, summarised in the preceding Five Propositions. The aim is to help the reader to be clear about what is (and what is not) being proposed, both in this book and by Keynes, so as to reduce the risk of sterile controversy. The subject of this Prologue is, accordingly, the things on which Keynes was either silent or cryptic, I think because of an implicit framework, which he inherited from Alfred Marshall and believed would be shared by his readers, perhaps wrongly as it turned out. The central chapters will then deal with his explicit statements within the context of the understanding developed in this Prologue.

An immediate illustration of the problem of mutual incomprehension is in the names given to different schools of thought. This text follows Keynes in using the term 'Classical' to denote what is now usually called the neo-classical orthodoxy, which may be described as the theory of value given the full employment of scarce resources, and which it was Keynes's primary object to challenge. Keynes by contrast used the term 'neo-classical' in a more limited sense, to denote specifically the strand of Classical thought which ascribed unemployment to monetary disequilibrium (*G.T.* 177, 183). Keynes's use of the term 'Classical' does not, from the perspective of modern heterodox economics, do justice to the strands of thought in Adam Smith and Ricardo that gave priority over supply and demand to the distribution of income in the formation of prices, let alone to the incorporation by Karl Marx and others into economic theory of social forces other than competition. From this point of view, Keynes was very neo-classical in the modern sense, and his analysis differs substantially from much Post Keynesian thought. At the other end of the spectrum, 'New Keynesian' theory is here treated as an analysis, within the Classical tradition, of disequilibrium defined in relation to a long-period equilibrium in which all scarce resources are allocated optimally and therefore fully employed. 'Old Keynesian' here means the income-expenditure interpretation of *The General Theory* known as the 'neo-classical synthesis' which dominated the discipline from the late 1940s until the mid 1970s, rather than pertaining to Keynes. So, even this simple attempt to classify the various schools of thought illustrates immediately the scope for confusion and the need for clarity and precision in the use of terms and concepts.

The following sections move through five key concepts of economic theory (equilibrium, competition, money, expectation and liquidity) and articulate the particular forms in which they are to some extent expressed, but for the most part implicit, in *The General Theory*. Each concept is open to a wide range of differing interpretations, so that any given statement by Keynes can make either perfect sense or nonsense, depending on the conceptual apparatus with which it is received. In accordance with the methodological hypothesis of this book, the interpretations put forward here are those which reduce the number of inexplicable statements in *The General Theory* to zero, or at least, to a very small handful.[1]

P.1 EQUILIBRIUM

There are several definitions of equilibrium in economics, including:[2]

1. a state of balance between countervailing forces or processes, notably supply and demand (usually interpreted as market clearing)
2. a state in which no party has both reason and power to change their position (a state of rest)
3. a state in which all parties make their preferred choices (implying that factor markets clear)
4. a state in which expectations are fulfilled.

It is possible for a state to meet all four criteria of equilibrium, but confusion arises when two states, meeting different criteria, are both referred to as states of equilibrium. This confusion is compounded when time and disequilibrium, being a departure from one or other criterion of equilibrium, are added to the mix.

Classical economists since Adam Smith have considered the concept of equilibrium between supply and demand central to economic theory; Keynes was no exception, and in this respect he differs from many of his Post Keynesian and other heterodox followers. For Walras, all four criteria are congruent; for Marshall, only the first three; and for Keynes, only the first two. Equilibrium theorists since Keynes have largely dropped the first criterion, to the detriment, I suggest, of the correspondence between theory and observation, and concentrated on one or more of the others: Old Keynesian and Post Keynesian economics on the fourth, modern Walrasian general equilibrium theory on the third, and game theory on the second. The core of *The General Theory* must be understood as an equilibrium theory in the 'mechanical' sense of the first two criteria and in the tradition of Marshall, although Keynes's detailed use of equilibrium analysis is highly original, quite unique and does not include the clearing of factor markets.

▶ **AP.1.1**

In the natural sciences, a state of equilibrium corresponds to our first criterion and means that the forces at work in a given situation offset each other, so as to induce no change in the observable state of their object. Simple examples include the archetypal balance in physics, osmosis in biology, and carbonated water under pressure in chemistry. In mechanics, equilibrium is furthermore a property of a body at rest (our second criterion), while dynamic analysis relates to a body in motion rather than in equilibrium, so that time as well as space is part of the equation. A state or position of equilibrium may be stable (egg standing on big end), unstable (egg standing on little end) or neutral (round ball on smooth table). Dynamic equilibrium, common in chemistry and biology, represents a steady state, where two or more dynamic processes offset each other (e.g. reversible chemical reactions, birth and death rates), and may refer to a steady rate of change, as well as to a static level.

Disequilibrium means a departure from equilibrium and is therefore always temporary, if that equilibrium is stable or the disequilibrium leads to a different equilibrium. Disequilibrium can be permanent only in the sense of periodic oscillation about a state of equilibrium, otherwise the new state is simply a trajectory produced by the loss of balance between the forces, and reference to equilibrium is no longer relevant. Disequilibrium always involves dynamics, a process through time. Disequilibrium is something quite different from a change in equilibrium, which results after a change in circumstances creates a new position of equilibrium. If someone grasps a stationary pendulum half-way along the string and pulls it to one side, the pendulum will soon find a new position of equilibrium. If the pendulum is then released, it enters a state of disequilibrium, until its oscillations die down over a period of time and it takes up the position of equilibrium normal for a pendulum free of interference.

Comparative statics is the comparison of different positions of static equilibrium, and comparative dynamics can be defined accordingly, in relation to different steady states. The path of an object towards equilibrium, either from a position of disequilibrium or from a previous position of equilibrium, both involve dynamic considerations. Such a convergence path or 'traverse' reflects a state of disequilibrium and may itself represent, although not necessarily, a series of positions of equilibrium of a different order at each point of time.

There are four aspects of equilibrium which must be taken into account in translating the concept from physics to economics: (1) the motive force moving variables towards, or keeping them in, an equilibrium position; (2) the observation of equilibrium positions; (3) the period over which equilibrium is established; and (4) the number and type of variables under consideration.

The motive force behind the economic equilibrium is competition, which is addressed in its own right in the next section. With regard to the second aspect, in mechanics, equilibrium is something which can be observed. However, in economics the relationship between equilibrium and disequilibrium has always been uneasy, since the earliest discussions of the trade cycle. The question is whether the observable measures of economic activity such as prices and quantities represent equilibrium or disequilibrium values. Keynes and Lucas (1981), I suggest, implicitly agree in insisting that equilibrium must in principle be observable and conversely that observable values must in practice be treated as equilibrium values, whether static or dynamic, if equilibrium theory is to be fruitful (although they would disagree on the meaning of equilibrium). If observable values are only ever disequilibrium values, equilibrium becomes something of a Platonic Idea with connotations of perfection and unattainability. The Idea of Equilibrium necessarily remains dominant even in the analysis of disequilibrium, since it is the benchmark against which disequilibrium is defined, and towards which the system is assumed to tend at any given instant.[3] If the equilibrium position is never in fact attained, or if ever attained, is not observable, the scientific value of equilibrium theory and its policy prescriptions is doubtful.[4]

The third aspect of equilibrium is the period of time over which any disequilibrium process converges to the equilibrium position. Again since Adam Smith, the distinction has been made between what Marshall called the market, short and long 'periods'. These periods correspond to what is taken as given or exogenous in the analysis of a particular problem, and have a major bearing on the relationship between equilibrium and disequilibrium. The periods are analytical devices for taming the many variables of a complex system, releasing one wandering beast at a time from Marshall's 'pound of *cæteris paribus*'. Market-period prices, which are the only prices observable at any time, are treated by Marshall and Keynes as equilibrium prices; both abstract entirely from market-period disequilibrium. A position of temporary equilibrium (where the supply of finished goods is given, during the market period) may be one of short-period disequilibrium. A position of short-period equilibrium (where the employment of labour and existing capital-goods by each firm can be adjusted so as to maximise expected profits, but the aggregate stock of producible capital-goods is given) may be one of long-period disequilibrium. The position of long-period equilibrium (in which the aggregate stock of producible capital-goods has been adjusted to its optimal position by the production of new capital-goods or the consumption of existing capital-goods) may itself move over the secular period, as the availability of non-producible factor services (labour and land) changes with population growth and new settlements. These different uses of equilibrium and disequilibrium, to describe the same current state of affairs from the perspective of different periods of reference, are serious traps for the novice or the unwary.

There are major difficulties with Marshall's treatment of time and his theoretical distinction between periods, which Keynes refers to in his biography of Marshall (*C.W.* X) as unfinished business and takes pains to address in *The General Theory*. The principal difficulty resolved by Keynes is how the equilibrium periods should relate to real or calendar time. In *The General Theory*, both the market and short periods correspond to the same period of calendar time, the 'day'. Whereas Marshall distinguishes between them in terms of the length of time ('several months or a year') over which production and employment can adjust so that market prices become equal to normal short-period supply prices, for Keynes the difference between the market and the short periods is that between realised and expected prices; between income and effective demand.

The production and employment decision involves two separate units of calendar time, which Keynes defines as the *day* and the *period of production*, which is a number of *days*. The day is Keynes's quantum unit of time, 'the shortest interval after which the firm is free to revise its decision as to how much employment to offer. It is, so to speak, the minimum effective unit of economic time' (*G.T.* 47, n1); the primary concern of *The General Theory* is the employment decisions of firms. This definition of a day is also the definition of the technical short period, in which entrepreneurs adjust the aggregate employment of labour associated with a given aggregate capital equipment to maximise their expected profits. The correspondence of the day with the market period again follows from the definition of the day, since it is the maximum interval for which the supply of finished output is limited to the stock on hand or producible on demand. Keynes's day need not correspond to a terrestrial day, but it does no harm to think of it as such, since the hours of over-time working can be, and often are, varied at such short notice. The *period of production* is the number of *days* 'notice of changes in the demand for [a product that] have to be given if it is to offer its maximum elasticity of employment' (*G.T.* 287). This definition is the macroeconomic counterpart of the period between starting and finishing an individual production process (*G.T.* 46), or *production period.*[5]

Keynes defines the long period in a unique and strictly *short-term* technical sense, to define the equilibrium on which the employment of labour and capital-goods will in theory converge if a new state of expectation persists for the full length of the period of production, allowing in particular for the production or depletion of raw materials and work-in-progress in line with the new pattern of production. This is very different from Marshall's concept of the long period ('of several years'), during which capital-goods are accumulated to the point where no new capital-good (and not only the marginal investment on a given day) yields more than the rate of interest, in a stationary state (or at least in a steady state of growth in line with secular growth in population and territory).

It is perhaps helpful to follow Joan Robinson in thinking of the terms market-period, short-period and long-period mainly as adjectives rather than substantives (Harcourt, 1995). That is not to deny the importance of their connection with intervals of calendar time. Each equilibrium period refers to a different type of adjustment: the market period mainly to market clearing, and income; the short period to the employment of labour and the other factors of production (including existing capital-goods), and effective demand; the long period to the employment of new capital goods, and the capital stock. Thus we need to distinguish the nature of the adjustment from the interval of time in which it takes place, as well as from the time horizon of the relevant expectations which prompt adjustment. The market-period adjustment of the demand for and supply of current output and existing stocks takes place 'instantaneously', on a single day, cleared by spot market prices – this is fairly standard. The short-period adjustment of employment also takes place on a single day but refers to short-term expectations of income that will arise at the end of the various production periods for different goods. The long-period adjustment of the capital stock takes place as a dynamic process over the period of production, and is contingent upon a given state of long-term expectation. Much of this book will be occupied with developing these central ideas in greater detail.

The fourth important aspect of equilibrium is the distinction between partial and general equilibrium. On the first criterion (of a state of balance) this should correspond simply to the analysis of the equilibrium position, on the one hand of one variable or part of a system in isolation, and on the other of a system of variables as a whole. However, the term 'general equilibrium' has come to mean equilibrium in the third sense (of a state in which all parties make their preferred choice), even when this does not correspond to equilibrium in the first two senses (including a state from which no party has both reason and power to change), as employed by Keynes. It is possible for each part of the system, and thus the system as a whole, to be in a state of competitive equilibrium even though not everyone is in their preferred position: entrepreneurs may have no reason to change their employment decisions and labour has no power to make them do so. Chapter 1 of this book will argue that the purpose of *The General Theory* is precisely to explain how this can be the case. Since it seems now impossible to reclaim the term 'general equilibrium' from its Classical usage without increasing confusion, this book will refer to *system* equilibrium as the still more general case, encompassing both Walrasian general equilibrium and Keynes's equilibrium of 'industry as a whole', with or without full employment.[6]

In the light of the above taxonomy, Keynes's *A Treatise on Money* (*C.W.* V–VI) can be seen to address the *disequilibrium* of employment as a deviation from a position of full employment equilibrium, on the 'neo-classical' hypothesis (in Keynes's sense, *G.T.* 177, 183) that it is in disequilibrium that the distinctive nature of a monetary economy becomes manifest. By contrast, *The General Theory* is a theory of employment *equilibrium* which takes seriously the historical nature of time. Classical authors (old and new) see the source of the disequilibrium of the *Treatise* in what would now be called 'real' or 'nominal' shocks to a long-period equilibrium based upon initial conditions including the availability and distribution of factor services, the technology of production, and the preferences of consumers and workers. In *The General Theory*, the level of employment at any time reflects a position of short-period system equilibrium conditional upon not only the standard Marshallian list of parameters but also upon, among other things, the state of psychological response of consumers and owners of wealth to an unknown future. The psychological factors, divided into the valuation of investment opportunities, the propensity to consume, and the preference for liquidity, are in Keynes's equilibrium analysis as exogenous as the Classical parameters. Furthermore, the psychological factors are independent *variables*, insofar as they are liable to sudden and substantial variation in the short term in a manner not shared, or fully determined, by the Classical parameters. Therefore Keynes's system is not 'closed' like the Classical system, in which the level of employment is fully determined by the parameters, some of which (in the Marshallian version) are taken as fixed in the short period and then released as the period of reference lengthens. Keynes's system is 'open' in the sense that the three key independent variables are not endogenous, that is, not part of the equilibrium theory. Nevertheless, *The General Theory* remains a theory of the level of employment as an equilibrium value.

Keynes is thoroughly empirical in his use of the concept of equilibrium. His primary interest is in the aggregate level of employment, which is observable and usually fairly stable, changing quite gradually from 'day' to 'day'. His theory offers an explanation of the aggregate level of observed employment, not of the more empirically elusive level of full employment, as a position of continuous system equilibrium. *The General Theory* is therefore an explanation of unemployment in terms of under-employment equilibrium, not unemployment disequilibrium, and this proposition will be expanded further in Chapter 1 of this book. For the most part it is a theory of short-period equilibrium, but there is also a detailed discussion (reviewed in Chapter 2) of the dynamic process of convergence, in which a series of positions of short-period equilibrium trace a path towards a position of long-period equilibrium in Keynes's sense. The short and long periods are not merely logical, but are embedded in calendar time, as are the processes by which equilibrium is established. *The General Theory* uses a statical, mechanical conception of equilibrium, in which a single determinate equilibrium level of aggregate employment at any time corresponds to a given state of the independent variables and initial conditions at the same point in time: this book will from this point onwards use the unqualified term 'equilibrium' in that specific mechanical sense unless stated otherwise. This does not prevent Keynes from considering variation in this state over time, in both the short and the long term, by the use of comparative statics, particularly in the application of his theory to questions of policy in *G.T.* Book VI. We shall find that Keynes's conception of equilibrium is considerably at odds with the received interpretation in terms of the fulfilment of expectations over time, and leads to quite different conclusions.

P.2 COMPETITION

In Classical theory and in Keynes, competition in supply and demand is the motive force which holds the economic system in equilibrium. The motto at the beginning of Marshall's *Principles* (1920) reads *'natura non facit saltum'* [nature makes no leaps] and is a direct reference to Darwin's *Origin of Species*.[7] There can be little doubt that Marshall saw competition as a force similar to natural selection and gravity, as certainly did Walras. Marshall preferred to refer to this social form of natural selection as a symptom of 'deliberateness', the pursuit of legitimate private interests or the considered exercise of liberty in the sense of Adam Smith. It is this purposefulness, or rational self-interest, combined with the assumptions of convex consumer preferences and production possibilities (diminishing marginal utility and returns, in Marshall's terms) that defines the point of equilibrium. The abstraction represented by the assumption of 'perfect' competition ▶ **AP.2.1** takes this purposefulness to its logical conclusion, by abstracting from the market power of individual firms and from the costs of making transactions and obtaining information about market prices. Decisions are reduced to a function of price alone. Firms themselves become Newtonian particles, each the centre of a web of contracts with consumers, investors and factors of production, including the abilities of the organising entrepreneur. ▶ **AP.2.2** Upon this foundation was developed the structure of the Classical economics addressed by *The General Theory*, and it is within this framework that Keynes's theory needs to be placed and understood.

If the mechanical conception of equilibrium (derived from the combination of our first two criteria) is to offer an explanation of prices at any time (a 'theory of value'), then prices must be taken to be in such equilibrium at all times. The market prices of Marshall's system are always equilibrium prices, even if they differ from the Normal prices corresponding to short- and long-period equilibrium. Disequilibrium is important to Marshall only in the sense of a departure from the Normal, and disequilibrium in the market period is given no theoretical significance. As Keynes notes, market-period equilibrium is a condition for output and money-income to possess a definite value (*G.T.* 64). This means that any tendency to diverge from market-period equilibrium is prevented by the countervailing forces of competition, and a change in the conditions of supply or demand leads not to disequilibrium, but to a change in the equilibrium price (market clearing). There are no queues or rationing: the accumulation or depletion of stocks is seen as an equilibrium decision to buy or sell, based on the spot and expected future market prices. The same elasticity conditions that permit an equilibrium position to exist also guarantee its stability and a smooth convergence from one position of equilibrium to another, as when Marshall's basin, containing a number of balls resting against one another, is tilted. As will be discussed in Chapter 3 of this book, Keynes's major contribution in this area is the identification of a marginal propensity to consume less than unity as a condition of the stability of the system as a whole.

Marshall thus approaches the question of the existence and stability of equilibrium from the premise that observed market prices are equilibrium prices (in the mechanical sense of our first two criteria) and that competitive responses to deviations in prices from Normal lead to changes in the supply and demand of quantities towards their Normal values, which represent equilibrium in our third sense, of full employment. By contrast, in the Walrasian auction, only the Normal is considered to be a position of equilibrium (in our third sense), and deviations from the Normal represent positions of simple disequilibrium. Nevertheless, for both Marshall and Walras, unemployment represents disequilibrium in one sense or other, which unimpeded competition must eventually eliminate. Keynes agrees with Marshall that market prices are equilibrium prices, but adds that the system is always in competitive equilibrium in our second sense (that no party has both reason *and* power to change their position, which allows for non-clearing factor markets), so that competition alone cannot eliminate involuntary unemployment.

Keynes's single cryptic reference to 'the degree of competition' (*G.T.* 245) has generally been interpreted as a reference to the degree of monopoly (*C.W.* VII, pp. 410–11). However, the degree of competition and the degree of monopoly are not the same thing. *The General Theory* assumes that the degree of monopoly is zero, so that individuals take prices as given and independent of their own actions: one element of the definition of perfect competition. The degree of competition is considered further below.

Together with its other elements, namely the absence of transaction costs and full information about market prices, perfect competition means that all finished goods, both consumption- and capital-goods, have perfect spot markets. Furthermore, this means there is no difference between new and old capital-goods in terms of convertibility into money, no difference in the degree of monopoly (or monopsony) facing sellers of second-hand goods. The assumption of perfect competition explains a number of important aspects of *The General Theory*, including its abstraction from financial and industrial structure and the distribution of income. ▶ **AP.2.3** Nowhere is Keynes's method more clear than in his treatment of capital-goods as if they were individually traded on the stock exchange. For the value of a capital-good thus to be independent of its situation in a particular firm or occupation requires the assumption that it can be transferred without cost or delay to whomever expects to make the best use of it. Thus all finished goods, of both types and of all vintages, have equilibrium market prices that can be realised at any time. The assumption of perfect competition has implications for the interpretation of the meaning of liquidity in *The General Theory*, which on this reading must mean more than convertibility.

So far we have noted that Marshall's and Keynes's system is always in market-period equilibrium, at the intersection of the supply and demand curves. These curves, strictly speaking, are graphical representations of partial derivatives at the point of equilibrium: for market price or quantity actually to change, the curves must shift. The observed prices in each market, being equilibrium prices, depend on each other and on the state of the system as a whole. What the supply and demand curves really show is the stability of the equilibrium, the signs of the relevant partial derivatives, and how the force of perfect competition corrects any infinitesimal divergence from the position of equilibrium. The divergence must be assumed infinitesimal in the sense of *ceteris paribus*, that any changes in price or quantity in a given market are too small to affect other markets or the system parameters. It is this which makes Marshall's partial equilibrium method determinate, legitimate and in fact superior to the Walrasian method in its treatment of time. Yet, without Keynes's modifications, this method can establish only the level of full employment, based on the labour available to firms, and not the actual level of employment. ▶ **AP.2.4**

Marshall's theory moves from the market period to the longer periods through shifts in the market-period supply and demand curves over time. The market-period supply curves in each industry shift, as firms change production in the short period of a few months or a year, and change the aggregate stock of capital-goods in the long period of several years, in response perhaps to an initial change in preferences or else to changes in technology, or in the factor endowment. These changes in supply may in turn provoke further changes in demand in individual markets as market prices change for given preferences, and these changes in turn may affect the supply of factor services. Meanwhile, the owners of producible capital-goods and specialised types of labour earn (positive or negative) quasi-rents, or wage differentials, if market prices and wages are struck above or below the Normal, and it is the competitive response to these quasi-rents which drives the changes in supply (this is also very much the method of *A Treatise on Money*). In fact, it is not necessary in Marshall's system that short-period or long-period equilibrium are ever reached, since the parameters of the system may change during the process of convergence, and expectations may well be disappointed (consider the pendulum hanging in the mill-race or being swung from side to side arbitrarily, Marshall, 1920, p. 288). The only equilibrium which unequivocally exists for Marshall, and can be observed in time and space, is the temporary market-period equilibrium at any time; Normal prices exist only in the minds of entrepreneurs. Nevertheless, Marshall assumes that, at least in theory, market prices will converge on equilibrium Normal prices, over periods of time which depend on the speed with which labour can become available for alternative occupations and entrepreneurs can enter or leave industries, and the time it takes to transfer, produce, wear out or scrap capital equipment. In the long period, competition between entrepreneurs brings marginal cost down to average cost, eliminating the excess of quasi-rents on existing capital-goods relative to those obtainable by new replacements, and competition between workers, in moving between different labour markets or acquiring scarce skills, eliminates temporary wage differentials.

Marshall's long period may be several years, because of the time needed to build new capital-goods (tangible and intangible) and for workers to change their occupations or skills, a period during which much change in parameters is possible and the target may move. Even with a given endowment, technology and preferences, long-period equilibrium may never be reached, if there are obstacles to the free movement of labour and capital-goods into or out of particular occupations and markets, such as 'closed shops' of either workers or entrepreneurs, or other social and institutional barriers to entry and exit. These obstacles may permanently prevent the erosion of market-period and short-period quasi-rents, and it is to these obstacles that the 'degree of competition' refers. ▶ **AP.2.5**

The microfoundations of *The General Theory* are laid squarely upon those of Marshall, and it was not in this respect that Keynes differentiated himself from the Classical school. He uses and develops Marshall's method to determine the level of aggregate employment at any time as a result of individual optimisation by price-taking agents, given the exogenous variables and parameters of the system as a whole. He achieves this by correcting the link between the equilibrium periods and units of calendar time, radically reducing the calendar length of the short and long periods, and by introducing the additional concepts needed to deal properly with time, including user cost and the three independent psychological variables. Perfect competition (meaning, of course, *flexible* prices) remains the motive force behind the equilibrium analysis of *The General Theory*, and it is important to remember, particularly in this respect, Keynes's claim in his preface (*G.T.* xxxi) that his book would be regarded as in essentially the Classical tradition. Nevertheless that tradition includes the approaches of both Marshall and Walras, who treat time and stability very differently: Keynes is firmly in the Marshallian camp.[8]

P.3 MONEY

If *The General Theory* is a theory of equilibrium under perfect competition, how and why does it differ from Classical theory in its treatment of money? In Classical theory, only relative prices matter in the allocation of resources and money is neutral in real terms (the 'Classical dichotomy'). Why does *The General Theory* not lead to the same conclusion, if it shares with Classical theory the concepts of equilibrium and competition?

The current orthodoxy is that Classical theory describes the long-run equilibrium, which would be reached immediately if prices were perfectly flexible and agents fully competitive, while Keynesian or 'business cycle' theory describes the short run, since prices are in practice sticky. The stickiness of prices reflects both nominal and real rigidities, the latter including obstacles to competition, slow adjustment of expectations, and in more recent theory, asymmetric information.[9]

We shall see in Chapter 1 of this book that Keynes's principle of effective demand also assumes competitive, flexible prices in goods and asset markets: only relative prices matter in the determination of employment; the problem (as Leijonhufvud pointed out in 1968) is that they are 'wrong', in the sense of our third criterion of equilibrium (preferred allocation). On the other hand, and this is the hardest thing for a Classical economist to swallow, factor prices are not market-clearing values: they are outside the equilibrium model, exogenous. The principle of effective demand can be (and is) worked out using wage-units (*G.T.* 41) as the unit of account: the employment of labour is determined completely independently of the price of labour. ▶ **AP.3.1** Keynes devotes most of *G.T.* Chapter 2 to refuting on entirely Classical grounds the idea that involuntary unemployment (of labour, although the argument applies equally to other factor services) is the result of a failure to allow money-wages (factor prices) to clear the market. Keynes's notion of system equilibrium does not include the clearing of factor markets; if it did, *The General Theory* would no longer be a theory of a monetary economy. The link between money and factor markets is explored further in Section 1.1 of Chapter 1 below.

The inconsistency is not in Keynes, but in Classical theory. The basic tenet of Classical theory is that money is neutral; yet how are markets to clear except through changes in money-prices? Relative prices (so-called 'real prices') are ratios of prices in more than one market, and there is no guarantee that a change in one price will leave prices in other markets unchanged (the stability problem explored initially by Hicks, 1939, and later by Arrow and Hahn, 1971). As Keynes points out (*G.T.* 12), the traditional solution is to introduce a *deus ex machina*, the quantity theory of money and prices. If the price-level is fixed by the quantity of money, changes in factor prices mean changes in their relative prices: yet the quantity theory assumes full (or fixed) employment. This is a circular argument that leaves no room for demand-deficient unemployment.

Keynes had no difficulty with the Classical quantity *equation* as a descriptive relation broadly applicable to the very long term (*G.T.* 306–9). The understanding of causation behind the quantity *theory* is an entirely different matter. His major concern was that the quantity theory of the general price-level, or the value of money, was 'on the other side of the moon' from the theory of value (or relative prices) as determined by supply and demand. In other words, Classical theory does not take supply and demand seriously enough. Far from neglecting money (as did Old Keynesian economics), *The General Theory* integrates it into the theory of value and employment. The relationship between the price-level and the quantity of money is found to be not one of bilateral uni-directional causation, but the resultant of a complex equilibrium system. ▶ **AP.3.2**

The perception of sticky factor prices (there is nothing in *The General Theory* to suggest sticky goods or asset prices) reflects their exogeneity from Keynes's equilibrium model. Exogenous wages are not rigid or sticky wages; on this point Keynes is quite explicit, both in *G.T.* Chapter 2 and the *whole* of *G.T.* Chapter 19. Yet, in a monetary economy, there has to be an anchor for the price-level if the price system is not to break down. Since the quantity theory assumes away the problem of involuntary unemployment, it cannot be invoked to explain the price-level. In a competitive economy, entrepreneurs set their prices in relation to factor cost, so that the price level and the 'cost-unit' (*G.T.* 302) move together. The cost-unit is Keynes's anchor, one of his independent variables, and while it is possible to make certain generalisations about the relationships between his independent variables and between them and employment (*G.T.* Book V is devoted to this), they are not endogenous equilibrium values, and this is what the Classical mind finds so hard to accept. Exogeneity means, not that the cost-unit is unaffected by the balance of supply and demand, but that if it is so affected, it moves from where it happens already to be as a result of past events, not from one position of equilibrium to another. There need be nothing preventing the adjustment of factor prices (especially the relative prices of heterogeneous labour and capital-goods), but such adjustment will not bring about the aggregate clearing of factor markets, which, in the Classical theory, would require changes in the 'aggregate' relative price. If factor prices responded solely to excess supply, they would fall to zero in circumstances of involuntary unemployment (technically, the factors of production would be free goods). Factor price stickiness is a condition of the stability of the market system, not of the existence of involuntary unemployment: however fast money-wages fall, such a fall cannot (directly) alter the relative prices that govern the level of employment in accordance with the principle of effective demand. Factor prices are in a quite different case from the prices of goods and debts, which are determined in *The General Theory* as equilibrium (market-clearing) values in the market period, by decisions to incur money-expense or to hold wealth in one form rather than another.

The principal form of real rigidity attributed to *The General Theory* is 'elasticity pessimism', meaning the claims that investment is inelastic with respect to changes in interest rates, and that interest rates are inelastic with respect to changes in the quantity of money. This may be supplemented by the absence of the 'real balance' effect, which may be described as an elasticity of consumption with respect to changes in the quantity of money expressed in wage-units, and which does not appear in *The General Theory*, for good reason as we shall see in Chapters 3, 4 and 5 of this book. Inelasticity is not the same as price stickiness, since markets may clear even if supply or demand is inelastic. Elasticity pessimism represents the '*ad hoc* critique' that *The General Theory* depends on behavioural assumptions which are inconsistent with rational long-term individual behaviour (this is considered in depth in Chapter 4 of this book). This can be understood as a rejection of Keynes's deliberate isolation of the three psychological independent variables from the closed loop of the Classical system, in order to leave them undetermined by the system parameters of technology and preferences, and to take them outside the realm of equilibrium theory (as with factor prices). The *ad hoc* critique neglects Keynes's reasons for adopting this open-ended model, which relate to his conceptions of expectation and liquidity, flowing from his recognition of the historical nature of time. The clarification of these reasons, which are of the utmost importance, is the major analytical task of this book.

P.4 EXPECTATION

Our first three propositions support Keynes's claim (*G.T.* xxxi) that *The General Theory* is an extension of the study of the competitive equilibrium of supply and demand in the Classical tradition so as to integrate money into the theory of value. His extension of Marshallian analysis falls into two main areas, the modelling of system as well as partial equilibrium, and the understanding and treatment of time. Keynes takes time seriously, as a one-way, irreversible sequence of historical events, and recognises that decisions are always made in the present, based on the unchangeable past and the unknown future. It is time which gives money its 'essential and peculiar' character, and makes a monetary economy

> ... one in which changing views about the future are capable of influencing the quantity of employment and not merely its direction. But our method of analysing the economic behaviour of the present under the influence of changing ideas about the future is one which depends on the interaction of demand and supply, and is in this way linked up with our fundamental theory of value. We are thus led to a more general theory, which includes the Classical theory with which we are familiar, as a special case. (*G.T.* xxii)

The understanding of time as irreversible has profound implications for equilibrium analysis. If today's decision to produce, consume or invest is to be described as an equilibrium outcome, the competitive forces bringing about this equilibrium must also act today, in the present. Past decisions and future outcomes are strictly irrelevant. For Marshall, the present corresponds to the market period, during which a given stock of finished goods and endowment of factor services are traded, and the supply and demand for the product of each industry are held in equilibrium by competition. The clearing of the markets for factor services in Marshall assumes that any offer of services at the market price will be accepted, but at this point nothing has been introduced to suggest this will not occur under perfect competition.

However, most production takes time. The decision to employ labour or invest in a capital-good today depends on the market prices that are expected to rule in the future (the 'expectations'), when the final output resulting from these decisions is finished and ready for sale. The Walrasian response to time is to postulate the existence of all necessary futures markets, so that the forward price of future finished output *at any date* can be determined today by the balance of supply and demand. This can be extended further to include contingent markets, so that the price implications of any future event, in any state of the world, can be fixed today. Under these strong conditions the future is reduced to the present, time disappears, and equilibrium remains a meaningful, if ideal, concept. Nevertheless, the forward market is an important concept that will prove helpful in understanding Keynes's thinking.

No-one disputes that not all futures and insurance markets exist, so the real question is whether competitive equilibrium theory can explain any important aspect of the world as we find it.[10] In the absence of a forward contract, decisions must be made on the strength of an expectation, something which already plays an important part in Marshall's system. ▶ AP.4.1 Marshall's market prices are qualitatively different from his Normal prices, the expectation of which in the short period induces firms to produce goods in a particular quantity, and in the long period induces investors to order new capital equipment. Marshall does not suggest that Normal prices as such are directly observable, but he does assume that competition tends to bring market prices into line with Normal prices in both the short and long periods, and conflates this process of convergence through time with the determination of Normal prices as equilibrium prices. Keynes accepts for theoretical purposes that market prices tend to converge towards Normal prices; but he changes the definition of the equilibrium periods in terms of calendar time, as well as the concept of a stationary or steady state that is necessary for this process of convergence also to generate Normal values as equilibrium prices. While Marshall's stationary or steady state refers to a physical allocation of resources, Keynes will allow only a given state of expectation that is independent of the physical parameters.

Keynes makes a subtle, but important, addition to Marshall's classification scheme by distinguishing between short-term expectation, which governs the level of production and employment, and long-term expectation, which governs the investment decision. Chapters 1 and 2 of this book will show how the state of short-term expectation can be represented numerically by the set of expected prices, or expectations, upon which production decisions are based. The corresponding representation of the state of long-term expectation is the combination of the schedules of the marginal efficiency of capital and of liquidity-preference, to be explored in detail in Chapter 4 of this book. The state of short-term expectation turns out to depend upon the state of long-term expectation, and it is often convenient to follow Keynes in referring simply to the state of expectation as a whole.[11] This use of the long and short term does not correspond to the technical long and short period, indeed Keynes's long period corresponds to his short term.[12] Periods are determined by the time postulated for competition to bring about equilibrium, and although they may be related to calendar time, in practice or by definition, this need not be so. Long and short term are also in one sense logical categories, relating to the time horizon over which expectations are formed, and in *The General Theory* to the perspectives respectively of the investor and the producer. However, as discussed earlier, both 'period' and 'term' are in *The General Theory* also connected with units of calendar time, the 'day' and the 'period of production', which are determined objectively by the social and physical conditions of production. Indeed, the need to link the periods of equilibrium analysis to units of calendar time is a prerequisite of treating observed values as equilibrium values.

Keynes's *long-period* equilibrium is based on *short-term* expectation, and relates to a state of expectation which remains unchanged long enough to allow the full adjustment of the aggregate stock of capital-goods and employment to that state of expectation. The horizon of short-term expectation is the period of production, the time required to produce the adjustments to the aggregate stock of capital-goods, and in the output of consumption-goods, to correspond to the long-period equilibrium level of employment. Although Keynes's long-period equilibrium is important for theoretical completeness, it is even less likely to be observed in practice than Marshall's stationary state, since the state of expectation is liable to constant change, even more so than the parameters of the Classical system. Nevertheless, as we shall see in Chapters 1 and 2 of this book, however much it may change from day to day, today's state of expectation determines *in the present* the point of effective demand, and the level of employment, as a position of short-period equilibrium. It is of less practical importance that the state of expectation also defines today a position of long-period equilibrium, on which the short-period equilibrium will converge if today's state of expectation continues unchanged; the limited likelihood of such stability explains Keynes's persistent emphasis on the short period.

Keynes treats the state of short-term expectation as reliable, or at least discoverable by trial and error, given the state of long-term expectation; but the state of long-term expectation itself is an entirely different matter. Keynes does not assume long-term expectations are fulfilled even in his long-period equilibrium (where they are merely unchanged), and indeed considers disappointment more than likely when expectations are not based on the rents of natural resources or monopoly. The period over which competitive equilibrium analysis is of scientific value relates directly to the time horizon within which expectations can reasonably be treated as determinate. The method cannot be applied to the long term, thus wholly undermining the Classical concept of long-period competitive equilibrium, whether static or dynamic.[13]

To assume so-called 'rational expectations' in the long term is heroically to assume a very unheroic world, in which the future can reliably be predicted from knowledge of the present and the past. ▶ **AP.4.2** The state of long-term expectation is as exogenous in *The General Theory* as the endowment and other Classical system parameters, meaning that it is beyond the reach of equilibrium theory. It is a close cousin to the propensity to consume and the preference for liquidity, both of which also reflect the historical nature of time. In the course of this book, it will become clearer why these three psychological states represent rational (by which I mean reasonable, not optimal in some objective sense) responses by purposeful individuals to the problems of time, in the real world where the Classical long-period equilibrium is logically unattainable, and therefore an objectively optimal response is physically impossible.[14]

P.5 LIQUIDITY

These days, a liquid asset is understood to be one that can readily be exchanged for money, meaning general purchasing power, at a well-defined market price. The claim of this book is that this does not capture the full meaning of liquidity in *The General Theory*, and that Keynes distinguishes between the attributes of convertibility and liquidity. There is more to his conception of liquidity than convertibility. In principle, an asset with low convertibility may have high liquidity, and *vice versa*, however counter-intuitive this may now seem. Liquidity is intimately related with expectation in *The General Theory*, and its meaning is fundamental to the understanding of the book as a whole.

How could Keynes be so perverse in his use of language as to make this interpretation tenable? In the opinion of Sir John Hicks (1972), the financial use of the term 'liquidity' originated with Keynes himself in *A Treatise on Money* and the 1931 Macmillan Report, so that perhaps the fault lies rather with his interpreters. Kaldor notes that

> Mr Keynes, in certain parts of *The General Theory* appears to use the term 'liquidity' in a sense which comes very close to our concept of 'perfect marketability'; ie goods which can be sold at any time for the same price, or nearly the same price, at which they can be bought. Yet it is obvious that this attribute of goods is not the same thing as what Mr Keynes really wants to mean by 'liquidity'. Certain gilt-edged securities can be bought on the Stock Exchange at a price which is only a small fraction higher than the price at which they can be sold; on this definition therefore they would have to be regarded as highly liquid assets. In fact it is very difficult to find satisfactory definition of what constitutes 'liquidity' – a difficulty, I think, which is inherent in the concept itself. (Kaldor, 1939, p. 4, n5)

The paradox of *The General Theory* is that Keynes so emphasises the liquidity of money within a theoretical framework, based on perfect competition, in which *all* assets are equally marketable or convertible. Why does he then discuss *degrees* of liquidity (*G.T.* 226) and, furthermore, suggest that in certain historic environments *land* has 'ruled the roost' in the hierarchy of liquidity (*G.T.* 241)? If the assumption of perfect competition is to be qualified in practice so that differences in the liquidity of assets are allowed, as a function of their degree of convertibility, this suggestion is startling. Land can never have been preferred for its convertibility, let alone as the medium of exchange. Keynes claims that historically it has possessed high liquidity, despite low convertibility. Conversely, in his discussion of organised investment markets, which come closest in practice to the ideal of perfect competition in terms of transaction costs and uniformity of price, he treats their 'liquidity' (note the inverted commas) as an illusion and something distinct from true liquidity. Listed equity securities have high convertibility, but low liquidity.

Unfortunately, Keynes does not provide a simple definition of liquidity in *The General Theory*, although he comes close towards the end of *G.T.* Chapter 17. In *A Treatise on Money*, Keynes defines (in passing) a liquid asset merely as one that is 'more certainly realisable at short notice without loss' (*C.W.* VI, p. 59). The understanding of liquidity put forward here, as Keynes's implicit definition in *The General Theory*, places the emphasis on the words 'more certainly' in the *Treatise* definition, as the degree to which the value of an asset, measured in any given standard, is independent of changes in the state of expectation.

Liquidity risk is therefore the possible (*not* probable or expected) loss of value as a result of a change in the state of expectation, which includes the state of confidence. In *The General Theory*, there is a hierarchy of liquidity risk, in which bonds are superior to capital-goods, and money is superior to bonds (see Chapter 4 of this book). This hierarchy is of crucial importance to Keynes's division between consumption and different types of investment decisions, which later theory has neglected. Keynes's conception of liquidity is intimately bound up with his conceptions of the state of expectation and of the historical nature of time. Liquidity has value only because the future is unknown, and its value increases with our fear of what might happen that we cannot prevent or insure against. In *The General Theory*, money is *the* liquid asset and dominant store of value, as well as the standard of value, and money's liquidity is the foundation of its non-neutrality. ► **AP.5.1**

NOTES

1.   There are some drafting and printing errors in *The General Theory*. The more substantial ones are dealt with in Sections A2.1.4, A5.3.1 and A5.4.1. In addition, the context requires

that on p. 250 (line 10 up) the word 'producing' should appear before 'its', and on p. 291 (line 14) 'greater' should be 'less'. Furthermore, in *C.W.* VII, on p. 286 (line 6) for 'or' read 'of', and on p. 236 (line 19) for 'closely' read 'slowly', as in the first edition. The presentation of aggregate supply and demand on p. 29 is satisfactory from the perspective of this book (contra Moggridge, *C.W.* VII, p. 385).

2. For a recent discussion of the different usages of equilibrium see Backhouse (2004).
3. Consider the phrase 'the long-run equilibrium around which the economy is fluctuating' (Mankiw, 2003, xxv) and the consequent view that the purpose of monetary and fiscal policy is to 'stabilise' the economy, rather than to shift its equilibrium position.
4. By scientific, I mean an explanation of the world that is open to empirical investigation and rigorous in the old sense of being in conformity with inter-subjective observation as well as internally consistent (Weintraub, 2002). For a scientific theory to have explanatory power does not require that it has predictive power (Lawson, 1997, 2003). See also Runde (1998) on the methodology of assessing competing causal explanations.
5. The consensus about Keynes's use of time periods, from which this book departs, is that Keynes's day and production period coincide, and correspond to a Hicksian week (Chick, 1983; Amadeo, 1989), an equation which tacitly assumes a uniform production period for all goods. Daily employment thus differs from the short-period employment equilibrium in which expectations are fulfilled (Casarosa, 1984).
6. The attempt to reconcile *The General Theory* with the third (Walrasian) criterion of equilibrium leads through Clower to Leijhonhufvud (1968), and other alternative models of equilibrium involving quantities (associated with Hicks, Patinkin, Barro and Grossman, and also the French authors Malinvaud, Grandmont, Benassy and Dréze). These models were thought to show promise for a brief period in the 1970s, but were largely swept away by the 'rational expectations' counter-reformation. Kornai (1971) re-defines general equilibrium in terms of information systems, replacing price-competitive concepts of supply and demand with 'pressure' and 'suction' within an institutional context.
7. See Fishburn (2005) for a fascinating discussion of Marshall's use of *natura non facit saltum*.
8. See Ambrosi (2003) on the relationship between the work of Keynes and Pigou.
9. See Mankiw (2003, viii, xxv). The case made for Keynesian business cycle theory by New Keynesians is that it is more realistic (ibid., pp. 11–12), although the harder line New Classical 'real business cycle' theorists would dispute this (ibid., p. 500). On the present reading, in this respect, Keynes is closer to the New Classicals than the New Keynesians.
10. Hahn (1973) argues that competitive equilibrium theory serves a useful purpose partly by showing precisely how and why the economy does not achieve Walrasian equilibrium.
11. Kregel (1976) associates 'short-period expectations' (sic) with particular individual expectations and 'long-period expectations' (sic) with the general state of expectation, rather than with production and investment decisions respectively (*G.T.* 47), leading to a quite different reading.
12. Keynes does sometimes use the substantive 'long period' to mean 'long term' (*G.T.* 93, 110, 279, 306, 318, 340). My argument depends mainly on his definition and discussion of long-period employment and the related dynamics (*G.T.* 48, see Section 2.2), and his consistent use of the adjective 'long-period' in the technical sense of an equilibrium period. The short 'run' lacks the link of the short 'term' to a definite interval of calendar time, the period of production. In Mankiw, the short run and the long run really refer to different models (2003, p. 240), and we are presumably always in the short run and in long-run disequilibrium.
13. Harrod did not accept that our ignorance of the future made long-term equilibrium theory pointless and regarded the absence of dynamic equilibrium from *The General Theory* as a weakness. He envisaged (and subsequently contributed to) the development of a theory 'concerned not merely with what size, but also what rate of growth of certain magnitudes is consistent with the surrounding circumstances. There appears to be no reason why the dynamic principles should not come to be as precisely defined and as rigidly demonstrable as the static principles' (1937, p. 86). This appears to be the basis of Barens and Caspari's rejection of *G.T.* Chapter 17 and of Keynes's treatment of the state of expectation as

exogenous (1997, p. 303, n48). It is also the view ultimately embodied in modern Classical dynamic general equilibrium theory based upon the concept of long-term long-period equilibrium that Keynes fundamentally rejected. Theories of accumulation and technical change are possible but they should not be equilibrium theories.

14. In this book I normally use the term 'rational' in its ordinary language sense of reasonable in relation to the available evidence, rather than meaning optimal in relation to objectively given circumstances. The main exception is as part of the phrase 'rational expectations', which has, for better or worse, become part of our vocabulary in the latter sense. See Dow and Dow (1985), Hoover (1997), Howitt (1997) and Dequech (1999, 2003). Shackle (1974) describes Keynes's concept of equilibrium as 'kaleidic', which should not be interpreted as necessarily unstable. The term 'kaleidic' refers to the possibility of instantaneous change in the compound psychological state that determines employment as an equilibrium value, and does not mean that this state of mind is inherently unstable or irrational.

Appendix to the Prologue

AP.1 EQUILIBRIUM

AP.1.1 Keynes and Marshall

Marshall's commitment to the use of equilibrium analysis is far from uncritical, and he is more conscious of the difference between animate and inanimate material than Walras, who writes:

> Equilibrium in production, like equilibrium in exchange, is an ideal and not a real state. It never happens in the real world ... yet equilibrium is the normal state ... towards which things spontaneously tend under a regime of free competition in exchange and production ... The law of supply and demand regulates all these exchanges of commodities just as the law of universal gravitation regulates the movements of all celestial bodies. Thus the system of the economic universe reveals itself, at last, in all its grandeur and complexity: a system at once vast and simple, which, for sheer beauty, resembles the astronomic universe. (Walras, 1926, pp. 224, 374)

Although the formal theory of Marshall's *Principles* employs the mechanical notion of equilibrium, he is diffident about the use of the stationary state and emphasises its value as a tool for analysis, rather than as a description of the world. He is attracted to biological notions of dynamic equilibrium, such as the continuous growth and decline of firms, but can capture them only by the static notion of the 'representative firm' (Marshall, 1920, pp. 264, 285). He is certainly conscious of the problem of time and the limitations of the essential *ceteris paribus* condition.[1]

Keynes is at the same time more, and less, ambitious than Marshall. He is less ambitious because he circumscribes the application of equilibrium theory. He confines equilibrium analysis to the short term, and regards the long term as open only to historical generalisation. He also regards variables such as the money-wage and the rate of interest as incapable of reduction to the parameters of the Classical system, as independent of preferences, technology and endowment. He is more ambitious, in his analysis of the system as a whole, and in defining functional relationships between measurable economic variables to capture aspects of psychology and probability that are intrinsic to the correct treatment of time. He articulates an explicit dynamic analysis of the relation between the short and the long period, but places more emphasis on shifts in equilibrium positions than on convergence to them.

Keynes is largely silent on the role of the political, social and institutional forces given priority by modern heterodox economics. His implicit position is that he regards competitive market forces as the dominant influence on prices and incomes in the short term, within a given social framework embodied in the parameters of his system. He leaves open the questions of what determines the relationship between capital and labour, the preferences of consumers, the progress of technology and the distribution of wealth. Keynes avoids, on one side, the paternalism of Marshall and Pigou towards the improvement of the working classes, and on the other, the revolutionary's condemnation of private property, yet he does not hesitate to offer proposals for radical reform, where practical reason suggests them.

AP.2   COMPETITION

AP.2.1   Perfect competition

Marshall uses the term 'perfect competition' in his *Principles* only once, in the context of labour supply and somewhat disparagingly, and mainly discusses 'free competition' and 'perfect markets' (1920, pp. 448, 284, 270). The primary characteristic of a perfect market is a uniform price *ex works*, and perfect information refers only to knowledge of market prices (1920, p. 278), in those markets that actually exist. Even the term 'price-taking' hardly does justice to Marshall, since he is well aware that prices must be set by firms and not, in general, by an auctioneer. 'Price-following', without a single price-leader, may be nearer the mark, but this would be an unfamiliar usage. Pigou uses, with reference to firms, the term 'simple competition', defined as 'conditions such that each seller produces as much as he can at the ruling market price, and does not restrict his output in the hope of causing that price to rise' (1932, p. 213). In the context of workers he refers to 'perfectly free competition among work-people and labour perfectly mobile' and here also makes a link between the imperfection of competition and the frictional resistances that prevent the instantaneous adjustment of wages to the demand for labour (1933, p. 252).

Joan Robinson (1934) notes that Chamberlin (1933) preceded her in criticising explicitly the use of the term 'perfect competition' (notably by Knight, 1921) to mean a frictionless, risk-free world. Chamberlin coined as an alternative the term 'pure competition', which was noted by Lerner in his definition of the 'degree of monopoly' (1934) and is generally insisted upon by Davidson. Chamberlin associates perfect competition with smooth adjustment and perfect foresight, while pure competition means simply price-taking, the assumption that agents take prices as parametric, that is, independent of their own quantity decisions. He contrasts pure competition with monopolistic competition, regarding Robinson's term 'imperfect competition' as confusing the issue. 'Monopoly ordinarily means control over the supply, and therefore over the price. A sole prerequisite to pure competition is indicated – that no one have any degree of such control' (1933, p. 7). This is an important definition.

Hicks follows Robinson in defining perfect competition as a neglect of 'the influence on supply which may arise from calculations made by sellers about the influence on prices of the sales they make themselves. (Similarly for demand.)' (1939, pp. 6–7). He emphasises that 'a general abandonment of the assumption of perfect competition, a universal adoption of the assumption of monopoly, must have very destructive consequences for [the determinacy of] economic theory' (ibid., p. 83). He then writes

> It is, I believe, only possible to save anything from this wreck – and it must be remembered that the threatened wreckage is that of the greater part of general equilibrium theory – if we can assume that the markets confronting most of the firms with which we shall be dealing do not differ greatly from perfectly competitive markets. (ibid., pp. 83–4)

At the time that Hicks was writing, Keynes also wrote in a similar vein about the empirical evidence against short-period diminishing returns that 'Mr Dunlop, Mr Tarshis and Dr Kalecki have given us much to think about, and have seriously shaken the fundamental assumptions on which the short-period theory of distribution has been based hitherto' (*C.W.* VII, p. 411).

Joan Robinson's aim was to define perfect competition solely in terms of demand, as 'a situation in which a single seller cannot influence price', and to undermine and dismiss the traditional idea of perfect competition as 'a situation in which a single seller cannot make more than normal profits', associated with the free movement of resources (1934, p. 104). Post Keynesians along with all other modern economists have followed Robinson, while Keynes remained on the side of tradition, which proves important when we come to consider the 'degree of competition'. Robinson's complaint was that the two different notions of perfect competition were 'very closely linked in many minds and lumped together' (ibid.). What we now call price-taking was certainly bound up closely with arguments that competition would allocate resources to their socially optimal use in the absence of frictional resistances:

> the free play of self interest, so far as it is not hampered by ignorance, tends in the absence of costs of movement, so to distribute resources among different uses and places so as to render rates of return everywhere equal ... [and where there are costs of movement, so as to] raise the national dividend and, with it, the sum of economic welfare to *a* maximum. (Pigou, 1932, pp. 142–3, original emphasis)

There is much to be said for following Chamberlin in preferring the term 'pure competition' when price-taking alone is meant, except that it is not in common use. Certainly Arrow and Hahn (1971, pp. 16, 33), masters of precision, follow Robinson and Hicks in using the term 'perfect competition' to mean only price-taking and are explicit that it does not automatically mean the assumption of all the futures markets necessary for Knight's perfect foresight.

Sections **AP.2.3** and **AP.2.5** develop the argument that *The General Theory* assumes perfect competition (in the above sense of price-taking) in the markets for current output and for existing capital-goods, with the degree of (imperfection of) competition understood to refer to long-term obstacles to the free movement of resources into and between industries and occupations. Some have interpreted Keynes as assuming (or needing to assume) quite the opposite of perfect competition;[2] nowhere does he state unequivocally what he assumes. Perfect competition (in both Robinson's senses) was the benchmark assumption of Marshallian economics, even after Robinson's and Chamberlin's books were published in 1933, so clearly Keynes might just have taken it for granted that an explicit statement was necessary only when departing from the standard case – he claimed, after all, to be writing essentially in the Classical tradition (*G.T.* xxxi).

Keynes's single reference in *The General Theory* to the term 'perfect competition' contrasts it with imperfect competition in a phrase that echoes Pigou's *Economics of Welfare* (1932):

> Again, if we have dealt otherwise with the problem of thrift, there is no objection to be raised against the modern classical theory as to the degree of consilience between private and public advantage in conditions of perfect and imperfect competition respectively. (*G.T.* 379)

In his post-publication correspondence with Ohlin, he writes 'The reference to imperfect competition is very perplexing. I cannot see how on earth it comes in. Mrs Robinson, I may mention, read my proofs without discovering any connection' (*C.W.* XIV, p. 190); and to Pigou: 'Imperfect competition and associated problems is the only *other* branch of theory which is interesting people at the moment, judging from what reaches me' (*C.W.* XXIX, p. 176, emphasis added). Together these comments provide circumstantial, if not conclusive, evidence that Keynes did not depart from the standard assumption of price-taking as defined here.

The first piece of textual evidence that *The General Theory* assumes price-taking is Keynes's acceptance of the first Classical postulate (that the wage is equal to the marginal product of labour, *G.T.* 17) of which the corollary is that, 'subject only to the same qualifications as in the classical theory', price equals marginal cost so that the degree of monopoly is zero. These 'qualifications' play no part in *The General Theory*, since Keynes's purpose was to demonstrate his point of departure from the Classical system, not to rehearse familiar arguments (see the above quotation from *G.T.* 379).

Further direct evidence is the equation of marginal proceeds with marginal factor cost (*G.T.* 55), definition of short-period supply price as the sum of the marginal factor cost and marginal user cost, or marginal prime cost (*G.T.* 53, 67–8), definition of long-period supply price as long-period average cost, including supplementary, risk and interest costs (*G.T.* 68), and reference to aggregate supply functions as embodying the *physical* conditions of supply (*G.T.* 246, original emphasis). The ambiguity that these references could be construed as equating supply price (in the above competitive sense) to marginal revenue when there is a degree of monopoly, rather than to demand price, is settled conclusively by the statement that: 'In a single industry its particular price-level depends partly on the remuneration of the factors of production which enter into its marginal cost, and partly on the scale of output' (*G.T.* 294). This view is corroborated by the definition of the elasticity of output (*G.T.* 283).

Further indirect textual evidence, in the form of Keynes's abstraction from financial and industrial structure and the distribution of income, is considered in Section **AP.2.3**.

AP.2.2   Keynes's agents

The assumption of price-taking is open to challenge on both theoretical and empirical grounds. Price-taking can be distinguished from atomism, as Chick notes by her use of the term 'polypoly' (1983, p. 25, also used independently by Kahn, 1989), and atomism is not itself a sufficient condition for price-taking. Yet the legal corporation strongly resembles a Newtonian particle in its lack of spatial dimensions. The distinction between the corporation and its members, officers and servants is of great practical importance, as is the similar distinction made by the tax authorities between persons (both natural or legal) and their trades or businesses. The atomistic conception of the firm is not in this sense unrealistic.

What is open to debate is the degree to which the firm can in practice be treated as having a single mind embodied in the 'entrepreneur', and to which the firm is capable of maximising its market value. Agency and asymmetric information theory, together with all shades of institutionalism and the reality of the human capacity to choose 'to do otherwise', emphasise the extent to which firms are complex social structures whose behaviour cannot be reduced to unitary corporate self-interest or fiduciary duty, constrained merely by competition and technology. Nevertheless, the atomistic conception of the firm does less violence to reality than does the abstraction from the historical nature of time represented by the Walrasian inter-temporal auction.

Some clarification of Keynes's taxonomy of market agents is useful. Individuals derive their income from three sources, as entrepreneurs, rentiers and workers. These categories are not social classes as in Marx or Kalecki, since one person may combine all three roles even if in practice people tend to specialise, by choice or otherwise. Entrepreneurs operate firms, rentiers provide the services of assets including money, and workers provide labour services. Firms are divided into a number of industries that each produce a single homogeneous good, which may be either a consumption-good or a capital-good.

Firms and households are best thought of as domains of activity, of transformation of goods and services into, respectively, other goods and services (production for sale in the market) and into personal utilities (consumption of purchases made in the market). The terms 'production' and 'consumption' must be used carefully, since household consumption involves domestic production, and production by firms involves capital consumption. Keynes adopts the usual abstraction from domestic production for personal use but gives considerable attention to the consumption of capital by firms, which he calls 'user cost'. Keynes does not use the term 'household' and uses 'firm' and 'entrepreneur' interchangeably. There is no separate treatment of legal persons, notably corporations, which he treats as artificial entrepreneurs with no net worth in terms of assets or personal faculties, all such services being bought in, and whose entrepreneurial income flows to rentiers.

The ultimate factors of production are non-producible natural resources ('land'), which command a true rental for their services; hired labour for which the rental is termed a wage; and a stock of existing producible capital-assets (the 'capital equipment') that may earn quasi-rents: taken together, these are the 'resources' whose employment is the matter in question (*G.T.* 4). Money is broadly non-producible and commands interest as its rent through debt contracts. Labour is treated as homogeneous, so that skilled labour is reducible by some function to standard labour.

The recipients of all three categories of income exchange money for consumption-goods. Both entrepreneurs and rentiers also exchange money for physical capital-goods, which, in the context of investment as opposed to production, Keynes tends to call capital-assets. Capital-goods are defined by the property of offering a money yield, either directly through sale or rental, or indirectly through production. He often refers to the stock of capital-goods (sometimes 'stock of capital') as the capital equipment, perhaps to avoid the connotation of homogeneity associated with the concept of capital stock (*G.T.* 38, 186, n1). Although money forms part of an individual entrepreneur's capital equipment, it largely disappears upon aggregation and, whether in the form of debt or commodity, is not producible to any significant extent by labour. There are no consumer durables since these offer no money yield; a consumption-good is defined by its sale to a consumer (*G.T.* 61).

AP.2.3   Capital-goods and capital markets

Keynes's assumption of perfect markets for capital-goods means that the number and size distribution of firms in each industry is endogenous, determined by the existing capital-goods and the degree of competition. If one entrepreneur expects to make more profitable use of any or all the capital-goods of another firm than the second entrepreneur expects to, the first entrepreneur will place a higher value on the assets than the second, and it will be mutually profitable to transfer them in the short period, just as is assumed in the case of the employment of labour. Keynes places great emphasis on the independence of his definitions of income from the degree of integration of industry (*G.T.* 24, n2, 55, 66–7). Keynes is therefore silent on industrial structure (apart from the degree of competition, see Section **AP.2.5**), and in general makes no assumption about the number of firms or the distribution of the capital equipment among them, nor do these appear in his list of given parameters (*G.T.* 245).

The assumption of perfect competition also makes the distribution of income partly endogenous. Keynes takes as a parameter 'the social structure and other forces' (*G.T.* 245) which influence the distribution of the existing capital-goods and human talent, access to particular occupations, etc, as well as transfers by taxation. While these may represent departures from, or obstacles to, some ideal long-period equilibrium of a meritocratic property-owning democracy, Keynes does not consider such questions open to equilibrium analysis, although he does express some preferences (e.g. that 'the euthanasia of the rentier' is to be welcomed). Nevertheless, the assumption of short-period diminishing returns required by perfect competition means that in a comparison of two positions of short-period equilibrium, the higher level of output and employment will be associated with a lower real wage (since the price of consumable goods will be higher relative to the money-wage) and a larger share of income will go to the owners of capital-goods by way of quasi-rents, including to entrepreneurs by way of the difference between average and marginal cost (the latter being in equilibrium equal to the expected price). Keynes later expressed considerable concern about the implications for the Marshallian theory of value of the empirical evidence that real wages were positively, and not inversely, related to output and employment (*C.W.* VII, p. 411).

Keynes's abstraction from corporate financial structure has always troubled the Post Keynesian school (notably Joan Robinson, Davidson (1972) and Minsky (1975), who have placed great emphasis on differences in the marketability or convertibility of capital-assets and their titles).[3] Keynes's discussion of capital-assets throughout *The General Theory* reflects the standard Classical assumption that all assets are held directly by individuals (including workers, in principle) in their capacities as rentiers or entrepreneurs (note the inclusive definition of entrepreneur for this purpose on *G.T.* 46). Shares merely divide the entrepreneurial element of corporate income between rentiers. Rentiers and entrepreneurs alike invest in capital-assets, whose prices are dominated by the expectations of rentiers, who can, if they have the stomach, become entrepreneurs themselves. The investment decision is framed in portfolio terms that apply equally to both entrepreneurs and rentiers, and there is no systematic difference between them in their access to loans of money or to the hire of capital-assets (although there may be differences between individual entrepreneurs in their access to credit, *G.T.* 144–5). The difference between rentiers and entrepreneurs is that rentiers, like workers, receive an income fixed in terms of money for a given level of employment of their services, while entrepreneurial profit depends on future realised results.

Capital-assets are perfectly transferable among entrepreneurs and rentiers and as Pigou puts it 'the free play of self interest, so far as it is not hampered by ignorance, tends in the absence of costs of movement, so to distribute resources among different uses and places so as to render [current] rates of return everywhere equal' (1932, p. 142). Keynes in effect qualifies this only by inserting the word 'expected' before 'rates of return' (*G.T.* 141). In footnote 1, *G.T.* 151, he states explicitly that 'I should now [say] that a high quotation for existing equities involves an increase in the marginal efficiency of the corresponding type of capital.' The rate of interest is the price of parting with money for a period of time, and the marginal efficiency of capital can equally denote the expected profitability of decisions to acquire a stock of newly produced raw material that will be wholly used up in a single production period, to acquire a machine that will wear out over several production periods in a year or two, or to acquire a new building for rental over a period of many years. The nature of the legal contracts, in particular whether an asset is owned by a rentier and hired by an entrepreneur, or owned directly by an entrepreneur (who may or may not have borrowed money to finance the purchase), is not important. The value of an asset is in *The General Theory* a function of its physical efficiency in adding to aggregate income, together with the rate of interest, so that there is no distinction between value in use in production and value in the market, a consequence of the assumption of perfect competition. If individual expectations differ, arbitrage will move an asset to the holder with the highest expectations (as in the reference to the purchase of an existing enterprise at *G.T.* 151).

The discussion of new and old investments in the Appendix to *G.T.* Chapter 14 relates to the distinction between the efficiency of an asset and the rate of interest. The value of an old asset may be greater or less than its original supply price, so as to bring its efficiency into line with the corresponding rate of interest. Any such difference between value and original cost, apart from physical depreciation and changes in the term structure of interest rates, reflects a change in either expectations or liquidity-preference, not a difference of convertibility. For Keynes the essential difference between liquid and fixed capital (where liquid here means finished output or raw materials which can be sold) is solely that the yield of liquid capital consists of a single current term rather than a prospective series; there is no suggestion that it reflects the relative ease with which the value of their prospective yields can be converted to money (*G.T.* 73). Note that the holding period (*G.T.* 225) may be shorter than the economic life of a capital-asset. A divergence of the bid and offer prices at the end of the holding period would mean the prospective yield from an asset could not be defined independently of the intended holding period. The assumption of perfect competition allows the value of the asset to be defined uniquely in terms of the prospective yield over its economic life, abstracting from the circumstances of particular firms and investors.

AP.2.4 The independence of supply and demand

The determinacy of Marshall's analysis requires the independence of the supply and demand curves, and, on both sides of the market, of price and quantity. This requires two sets of conditions, one relating to individual markets and the other to the system as a whole.

The first (microeconomic) condition can accommodate the case of monopoly (and monopsony, a single buyer), but not oligopoly or imperfect competition, where the bids and offers of individuals depend on those of their competitors. For this reason perfect competition is always associated with atomism, meaning that firms and households are small enough for the quantity they individually supply or demand not to affect the market price. The Marshallian concept of the industry neatly reconciles the horizontal demand curve facing the individual price-taking firm with the downward slope required for a stable equilibrium. Atomism in turn requires a further assumption that individual firms face diminishing returns, so that the output of a firm is limited at any given price, and that individual households experience diminishing marginal utility, so that demand is limited at any given price.

The second (macroeconomic) condition for the determinacy of the Classical system is that the factors of production are fully employed. In the absence of production (during the market period), the aggregate quantity of goods reflected in the supply curve is fixed, so that equilibrium between supply and demand in one market also implies equilibrium in the choice between substitutes. When production is introduced (in the short and long periods), the constraint of a fixed aggregate quantity has to be replaced by another, and in the Classical system this constraint is the endowment of factor services. In particular, the level of aggregate employment is equal to the supply of labour made available by households to firms, and marginal rates of transformation or 'productivity' are added to the analysis in order to link together equilibrium in product and factor markets.

It is in presenting effective demand, rather than the endowment of factor services, as the constraint on aggregate production that Keynes differs from the Classicals. The virtue of Keynes's Marshallian method is that, if the total level of output is determined by effective demand, the theory of the individual industry and firm remains essentially intact, as Keynes suggests (*G.T.* 31–2). By contrast, no meaning can be given to a system equilibrium with less than full employment in a Walrasian context.

The parameters of endowment, technology and preferences must be fixed, or changing only in a steady manner, if the Classical supply and demand curves are legitimately to be drawn for the short and long periods as well as for the market period (as in Marshall 1920, p. 288, n1). For in Marshall's system, quite rightly, changes in employment and capital equipment take time, for which there is no axis in the market-period diagram (Marshall acknowledges this, 1920, p. 667, n2). The determination of Normal prices as equilibrium prices assumes that any divergence of market prices and quantities from Normal does not itself shift the Normal position of equilibrium. An increase in production, induced by a temporary increase in demand that subsequently abates, which then leads to a market price below Normal, must be reversible so that if production returns to Normal, market price will do so also. This condition can only be met in a stationary or steady state.

When challenged that since 'the economic world is subject to continual changes, and is becoming more complex, … the longer the run the more hopeless the rectification', Marshall concedes that the provisional treatment of 'variables as constants' is the best he can do (1920, p. 315, n1); it seems probable that he would have regarded modern Walrasian inter-temporal general equilibrium theory as achieving greater consistency by an *ignoratio elenchi* – by missing the point, namely the difficulties associated with time.

The 'top down' relation between aggregate effective demand and employment, in aggregate and at the level of the industry and the firm, is defined by Keynes as the 'employment function', which itself is related to the aggregate supply function. Keynes's important but neglected synthesis of the principle of effective demand and the theory of value is considered further in chapters 2 and 5 of this book and their Appendices.

AP.2.5 The degree of competition

In Marshall and Pigou, what Keynes calls 'the degree of competition' (*G.T.* 245) refers to the conditions of supply rather than to the slope of the demand curve faced by an individual firm. Joan Robinson wrote that 'Keynes did not accept the "perfect competition" of the text-books, but some vague old-fashioned notion of competition that he never formulated explicitly' (quoted in Sawyer, 1992; see Marshall, 1923, pp. 396–8). In my view, Keynes's given degree of competition refers to competition among entrepreneurs and workers, and is a matter of the obstacles to the free movement of resources (both capital-goods and labour) into and between industries and occupations, associated with what he calls 'closed shops' of either employers (*C.W.* XIII, p. 639, n1) or workers, together with the other social and institutional resistances connected with voluntary unemployment (*G.T.* 6). These long-period obstacles are to be distinguished from the temporary frictional delays that may prevent full adjustment in the short period and lead to the Classical form of (frictional) involuntary unemployment, from which Keynes abstracts in defining full employment (*G.T.* 15–16).

The degree of competition is quite different from Lerner's 'degree of monopoly', which measures (in monopolistic equilibrium) the extent to which a firm can influence the demand price for its output by varying its supply offer, and which for a price-taker is zero. A degree of imperfection in competition need not be associated with any degree of monopoly. If competition is less than perfect, in Marshall's sense, price-taking firms may be earning profits above the normal level in the long period because of obstacles to the introduction of additional capital equipment into the industry, but they cannot increase these profits by restricting their own output from a given capital equipment unless they can also act together as a cartel and achieve monopoly (in line with Chamberlin's definition, see Section **AP.2.1** above). Profit-maximisation in the short period with the industry's existing capital equipment means satisfying the first Classical postulate, so that labour receives its marginal product and unemployment cannot result from 'monopolistic practices on the part of employers'. Similarly, unionised workers may be able to restrict entry to a particular occupation and keep wages up accordingly, but a closed shop does not prevent increases in the employment of union labour by an individual firm. The first Classical postulate remains valid, even if trade unions restrict entry to occupations and keep wages in particular trades above the levels associated with the free movement of labour.

A measure of the degree of competition for a firm would be long-period average cost divided by long-period price (defined in Section **AP.2.1**), by contrast with the degree of monopoly defined as the ratio of the excess of short-period price over short-period marginal cost to the price $(p-mc)/p$; the degree of competition may be less than the long-period maximum (100%) even if the degree of monopoly is zero. For workers, a measure of the degree of competition would be the labour actually available to firms, divided by the aggregate labour individual workers are willing to offer at the going wage —

$S_u(\hat{w})/S(\hat{w})$. Whether any of these measures can be observed is another matter.

The General Theory is a development of the Classical tradition of its time to address the economics of the system as a whole. Keynes is clearly aware of the contemporary development of the economics of monopolistic competition by Robinson and Chamberlin, yet regards this development in the same light as the traditional theory of monopoly and monopsony, as relevant only to the analysis of individual markets. Since all such analyses must take the demand curve as given, they can only describe the distortion of price and quantity in a particular market once the level of aggregate employment is given, and necessarily invoke the *ceteris paribus* condition. Keynes's method appears to be to specify the general case for the system as a whole in terms of perfect competition, while leaving the analysis open for theoretical purposes to departures from perfect competition in particular cases at industry and firm level, in accordance with established principles. ▶ **A5.3.4** Keynes's approach is consistent with his principal objective of demonstrating that involuntary unemployment (in his sense) does not reflect obstacles to competition.

AP.3   MONEY

AP.3.1   Unit of account, store of value and means of payment

The General Theory is a theory of the monetary economy. Not only are prices and incomes expressed and determined in terms of money, it has a significance beyond that of a simple counter, numeraire or 'money of account'. Nevertheless, the paramount importance of money (as unit of account and store of value) in the determination of employment must not be confused with the role of money (as means of payment) in the finance of expenditure, even if that former importance ultimately derives from its latter role as means of payment.[4] For the reasons elaborated in Chapter 2 of this book, it is essential to follow Keynes in keeping money payments and money-income at one remove from each other. Apart from the exceptional case of the production of commodity money (e.g. gold-mining), in accounting terms money belongs to the balance sheet and money-income to the income statement: they have entirely different domains. This means, in particular, rejecting the idea that the importance of income is as a source of *finance* for expenditure, notably consumption: the question of finance is entirely secondary and Keynes largely abstracts from it. The concept of the circular flow of income and expenditure, while valid if understood as a snapshot representation of static equilibrium at a point in time (provided that income and expenditure refer to accruals, not receipts and payments), is highly misleading when used to suggest a sequence of events over time and the circulation of means of payment, as will become clear when we come to discuss Robertson's version of loanable funds theory. ► **A2.3.3** The separation of the domains of money and money-income does not, of course, detract from the central role played by money (as a store of value) in the inducement to invest.

AP.3.2 Endogenous money

Part of the Post Keynesian response to the renaissance of the quantity theory has been to emphasise the endogenous nature of money creation by the banking system and the ability of the central bank to control either the quantity of money or the short-term interest rate, but not both. This has led to some tension with Keynes's liquidity-preference theory of interest rates and to a questioning of the generality of Keynes's assumption in *The General Theory* that the quantity of money is an independent variable. Some points of clarification are useful here.[5]

Firstly, Keynes was well aware of the nature of bank money and had written extensively on it in *A Treatise on Money*. At several points in *The General Theory* he describes the creation of money by the banking system, and notes that the quantity of money may be a function of the price-level (*G.T.* 266), although he appears to bend over backwards to accommodate the Classical position by allowing that the quantity of money may be 'virtually fixed'. Secondly, he accepted subsequently the case for making the finance motive an explicit part of the transactions demand for money, and noted the practical importance of overdraft finance in allowing the banking system to meet this demand without an increase in interest rates. Thirdly, the rate of interest in *The General Theory* is to be understood mainly as the interest differential between long-term bonds and short-term bills or deposits.[6]

Long-term bonds are the relevant benchmarks for investment in durable capital-goods with a similar life, such as housing, transport and utilities systems. It is this form of investment that Keynes regards as sensitive to monetary policy and of greater importance for employment than industrial investment (*G.T.* 106, 163–4). A major concern of *The General Theory* is to explain, in terms of liquidity-preference rather than time-preference, why the interest rates on long-term bonds do not fall to zero.

Liquidity-preference remains relevant to the extent that long-term capital-goods have to be financed, directly or indirectly, by individuals, corporations and institutions other than banks. If all capital-goods could be financed entirely by bank loans, the problem of liquidity-preference would not arise. *The General Theory* abstracts from financial structure, but as noted above, the tacit framework is that capital-goods are owned by entrepreneurs and rentiers (whether individual or corporate), funded by accumulated income and by debts both to banks and to other rentiers (i.e. bonds). ▶ **AP.2.2**

Keynes is explicit that, as a rule, he assumes that money is co-extensive with bank deposits but that this is not fundamental (*G.T.* 167, n1). He does not address the determination of the short-term interest rates at which banks lend and accept deposits, although these must be assumed respectively to lie between the bounds set, on the one hand, by bonds or bills of similar maturity to bank loans and, on the other, by the zero rate on currency. The theory of liquidity-preference addresses the differential between the short-term interest rates, if any, on money, so defined, and the complex of rates of interest for non-bank debts of different maturities (*G.T.* 167, n2).

The quantity of money is accordingly a function of the terms on which reserves are made available by the monetary authority, the attitude of the banking system towards reserve ratios (which partly depends on the state of confidence), and the demand for bank loans, which in turn depends on the short-term rates of interest at which banks lend. This composite function may be regarded as the state of banking policy (*G.T.* 327, 378). The quantity of money may be endogenous to the banking system, insofar as the banks may decide the volume of their lending after taking into account the price at which they can borrow reserves from the monetary authority, yet it remains under the control of the banking system (as distinct from the monetary authority), and not of the entrepreneurs who apply for bank loans. The quantity of money remains independent of the employment decisions of entrepreneurs, even if the quantity of money can be altered by the financial decisions of the banking system.

The trade-off for the banking system, between the loss of income from holding idle reserves and paying a penalty rate for borrowed reserves, may partly reflect speculative liquidity-preference in a more specialised sense. The extent to which the monetary authority can control the banking system may vary, especially between the up-swing and the down-swing. Yet the main issue for Keynes is the liquidity-preference of the rentier public in relation to the quantity of money created by the banking system and the interest rates offered by long-term bonds.

AP.4 EXPECTATION

AP.4.1 Expectation and expectations

In Keynes's Marshallian framework, an 'expectation' is usually associated with an expected price, including a rate of return. The expected price is the price which 'if it were held with certainty, would lead to the same behaviour as does the bundle of vague and more various possibilities which actually makes up [the entrepreneur's] state of expectation when he reaches his decision' (*G.T.* 24, n3). A 'state of expectation' can in turn be associated with a set of expected prices.

Keynes's use of the term proceeds rather than price has led some to understand him to extend 'expectations' to quantities, in the sense that firms are assumed to estimate demand curves, whether at the industry or aggregate level. Such a 'price-making' approach would have been quite inconsistent with the Marshallian method, and Keynes certainly gives no explicit indication of having made such a radical departure. Expected prices are sufficient under perfect competition, given the capital equipment and other short-period parameters, to determine the level of employment (and the expected proceeds, to which the above footnote in fact refers), so that short-term expectations can be taken to refer solely to the prices relevant to production decisions. It is true that to work out the prospective yield of a new capital-good requires an expectation not only of price, but of income over the economic life of the asset, but once again, this series of income is in principle determined by future prices, given the future capital equipment, technology, degree of competition and indeed all of Keynes's short-period parameters in each future period, as well as future levels of effective demand based on future states of long-term expectation, liquidity-preference and the propensity to consume (*G.T.* 147). Given all these future conditions, it comes as no surprise that long-term expectations are tentative, and not often in practice arrived at by calculation in this manner. The particular point at issue here is that both future price and future supply and demand conditions are treated as parametric by the individual firm. There is no suggestion that firms take into account the production decisions of other firms or the effect of their own production decision on the future market price.

AP.4.2 Expectation and probability

Keynes's approach to long-term expectation in a world subject to unforeseen change appears to be informed by his distinctive and highly developed understanding of probability.[7] In *A Treatise on Probability* (*C.W.* VIII) he treats Classical frequentist probability theory as a special case within a branch of philosophical logic that deals with arguments that are doubtful, but neither demonstrably certain nor logically impossible. He understands probability as an argument or logical relation between one set of propositions (the conclusions) and another set (the evidence). Mathematics deals with analytic relations between propositions that must be either true or false. In matters of metaphysics, science and conduct, an argument is considered 'probable' to the extent that it warrants a degree of rational belief. Such a probability relation is objective, in the sense that any rational judge would reach the same conclusion upon the same evidence. Probability is not in general numerical, as in frequentist theory, but arguments can be, and often are, compared. An archetypal case is the verdict reached in a court of law.

Although Keynes treats investors as forming single-valued expectations of prospective yield, these estimates bear a complex relation to the 'bundle of vague and more various possibilities' (*G.T.* 24, n3) which actually make up their state of expectation when they reach their decisions, a relation which cannot be reduced to calculations based on relative frequency. The expected value of Classical probability theory is known (i.e. certain) as soon as the population frequency distribution is known, while an expectation in terms of Keynesian probability reflects the balance of available evidence but remains uncertain. The confidence with which an expectation is held depends on the weight of the evidence compared with the conclusive evidence of hindsight (or perfect foresight).

These ideas can be expressed in the mathematical symbols of *A Treatise on Probability*, with a view to clarifying precisely the difference between the Classical and Keynesian views of probability. Using Keynes's terminology, the expectation $\hat{x}$ of the outcome x is the value of $\hat{x}$ which satisfies

$$(x \geq \hat{x})\big|\Omega = (x \leq \hat{x})\big|\Omega \qquad \text{(AP.1)}$$

where this expression means that the probability (in Keynes's sense) that the outcome x lies at or above the expectation $\hat{x}$ equals the probability that the outcome lies at or below the expectation, given the available evidence Ω, including relevant propositions for and against each conclusion. Ω is a subset of $\overline{\Omega}$, the complete 'perfect foresight' information set from which x might be known with certainty, i.e. $x\,|\,\overline{\Omega} = 1$.

The 'expected value' $\mathrm{E}[x]$ of Classical probability theory is in similar fashion given by the centre of gravity of the population relative frequency density function $\varphi(x)$ (I use the term 'relative frequency' to distinguish probability based on frequency from Keynesian probability) such that

$$E[x] = \int_{-\infty}^{+\infty} x\varphi(x)\,dx \qquad \text{(AP.2)}$$

whence it follows that

$$\int_{-\infty}^{E[x]} \varphi(x)\,dx = \int_{E[x]}^{+\infty} \varphi(x)\,dx = 0.5 \qquad \text{(AP.3)}$$

Equation (AP.3) is the Classical equivalent of equation (AP.1), in that x is as likely to fall above $\hat{x} = E[x]$ as below it, with the difference that, if we *know* $\varphi(x)$, we *know* that, in the limit, half the 'drawings from the urn' will fall on one side and half on the other of the expected value $\hat{x}$. In Keynes's terms, $\hat{x}|\varphi(x) = 1$; the *expectation* (although not the outcome itself) is *known* with certainty (as opposed to merely probable in Keynes's sense) as soon as the frequency density function is *known*, since the conclusion follows from the evidence as a matter of strict logical implication: expected value is simply a mathematical transformation of the frequency density function. By contrast, in equation (AP.1), the information set Ω does not permit conclusive determination of the expectation $\hat{x}$ (let alone, *a fortiori*, the outcome x); or put another way, the two sides of equation (AP.1) do not 'sum' to unity (although strictly these Keynesian probabilities are not in general of the numerical form necessary for addition).

While each side of equation (AP.1) depends on the balance of the evidence for and against each conclusion, the 'weight' of the argument for the expectation $\hat{x}$ depends on the relation between the available information Ω and the complete information $\overline{\Omega}$. Although no numerical comparison is possible between Ω and $\overline{\Omega}$, it is clear that if Ω is very scant, little confidence will be placed in the expectation; while if $\Omega = \overline{\Omega}$, there will be complete certainty and therefore absolute confidence. Thus the degree of confidence in the expectation $\hat{x}$ will depend, although not by a numerical functional relation, upon the weight of the evidence in Ω relative to the complete information set $\overline{\Omega}$, which in practice can only be known in retrospect.

This understanding of Keynes's view of probability explains why he makes no reference to statistical variance anywhere in *The General Theory*. The concept of an expectation is of great importance to Keynes and in the above terms is represented by $\hat{x}$, the value which is most likely on the balance of the evidence, and to which Keynes refers as the 'actuarial' value. What is missing from *The General Theory* is the extra assumption that an expectation can be justified in statistical terms based on observable frequency distributions. A corollary is that Keynes does not assume that uncertainty can be enumerated by a measure of dispersion such as variance. Thus the Old Keynesian reduction of uncertainty to variance by Tobin (1958) fundamentally undermines the meaning of liquidity-preference.

When Keynes refers to 'actuarial' risk, he means the expectation of loss on a portfolio of assets, most likely on the balance of evidence and perhaps indeed based, at least in part, on frequency tables, in the sense of the insurance underwriter. He expresses great scepticism about such calculations, despite being (indeed, because he was) the author of a treatise on probability and the chairman of an insurance company. These fields of expert knowledge are the grounds of his scepticism, since any acquaintance with the operations of Lloyd's reveals that the underwriter is far more a book-maker than a mathematician. This scepticism applies *a fortiori* to more sophisticated formulations of statistical risk in terms of 'states of the world', which do not necessarily assume a normal or other standard probability distribution whose dispersion can be fully described by the single measure of variance, but do require that each state of the world can be defined so that it is certain that one of these states will prevail (the two sides of equation (AP.1) sum to unity).

So the uncertainty and consequent risk on which Keynes places such emphasis in *The General Theory* are something rather different from random error and the corresponding loss function. Some authors accordingly prefer to limit the use of the term uncertainty to refer solely to this quite different concept associated with Keynes and also Knight (1921), but both Keynes and Classical authors tend to use them interchangeably in their own contexts and to mean different things, adding to the reader's confusion. Furthermore it is important not to identify risk with uncertainty itself, rather than with the loss to which uncertainty exposes us. Keynes makes *confidence* ('how highly we rate the likelihood of our best forecast turning out quite wrong' *G.T.* 148) the main measure of uncertainty, in the above terms the relation between Ω and $\overline{\Omega}$. Confidence is the converse of liquidity-preference, so that Tobin comes close when he defines 'liquidity-preference as aversion to risk': but the risk in question is Keynes's liquidity risk, and not the actuarial risk represented by variance.

AP.5   LIQUIDITY

AP.5.1   Fundamental uncertainty

There is no liquidity risk in Classical theory because expectations are reliable within the limits of random error. Classical theory struggles to find a role for money in the Walrasian general equilibrium system. The concept of liquidity is inextricably bound up with the concept of probability, and modern Classical economic theory has reduced uncertainty to random error by incorporating into its system the Classical frequency theory, rather than Keynes's logical theory, of probability. If uncertainty consists only of random error, the certainty-equivalent expectation can be discovered by repeated sampling. The expected value will converge on the population mean as the sample increases in size, and within the limits of merely statistical confidence the expected value becomes *certain*. The definition of uncertainty as no more than random error is the foundation of the so-called 'rational expectations hypothesis'.

It is his understanding that the world does not fit this modern Classical definition of uncertainty (which had not been fully developed in his time) that leads Keynes to write:

> Or, perhaps, we might make our line of division between the theory of stationary equilibrium and the theory of shifting equilibrium—meaning by the latter the theory of a system in which changing views about the future are capable of influencing the present situation. *For the importance of money essentially flows from its being a link between the present and the future.* We can consider what distribution of resources between different uses will be consistent with equilibrium under the influence of normal economic motives in a world in which our views concerning the future are fixed and reliable in all respects;—with a further division, perhaps, between an economy which is unchanging and one subject to change, but where all things are foreseen from the beginning. Or we can pass from this simplified propaedeutic to the problems of the real world in which our previous expectations are liable to disappointment and expectations concerning the future affect what we do today. (*G.T.* 293–4)

A theory of stationary equilibrium can describe not only a static stationary state, but also a dynamic steady state in which 'a steady increase in wealth or population may constitute a part of the unchanging expectation. The only condition is that the existing expectations should have been foreseen sufficiently far ahead' (*G.T.* 48, n1). The definition of uncertainty as random error leads to a theory of stationary rather than shifting equilibrium because, although 'our previous expectations are liable to disappointment' through random error, we can be confident that these errors will average out. Random error is a typical symptom of disequilibrium and is characteristic of many physical systems which are otherwise entirely predictable within the limits of experimental error. Thus the Classical treatment of uncertainty amounts to an assumption that its only source is unpredictable variations in the individual behaviour of atomistic agents and in the parameters of technology and preferences, generating random error exactly as in the physical case of Brownian motion.

A stationary state with the addition of a random disturbance term and perhaps a deterministic trend can be described as an 'ergodic' system (Davidson, 1996, following Samuelson). The ergodic hypothesis was originally conceived by Boltzmann in developing the kinetic theory of gases in physical chemistry, to explain the behaviour of macroscopic volumes in terms of the Brownian motion of individual particles. The rational expectations hypothesis can be understood as taking markets to generate equilibrium prices in the same way that equilibrium temperatures and pressures are generated by the random collisions of myriads of gas molecules in a closed vessel with a fixed volume. However, the real world is far from stationary, even in this stochastic sense.

The theory of shifting equilibrium (which is the analytical core of *The General Theory*) recognises that the knowledge upon which we base our expectations about the long-term future is very limited. The most cursory study of history and the warnings of financial regulators bear witness to how foolish it is, particularly in the matter of investment, to assume that the past and present are a reliable guide to the long-term future. As Keynes puts it eloquently:

> The outstanding fact is the extreme precariousness of the basis of knowledge on which our estimates of prospective yield have to be made. Our knowledge of the factors which will govern the yield of an investment some years hence is usually very slight and often negligible. If we speak frankly, we have to admit that our basis of knowledge for estimating the yield ten years hence of a railway, a copper mine, a textile factory, the goodwill of a patent medicine, an Atlantic liner, a building in the City of London amounts to little and sometimes to nothing; or even five years hence. (*G.T.* 149)

By uncertain knowledge, let me explain, I do not mean merely to distinguish what is known for certain from what is only probable. The game of roulette is not subject in this sense to uncertainty...Or, again, the expectation of life is only slightly uncertain. Even the weather is only moderately uncertain. The sense in which I am using the term is that in which the prospect of a European war is uncertain, or the price of copper and the rate of interest 20 years hence, or the obsolescence of a new invention, or the position of private wealth owners in the social system in 1970. About these matters there is no scientific basis on which to form any calculable probability whatever. We simply do not know. (*C.W.* XIV, pp. 113–4)

The very real possibility of a change, in what we believe to be the most probable forecasts of what the future holds, is what undermines our confidence and causes us, in the absence of an incentive to do otherwise, to seek security by keeping our wealth in the form that we most expect to maintain its value, whatever the future may bring.

NOTES

1. The continuity between Marshall and Keynes and the importance of the differences between Marshall and Walras have been emphasised by a few writers, including most recently by De Vroey (2004). The Marshallian firm was at the centre of some of the earliest expositions of Keynesian analysis, such as Tarshis (1947), before the competitive microeconomics of Keynes came to be neglected. See also Reisman (1986), Rogers (1997) and Toye (1998).
2. Notably Dutt (1987) and Marris (1997), but see Trevithick (1992), Kahn in Marcuzzo (1994, p. 32) and Sardoni (2002) for examples of the contrary view.
3. The main purpose of this book is to explain *The General Theory*, so discussion of industrial and financial structure arises only in Section E.2 of the Epilogue, where I offer my own extension of some of his ideas.
4. Rogers (2006) has drawn out the practical dangers for central banking policy of confusing these subtle theoretical concepts. He emphasises that an electronic money system, in which the means of (final) payment plays a limited role, is by no means the same as the clearing house of a Walrasian auction. The perverse conclusion of Walrasian theory, that money reduces efficiency, reflects the non-monetary nature of the theory, in exactly the sense that concerned Keynes. The means of exchange need not be the means of payment, even if the means of payment is always acceptable as the means of exchange. Mankiw does not adequately distinguish these two from each other (2003, p. 77).
5. I use the term 'independent' rather than 'exogenous', mindful of the debate over the meaning of the latter in this context (Dow, 1997), although in my usage either would do. By exogenous I mean only outside the equilibrium model, which implies nothing about the distinction between independent variables and given parameters, nor about the use of the term in a looser sense, such as 'exogenous to the private sector'. For a recent introduction to the debate between 'horizontalists' and 'structuralists' see Fontana (2004).
6. Mankiw concentrates on the transactions demand for money and therefore on short-term rates (2003, pp. 271–3). In his model, the long-term (or long-run) rate of interest is determined by the supply and demand for loanable funds and not by liquidity-preference.
7. An extensive literature has explored the case for continuity in Keynes's thought between *A Treatise on Probability* and *The General Theory*. See Dequech (1999, 2003).

1.   Two Theories of Employment

The General Theory is not primarily a theory of the determination of the level and distribution of income, and it is certainly not a theory of growth through the accumulation of wealth or the advance of technology. As its title indicates, *The General Theory of Employment, Interest and Money* is first and foremost a theory of employment. Employment here means wage labour, the hire of labour for a sum of money, and not merely occupation or self-employment. A theory of employment is then a theory of the decisions of employers to hire labour and of employees to offer their services.

A theory of self-employment is rather different, since there is no hiring decision. In an economy composed of self-employed farmers and artisans the employment decision is simply a production decision, how much effort to exert to obtain goods other than leisure.[1] A decision by a self-employed worker to produce for sale (rather than for stock or for personal consumption) may involve money, as the medium of exchange for other goods, but money does not enter directly into the production process. Where an economy is based on employment, production requires the payment of a money-wage, and this arrangement can be described as an 'entrepreneur' or 'monetary production' economy.[2]

Keynes argues that *The General Theory* is necessary in order to explain how unemployment can arise from a lack of aggregate demand. The Classical theory is essentially a theory of self-employment in which, if prices are perfectly flexible, involuntary unemployment can arise only from frictional delays in the physical change-over from serving one market to another. In the Classical theory, the level of (self-)employment is limited only by the supply of labour available at a given real wage, so that 'non-employment' is either voluntary or frictional.

In modern Walrasian theory, the distinction between firms and households is merely convenient, not essential. It is convenient in order to analyse production and consumption activities separately, but the distinction is really between these types of activity, not the domains in which they are carried out. Households can be assumed to both produce and consume without altering the basic result, and there is no intrinsic need for a market for labour, as opposed to goods produced by the self-employed household. The implication is that nothing fundamental changes if households supply labour services as one, or indeed their only, produced output. It is simply a matter of choice and endowment. Not only money, but wage labour, are inessential to the Walrasian scheme.

The General Theory takes 'the skill and quantity of available labour' as one of its initial conditions and does not consider the weighty question of why a wage-dependent labour force exists. The distinction between entrepreneurs (employers) and workers (employees) is essential, but taken as given. Entrepreneurs alone, and not workers, sell to product markets and decide what, and how, to produce. Entrepreneurs and workers necessarily bargain over money-wages and not real wages. The idea of real wage bargains is based on the self-employment model, and for it to be generally valid, all firms would have to be producer co-operatives, in which labour was paid according to the sales value of its output. Although this type of firm does exist, as a species of collective self-employment, along with skilled artisans from plumbers to barristers, the main concern of *The General Theory* is with employers and employees, who put a price on labour time that must necessarily be arrived at independently of the value of the subsequent output to which the labour may give rise. In a co-operative or self-employed economy, given competitive product markets, the exertion of labour to produce saleable output will generate revenue. If the product price is low, the revenue may not be worth the effort, and leisure may be preferred (i.e. may offer higher utility at the margin). The difference between an economy of self-employed households in perfect competition and Robinson Crusoe lies only in the division of labour. In a monetary production economy, by contrast, labour cannot insist on being employed, even if its marginal revenue product and real wage exceed the marginal disutility of that amount of employment (*G.T.* 291). Entrepreneurial firms exist, not to hire labour, but to make profit. By definition, wage-labour does not make the hiring decision, and the primary purpose of *The General Theory* is to explain how firms can find it unprofitable to employ labour, even though unemployed labour is for hire at the going rate.[3]

The following sections consider in turn the first three *G.T.* Chapters, beginning with Keynes's claim to offer a *general* theory in *G.T.* Chapter 1; his critique of the Classical theory of employment in *G.T.* Chapter 2; and finally, the core of Keynes's own theory, the principle of effective demand, set out in *G.T.* Chapter 3.

1.1   GENERAL THEORY OR SPECIAL CASE?

The modern Classical view is that contrary to Keynes's claim in *G.T.* Chapter 1, *The General Theory* is a special case of Classical theory. Keynes's involuntary unemployment is to be understood as a symptom of disequilibrium, of departure from full employment general equilibrium, associated with 'sticky' wages, interest rates and expectations. The New Keynesian variant of Classical theory emphasises that such disequilibrium may not be self-correcting, since the failure of prices to adjust may reflect permanent features of the real world, especially the asymmetric distribution of information among the bargaining parties. Nevertheless the diagnosis of the problem in terms of disequilibrium leads to a set of policy prescriptions that might have found favour with Professor Pigou, but not with Keynes (Darity and Young, 1997).

Although *The General Theory* cannot be reduced to the assumption of sticky interest rates, this point has some merit as will become clear in Chapter 4 of this book. What is surprising, as noted in the Prologue, is the continued widespread assertion that *The General Theory* depends on sticky money-wages. Although sticky money-wages may be a condition of the stability of the price system, that is not the same thing as a condition of under-employment equilibrium.

As noted above, Keynes assumes that workers do not supply product markets directly. Can this be regarded as a special case? In the purest Walrasian system, the decision to offer labour services rather than products, to be a worker rather than an entrepreneur, is a matter of endowment and choice. Yet Keynes was here no different from Marshall and Pigou and their predecessors, who recognised the distinctive character of wage-labour (along with the services of non-produced capital-goods such as land) as 'factors of production' requiring separate treatment from goods produced by entrepreneurs. *The General Theory* was addressed to the Marshallian form of Classical theory, so the assumption that labour works only for wages cannot be the point of departure.

Keynes himself emphasises Say's Law (as defined by Mill, Marshall and Ricardo, *G.T.* 18–19, 369) as the special assumption required for Classical theory to apply to the monetary production economy, creating a 'Neutral' economy. This implies 'a nexus which unites decisions to abstain from present consumption with decisions to provide for future consumption [i.e. invest]; whereas the motives which determine the latter are not linked in any simple way with the motives which determine the former' (*G.T.* 21). As Keynes puts it, 'An act of individual saving means – so to speak – a decision not to have dinner today. But it does not necessitate a decision to have dinner or to buy a pair of boots a week hence or a year hence or to consume any specified thing at any specified date' (*G.T.* 210, a clear reference to the intertemporal theory of consumption in Fisher, 1930).

Keynes's proposition has been formalised in modern Classical terms as the incompleteness of the necessary futures markets for all possible consumption plans. Provided at least one futures market exists (e.g. for money) a short-period full employment 'temporary equilibrium' (in the sense of Hicks, not Marshall) can still exist, so that the argument comes to centre on the relationship between saving (strictly, income not consumed) and investment, and on the rate of interest as the rate of time discount bringing non-consumption into line with investment opportunities.

The Neutral economy can also be interpreted as the assumption that no-one will hold money in the long term except for its convenience value as the medium of exchange. The disequilibrium strand of pre-Keynesian Classical theory (what Keynes called the 'neo-classical' strand, *G.T.* 183) had always been concerned with the problem of 'hoarding', the refusal either to consume or invest in new goods. Sooner or later, particularly if the price-level fell, people would prefer capital-assets or consumption to money hoards, and money would again become neutral. Since *The General Theory*, Milton Friedman among others has argued that even if money interest rates are sticky and new capital-assets remain relatively unattractive, consumption-goods (particularly durables) are preferable to sterile hoards, especially as the real value of base money increases (and of government debt, to the extent not offset by the prospect of an increased tax burden in real terms). The Pigou, or 'real balance', effect (Pigou, 1943) has become the core of the modern Classical theory of aggregate demand, even if for policy purposes it is recognised as more desirable to increase the money supply to offset serious 'monetary shocks', rather than attempt general wage cuts and put the financial system at risk through debt deflation. This amounts to a claim that, given the level of investment, consumption will in the long term rise to bring about the full employment equilibrium of the Neutral economy. Although Keynes recognises the influence of unexpected capital gains and losses, he deliberately ignores the Pigou effect, and regards an increase in wealth as more likely to reduce, rather than increase, the propensity to consume. The Pigou effect is discussed further in Chapters 3, 4 and 5 of this book.

It has thus become possible for modern Classical theory to reject Keynes's propensity to consume, along with liquidity-preference, as 'ad hoc', albeit on the rather thin foundation of the real balance effect (to which we shall return). *The General Theory* becomes a special disequilibrium case of 'elasticity pessimism', where consumption is inelastic to wealth, interest rates inelastic to money supply, and investment inelastic to interest rates. Behind this criticism ultimately lie two assumptions: (a) that flexible prices would tend to move a monetary production economy, trading at 'false' disequilibrium prices, to a unique and stable full employment equilibrium, and (b) that the psychological propensities of *The General Theory* have no solid long-term foundation in rational choice. The purpose of this book is partly to demonstrate that *The General Theory* does in fact answer this criticism and undermine the underlying assumptions upon which it is based, thereby substantiating Keynes's claim to generality.

1.2 THE CLASSICAL THEORY OF EMPLOYMENT

The purpose of *G.T.* Chapter 2 is to refute the Classical theory of employment and unemployment on both empirical and logical grounds. By *reductio ad absurdum*, Keynes demonstrates that the predictions of Classical theory do not accord with the observed response of workers to changes in real wages. Secondly, he challenges at root the assumption that bargains in money-wages determine real wages, so that unemployment is a matter of money-wages. This second point leads to the core proposition that only at full employment does the real wage determine (or rather, constrain) the level of employment, while in general it is the level of employment that determines the real wage. The rest of *The General Theory* offers an alternative explanation of the level of employment compatible with the possibility of involuntary unemployment, something that cannot logically exist in Classical theory.

Keynes's definition of involuntary unemployment in *G.T.* Chapter 2 is that 'Men are involuntarily unemployed if, in the event of a small rise in the price of wage-goods relatively to the money-wage, both the aggregate supply of labour willing to work for the current money-wage and the aggregate demand for it at that wage would be greater than the existing volume of employment' (*G.T.* 15). The reason for this convoluted definition is that it allows Keynes to identify his point of departure from the Classical theory of employment on its own terms. The clearer definition (in his own terms, of inelastic employment) has to await the definition of effective demand in *G.T.* Chapter 3.

In the Classical theory, the real wage is determined by the bargains between employers and workers, and the real wage in turn determines the level of employment. In *The General Theory*, the level of employment determines the real wage and has nothing directly to do with the bargains in terms of money-wages between employers and workers, taken in aggregate. In the Classical theory, observed levels of unemployment *reflect* a real wage (or strictly, labour cost) above the market-clearing level, and the solution lies in wage reductions, increased labour market flexibility, etc. In *The General Theory*, observed levels of unemployment are *associated* with a real wage above the market-clearing level, but employers and workers cannot reduce the real wage simply by agreeing lower money-wages.

Keynes's definition of involuntary unemployment in Classical terms is needed for an appeal to the facts of experience, a simple offer of empirical evidence against the Classical theory of unemployment. Leaving aside the question of how the real wage can be reduced, he drives the Classical theory to its logical conclusion, that if such a reduction takes place, the supply of available labour will fall below the amount actually employed before the reduction. This implies that 'all those now unemployed though willing to work will withdraw the offer of their labour in the event of even a small rise in the cost of living' (*G.T.* 13). This can be illustrated in a diagram plotting the real wage ω against the level of employment N (see Figure 1.1).

The point (N^*, ω^*) represents the point of market-clearing equilibrium given competitive Classical supply (S) and demand (D) curves for labour. Nothing hangs in this example on the particular elasticities. Unemployment exists in the Classical account because obstacles to competition in the form of restrictions on the movement of labour shift the supply curve to the left (S_U). This curve relates the amount of labour *actually available to employers* at a given real wage, which is less than the amount of labour individual workers are willing to provide in aggregate. The point of 'unemployment equilibrium' is given by (N_1, ω_1), and the level of unemployment is U_1. Note that at ω_1 the supply of labour is higher than at ω^*.

Keynes's *reductio ad absurdum* runs as follows. Given the restricted supply (S_U) and the demand (D) curves for labour, assume the real wage is reduced from ω_1 to ω_2. This defines a point of Classical disequilibrium (N_C, ω_2) where demand exceeds supply (by $N_K - N_C$ shown by the double-headed arrow), and employment is rationed by supply. N_C is less than N_1, so that some of the workers employed at (N_1, ω_1) withdraw their services *and so do all those unemployed* at ω_1, despite an excess demand for labour. If not *all* the unemployed represented by U_1 do so withdraw, employment must lie somewhere between N_C and N_K.

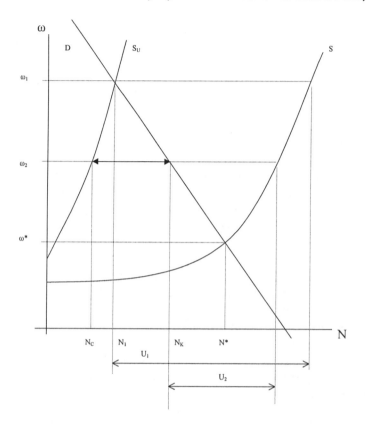

Figure 1.1 Employment and the real wage

The diagram also illustrates Keynes's definition of involuntary unemployment in Classical terms. This time we use the perfectly competitive labour supply curve (S). At (N_1, ω_1) the labour market is in disequilibrium, with supply exceeding demand, and employment is rationed by demand. U_1 is as before the level of unemployment. If now the real wage is reduced from ω_1 to ω_2, actual employment increases from N_1 to N_K, and unemployment reduces from U_1 to U_2, as a result partly of increased demand and partly of reduced supply. Keynes is not suggesting that the reduction in the real wage causes the reduction in unemployment, but that the two are associated. His argument is that his definition of unemployment is in accordance with the facts of experience, while the Classical definition leads to an absurd prediction.

The second aspect of *G.T.* Chapter 2 considers how changes in real wages come about. Up to this point, the argument has considered the empirical implications of such changes without enquiring into the adjustment mechanism. Keynes observes that the assumption that the real wage depends on the money-wage bargains between employers and workers is not obviously true, and appears to depend on the tacit assumption that the price-level is determined independently by the quantity of money; indeed the assumption clashes with the Classical view that money is neutral. The Classical relationship between the real wage and the level of (full) employment makes the tacit assumption that all offers of wage-labour at given product prices will be accepted, and rewarded by the marginal revenue product of each class of labour. This abstraction from the determinants of the hiring decision assumes that a monetary production economy can be treated for these purposes as a self-employed or co-operative economy, in which involuntary unemployment cannot exist. In equilibrium, the Neutral economy behaves like a self-employed economy and exhibits Say's Law, namely that an increase in production generates revenue at the given market prices and a corresponding increase in expenditure. Keynes's task is therefore to explain what determines the level of employment, if Say's Law is not assumed automatically to hold in equilibrium, and if the possibility is admitted, in circumstances of perfect competition, of a difference between the demand prices for the products of each industry and the supply prices necessary to induce firms to hire sufficient labour to employ all the labour available at a given real wage. This is the cue for *G.T.* Chapter 3, The Principle of Effective Demand.

After some 70 years, Keynes's critique of the Classical theory of unemployment remains valid, even though new forms of the Classical theory dominate both the academic and the policy agenda. Theoretical developments in terms of the agency model and asymmetric information continue to concentrate on the difference between S_U and S, as in a different way did Pigou in his works on welfare and unemployment. The focus of Anglo-American employment policy (and increasingly that of continental Europe) is on labour market flexibility and work incentives. Keynes might have approved of at least some of these policies, if understood as aimed at increasing the mobility, productivity and availability of labour, but Keynes's involuntary unemployment remains possible even if the S curve in our diagram is relabelled S_U. To the extent that modern monetary policy is effective in delivering a steady growth of aggregate demand, it may be thought of, from a Classical perspective, as successful in eliminating the disequilibrium departures from Say's Law, which used to be expressed as hoarding and dis-hoarding, while the 'natural rate of unemployment' remains a matter of (real) labour costs and obstacles to free competition. Only if one is convinced that long-term involuntary unemployment in Keynes's sense cannot exist, given stable growth of money demand and competitive conditions with flexible prices, can one disregard Keynes's *G.T.* Chapter 2 critique. Indeed such a conviction still appears at the present time, as in 1936, to be the open or tacit belief of most orthodox economists and policy makers; as a matter of scientific integrity, as Keynes puts it.

1.3   THE POINT OF EFFECTIVE DEMAND AS THE POSITION OF SYSTEM EQUILIBRIUM

The rather short *G.T.* Chapter 3 is the core of the book, and its brevity derives from the attempt to summarise a complex skein of ideas in a few words sufficient to orient the reader for what is to come. Unless its full significance is grasped, the rest will not really make sense; over the years the charge has repeatedly been made that *The General Theory* is unnecessarily obscure. The difficulty, Keynes maintains, is mainly in the hold of pre-existing ideas on the mind of the reader, and the manifold interpretations of the text are themselves conclusive evidence of the difficulty of conveying unambiguous meaning. Inevitably Keynes must in *G.T.* Chapter 3 draw upon concepts and ideas that he has not yet fully defined, which can lead readers to pursue all manner of wild geese, if they do not work through the detailed articulation of the later chapters.

There are several major preconceptions which the modern reader must put aside in approaching *G.T.* Chapter 3. First, the principle of effective demand defines a system equilibrium in which factor markets may not clear, although all goods and asset markets do so. Equilibrium is defined in terms of the decisions of employers, consumers and investors, rather than of the owners of factor services, because the owners of factors do not (in that capacity, although employers also own factors) make the hiring decisions in a monetary production economy. The principle of effective demand is a theory of short-period system equilibrium, which may converge to a long-period position, but only in the short-term sense of Keynes and not in the long-term sense of Marshall. The Classical reader must accept that it is legitimate for Keynes to define the point of effective demand, not as a position of disequilibrium in relation to the Classical general equilibrium, in which all parties make their preferred choices, but as a position of equilibrium, both in the short and the long period, in which no party has both reason and power to change their position.

For the Old Keynesian and Post Keynesian reader, particular difficulties arise in the interpretation of income, aggregate and effective demand. The Post Keynesian notes the difference between aggregate and effective demand, but both traditions treat effective demand as equilibrium income, in the sense of our fourth criterion, that short-term expectations are fulfilled.[4] This book claims, by contrast, that in *The General Theory* the level of income, whether realised or expected, bears no simple relation to effective demand, and the equilibrium level of income in the (Post) Keynesian sense is conceptually different from the point of effective demand. Income, aggregate and effective demand are three entirely distinct and separate concepts. Income is linked to current output, and effective demand is linked through future output to current employment: both are equilibrium values in the mechanical sense we have defined, but the relation between them is subtle and indirect.[5]

Picking up the earlier cue, the purpose of *G.T.* Chapter 3 is to explain how differences can exist, in circumstances of perfect competition, between the demand prices for the products of each industry and the supply prices necessary to induce firms to hire sufficient labour to employ all the labour available at a given real wage. The analytical framework is a direct extension of Marshall's supply and demand apparatus, based on perfect competition and price flexibility, for use at the macroeconomic level, or in other words, to analyse system equilibrium. The aggregate demand function (*D*) relates the total money-income expected by industry as a whole to the total level of employment (*N*), where the direction of causation runs from employment to income. The aggregate supply function (*Z*) relates the total expected money-income to the total level of employment (*N*), where the direction of causation runs from expected income to employment. The intersection of the aggregate demand and supply functions determines as equilibrium values the effective demand (let us call it *D**) and the level of employment (let us call it *N**).

This definition of effective demand can be summarised (and Keynes does so) as the solution to three equations:

$$D = f(N) = D_1(N) + D_2 = \chi(N) + D_2 \tag{1.1}$$

$$Z = Z(N) = \phi(N) \tag{1.2}$$

$$D = Z \tag{1.3}$$

where D_1 reflects the propensity to consume and is mainly a function of aggregate employment, and D_2 reflects the inducement to invest and is independent of D_1, and largely of N. These three equations define an equilibrium level of aggregate employment N^* which may be less than, or equal to, the supply of available labour.

It is then possible to plot, as an exercise in comparative statics, a further functional relation between the equilibrium values of effective demand D^* and aggregate employment N^*, such that $N^* = F(D^*)$, corresponding to different states of the independent variables of the system, namely the three psychological factors (the propensity to consume, and the schedules of the marginal efficiency of capital and of liquidity-preference) together with the quantity of money and the wage-unit. This relation between D^* and N^* (the 'employment function') is the backbone upon which the skeleton of *The General Theory* is constructed. Book II articulates the definitions and concepts anticipated in *G.T.* Chapter 3. Book III considers the propensity to consume $\chi(N)$ and Book IV the determinants of the rate of investment D_2. Book V unpacks the aggregate supply function $\phi(N)$ and considers the relationship between effective demand, money-wages and the price-level.

The principle of effective demand is part of the theory of value and, in moving from the consideration of the individual industry to industry as a whole, there is no suggestion by Keynes that supply and demand have ceased to determine the prices and quantities of each product. Apart from improvements such as the introduction of user cost to deal with the element of supply price attributable to the use of existing capital-goods, Keynes's theory of value remains essentially that of Marshall and Pigou. However, the principle of effective demand solves the problem that supply and demand in each industry depends on the output of industry as a whole, and brings precision to Marshall's claim that short-period and long-period *expected* prices, and not only the spot prices of the market period, can realistically be treated as determined by the equilibrium of supply and demand.

Most production takes time, so that today's employment will result in final output of finished goods only at a later date, at the end of the production period for each kind of good. Marshall recognises that employment is based on short-term expected prices, so that his short-period supply and demand curves must strictly be understood as relating expected, not spot market, prices to quantities. Each day firms must decide how much employment to offer today, based on their expectations of the market prices they will receive for the different kinds of final output that will emerge at the end of the various production periods. These expected prices may reflect, but are logically quite different from, the market prices which output finished today will fetch if sold in the spot market at once, and which determine the value of today's income.

Keynes's effective demand relates directly to this Marshallian conception and is the expected present value of the final output resulting from the employment that firms choose to offer. Effective demand is accordingly an expectation of income (income being the value of output, *G.T.* 63), yet the expected income represented by effective demand does not correspond to the income expected on any one future day, but is spread over a number of days. This idea is more difficult to convey than those behind the Keynesian cross (see Section **A1.3.1** for a formal approach), but Figure 1.2 illustrates the central concepts, on the assumption that there is one production method which takes five days and is started up each day, so that there are five processes running in parallel at any time, say the construction of five log-cabins. There are no producible capital-goods other than work-in-progress, which is identifiable by date of production. The gross value of output on day *t*, before allowing for the value of work-in-progress depleted (user cost), is made up from the money-value A_1^t of the output of finished goods in process 1, together with the money-value of the addition to the work-in-progress in processes 2–5, represented by $-U_j^t$. The symbol U is a reference to user cost, which is the inverse of investment (the value of capital-goods produced), so that $I_j^t = -U_j^t$. The money-value of the outstanding work-in-progress, on which the production decisions of day *t* are partly based, is represented by all the cells for days prior to *t*, which may be written $^tG^{t-1}$, where the prefix *t* means that work-in-progress brought forward is valued at market prices on day *t*. The level of income on day *t* (Y^t) is given by the shaded area, which represents the value added in completing the first log-cabin after *deducting* the value already embodied in the work-in-progress, and so the value of consumption (one log-cabin delivered to consumers); together with the addition to the value of the work-in-progress on the other four cabins, being the value of investment. By contrast, the level of effective demand on day *t* (D^{*t}) is represented by the entire grid, treating cells as positive or negative as appropriate.

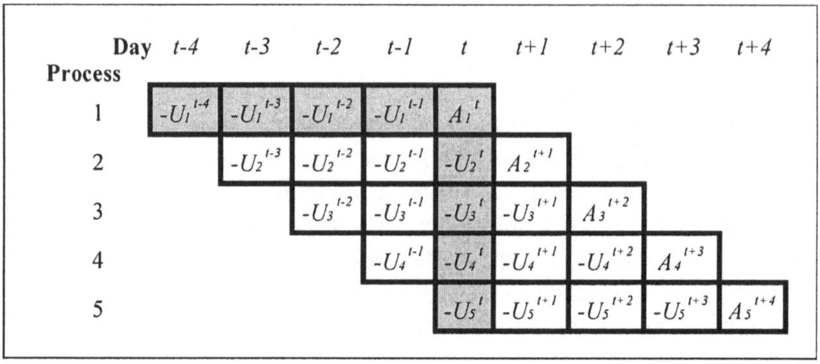

Process \ Day	t-4	t-3	t-2	t-1	t	t+1	t+2	t+3	t+4
1	$-U_1^{t-4}$	$-U_1^{t-3}$	$-U_1^{t-2}$	$-U_1^{t-1}$	A_1^t				
2		$-U_2^{t-3}$	$-U_2^{t-2}$	$-U_2^{t-1}$	$-U_2^t$	A_2^{t+1}			
3			$-U_3^{t-2}$	$-U_3^{t-1}$	$-U_3^t$	$-U_3^{t+1}$	A_3^{t+2}		
4				$-U_4^{t-1}$	$-U_4^t$	$-U_4^{t+1}$	$-U_4^{t+2}$	A_4^{t+3}	
5					$-U_5^t$	$-U_5^{t+1}$	$-U_5^{t+2}$	$-U_5^{t+3}$	A_5^{t+4}

Figure 1.2 Income and effective demand

The level of employment N^{*t} that entrepreneurs find it worthwhile to offer today depends on the expected sales values $'A_j^{t+n}$, the expected costs of future construction work $'U_j^{t+n}$, and the value of the work-in-progress to date $'G^{t-1}$. It is clear from the diagram that the shapes of Y and D^* are quite different; income and effective demand at time t coincide only in the case of process 1 in isolation, and only then if prices have not changed during the production period. The income of the factors of production hired by an entrepreneur is indeed fixed when they are employed, and we shall see that this is important in allowing Keynes to switch from employment to income as the determinant of consumption, but here we are concerned with the expectations of the entrepreneur.

Many have been puzzled by the definition of aggregate demand as 'the proceeds which *entrepreneurs* expect to receive from the employment' (G.T. 25, emphasis added see also G.T. 28–9, 89), rather than in terms of the expenditure of consumers and investors, the aggregate demand of Old Keynesian economics. Yet this paradox is already implicit in Marshall's claim that Normal prices, which are prices expected by entrepreneurs *today*, are determined by the equilibrium of supply and demand. My answer is that Keynes's entrepreneurs must be understood as fulfilling two separate functions on either side of the market, as employers of labour on the one hand, and as self-employed wholesale and retail dealers on the other (see Marshall 1920, p. 283; C.W. XIII, p. 616).[6] Employers are specialised in managing the risks of production, and dealers in managing the risks of marketing finished goods; a division of enterprise commonly observed in practice. In this construction, production takes place when an employer receives an order, usually from a dealer or another employer. Production to order implies, under perfect competition, the existence of a set of forward markets, for each good that is producible today, for delivery at the end of its production period. Competition between employers establishes a unique supply price for any given quantity, and competition between dealers, whatever their individual expectations about future spot prices, establishes a demand-price at which each dealer's demand is in equilibrium. If any speculation about future spot prices by employers is treated as a dealer activity, the equilibrium forward prices of current output become shared short-term expectations, which permits unique definition of 'the' state of expectation.[7]

The point of effective demand is a short-period equilibrium position, meaning that entrepreneurs as a whole adjust their employment of labour to maximise their expected profit with a given aggregate stock of capital-goods. Since Keynes's short period is his day, and the day is the quantum unit of time, this means that aggregate demand and supply are in static equilibrium at all times (every day); the equilibrium process of finding the point of effective demand described at *G.T.* 25 takes place on a single day, the present day. The equilibrium price of the output of each industry corresponding to *today's* aggregate employment is determined *today* as the price which clears the supply offers by employers and the demand bids by dealers in the forward market for delivery at the end of the production period. Each day employment moves directly to the equilibrium position corresponding to the set of forward prices, so that within the quantum limit of the day as the unit of time, employment is in continuous equilibrium.

The set of equilibrium expected prices that determines effective demand also corresponds to the state of short-term expectation (*G.T.* 46), so that it can properly be said that expectation determines output and employment, the title of *G.T.* Chapter 5, which we will consider further in the next chapter.

1.4 SUMMARY

The Classical theory describes an economy in which there is either no wage labour or no demand for money as a long-term store of value. The money-wage is the distinctive feature of the entrepreneur or monetary production economy, in which workers must be paid in money and not with a share of output. The Classical theory of employment can describe a self-employed or co-operative economy in which there is no decision to hire labour, only offers of labour, and involuntary unemployment in Keynes's sense is impossible.

Alternatively it describes a neutral economy in which there exists no long-term option to abstain from either consumption or investment, and involuntary unemployment is part of disequilibrium business cycle theory.

Keynes criticises the Classical theory of employment on both empirical and logical grounds. Unemployed workers do not behave as the theory predicts, and as a matter of logic, aggregate real wages cannot be determined by money-wages. In order to replace the Classical theory, Keynes extends Marshall's analysis of competitive supply and demand from partial to system equilibrium, by introducing the principle of effective demand. The position of competitive equilibrium of a monetary production economy is the point of effective demand, and does not automatically correspond to full employment. The distinctions between income, effective demand and aggregate demand are of great importance.

Keynes's Marshallian approach to system equilibrium differs from the Walrasian, not only in the comparative realism of its theory of price adjustment as a process in time, but also in the separate treatment of the factors of production. The modern Classical theory of aggregate demand, as summarised in text-book AD-AS analysis, is a new form of the quantity theory, in which the Pigou effect continues to deliver Say's Law in the long term; aggregate supply continues to be determined in the labour market by the choice between work and leisure; and money remains neutral in the long term, even if 'neo-classical' short-term disequilibrium is possible. *The General Theory* continues to be misinterpreted by Classical theory as a special case of fixed or sticky price disequilibrium, partly because of Keynes's entirely different concept of system equilibrium in terms of the decisions of employers, consumers and investors, rather than of the owners of factor services.

NOTES

1. Weitzman (1982) is a good example of such a theory, which produces a form of involuntary unemployment by dropping the Marshallian assumption of diminishing returns. Increasing returns may partly explain the existence of a wage-dependent labour force, but it is not the question addressed by Keynes.
2. See Torr (1988) for a full discussion of Keynes's use of the terms co-operative, neutral and entrepreneur economy in the drafts of *The General Theory* (*C.W.* XXIX, pp. 76–9).
3. The definition of a monetary production economy as one involving wage-labour is more specific than Pasinetti's (1997, 2001) but shares an emphasis on the decision to produce, rather than to spend, as the essence of the principle of effective demand. Pasinetti's broader 'pre-institutional' definition encompasses the possibility in a self-employed monetary economy of deficient demand such that actual production falls short of productive capacity, with involuntary under-employment rather than unemployment of wage-labour. By

contrast, a monetary production economy cannot properly be represented by a non-monetary 'corn model'.

4. Kregel (1976) associates the concept of equilibrium income (as here defined) with Keynes's stationary equilibrium (*G.T.* 293), emphasising that the disappointment of individual expectations does not affect the position of the point of effective demand based on a given 'state of general expectations' (i.e. what Keynes calls the state of expectation). He notes Keynes's rejection of the Swedish method of *ex ante* and *ex post*, but attributes this to the effect on the state of general expectations of the disappointment of individual expectations, an interaction which he associates (wrongly, if I am correct) with Keynes's shifting equilibrium (ibid.).

5. Keynes writes in the 1934 draft: 'But finally I have come to the conclusion ... to call the actual sale proceeds income and the present value of the expected sales proceeds effective demand. Thus it is the present value of the expectation of income which constitutes the effective demand; and it is the effective demand which is the incentive to the employment of equipment and labour ... the excess of income over effective demand is entrepreneur's windfall profit' (*C.W.* XIII, p. 425).

6. Employment by dealers is exogenous in the short period, and may perhaps be regarded as attached to the capital equipment and as capable of variation in the long period.

7. Chick (1983, 1992b) offers perhaps the most sophisticated development of the received idea that the equilibrium point of effective demand is discovered by the fulfilment of expectations. She (and Casarosa, 1981) distinguish between D^e, aggregate demand in terms of entrepreneurial expectations (which may be entirely individual to each firm, and thus does not permit definition of a unique and common state of expectation), and D, meaning aggregate demand in terms of expenditure. The point of effective demand is then defined by the intersection of Z and D^e, but equilibrium is not reached in terms of fulfilled expectations until (if ever) D^e coincides with D. A difficulty with her interpretation is that it leaves no room for Keynes's long-period employment, which various other authors have also found problematic (Asimakopulos, 1984, 1989; Hansson, 1985; Carvalho, 1990).

Appendix to Chapter 1

A1.2   THE CLASSICAL THEORY OF EMPLOYMENT

A1.2.1   Involuntary unemployment

Lucas (1978) rejects the distinction between voluntary and involuntary unemployment as meaningless, but justifies this claim only by conflating the two separate concepts of frictional and voluntary unemployment. In Lucas's account frictional unemployment is voluntary, because unemployed workers 'can always find *some* job at once', but do not choose to take it, because they think they can do better by job search. However, the definitions of frictional and voluntary unemployment in *The General Theory* (*G.T.* 6) are quite distinct and they are the products of Classical theory, not Keynes's. The difference between Lucas and Keynes has its roots in the difference between Walras and Marshall.

There are three separate concepts here, not two; frictional and voluntary unemployment are not interchangeable, either with each other or with Keynes's involuntary unemployment. Classical frictional unemployment can exist in the Marshallian short period, even if there is only one standard type of labour (so that under competitive conditions in particular labour markets there is no net advantage to be gained by refusing the first job that comes along), provided that costs of movement and information prevent workers being immediately matched to jobs in different labour markets. This Classical *involuntary* unemployment is explicitly recognised and differentiated from the *voluntary* unemployment resulting from the individual search for a better job or from collective bargaining, etc, by Pigou (1933, see also *G.T.* 5, n1). Frictional unemployment for Pigou and Keynes means (micro) labour rationing in particular markets in the Marshallian short period, not the refusal of available work in the hope of something better. In defining involuntary unemployment to exclude frictional unemployment (*G.T.* 15), Keynes recognises that frictional unemployment is also involuntary, but that it is simply convenient to separate what would now be called the microeconomic and macroeconomic problems. In abstracting from both frictional and voluntary unemployment, Keynes abstracts from Classical short-period unemployment arising from the heterogeneity of workers and labour markets. He treats the remaining involuntary unemployment as the (macro) rationing that workers would face even if they were all perfect substitutes in a single competitive labour market.

The Walrasian approach adopted by Lucas leaves no room for the further category of short-period involuntary frictional employment as the 'Classical' labour rationing accepted by Pigou in the Marshallian tradition of realism. *A fortiori*, if frictional employment is excluded, there can be no involuntary unemployment whatsoever, exactly as Keynes argues must be the case in Classical theory (*G.T.* 16). By contrast, Keynes's macroeconomic definition of involuntary unemployment as labour rationing in the aggregate works with standard labour units and deliberately abstracts from the microeconomic complications of frictional and voluntary unemployment, in order to isolate his point of departure from Classical theory. Lucas conversely abstracts from the very problem that Keynes seeks to address.[1]

A1.3 THE POINT OF EFFECTIVE DEMAND AS THE POSITION OF SYSTEM EQUILIBRIUM

A1.3.1 The relative prices of the principle of effective demand

Since the modern reader is likely to be accustomed to the idea that Keynes neglects competition and relative prices, it may be helpful to expand Keynes's summary in *G.T.* Chapter 3, partly anticipating *G.T.* Chapter 20 by bringing in the distribution of employment. This is in the spirit of Davidson and Smolensky, which sought to offer 'a treatment of Keynesian theory into which price theory has been directly incorporated' (1964, p. xi). Following Keynes, the verbal argument of the main text of this chapter is here expressed, in an attempt to aid exposition, in mathematical terms broadly following the nomenclature of Arrow and Hahn (1971); but non-mathematical economists should rest assured that the only mathematical concepts employed are those of simultaneous equations and (going just one step further than Keynes) the use of vector as well as scalar quantities. There are no subtle proofs.

Recall Keynes's own mathematical exposition of the point of effective demand (*G.T.* 25–9) as the solution to three equations:

$$D = f(N) = D_1(N) + D_2 = \chi(N) + D_2 \tag{A1.1}$$

$$Z = Z(N) = \phi(N) \tag{A1.2}$$

$$D = Z \tag{A1.3}$$

where D_1 reflects the propensity to consume χ and is a function of aggregate employment, and D_2 reflects the inducement to invest and is independent of D_1, and largely of N. It is convenient for the avoidance of doubt to write the solution to this system with asterisks as (D^*, N^*), although Keynes chooses not to do this, perhaps because as a strict Marshallian he treats D and N as always in equilibrium.

To make the relative prices and the supply and demand for the products of individual industries explicit, Keynes's system of equations can be expanded to

$$D = D(\mathbf{n},\bar{\mathbf{x}}) = (\mathbf{x} - \bar{\mathbf{x}})' \mathbf{p}^d \tag{A1.1a}$$

$$\mathbf{x} = \chi(\mathbf{n},\bar{\mathbf{x}},\mathbf{p}^d) + \Theta(\mathbf{p}^d, \Omega, r) \tag{A1.1b}$$

$$Z = Z(\mathbf{n}) = \mathbf{y}'\mathbf{p}^s \tag{A1.2a}$$

$$(\mathbf{y},\mathbf{p}^s) = \Phi(\mathbf{n},\bar{\mathbf{x}}) \tag{A1.2b}$$

$$D = Z \tag{A1.3}$$

where column vectors are defined as follows:

n   quantities of homogeneous labour employed today in each industry n_i

x   quantities bid by dealers today x_i for delivery of a dated good i at the end of its production period, where goods include both consumption- and capital-goods produced by an industry. Each good may have a different production period, so that output is heterogeneous both by industry and by date of delivery.

$\bar{\mathbf{x}}$ today's opening stock of producible capital-goods (Keynes abstracts from storage of consumption-goods by their definition). Capital-goods are held by rentiers and entrepreneurs of either type.

y   quantities offered by employers today y_i for delivery of a dated good
i at the end of its production period. Negative elements of **y** represent
bids by employers for the output of other firms and for existing
capital-goods (user cost).

p^d   forward bid prices corresponding to **x** in terms of numeraire, say
wage-units.

p^s   forward offer prices corresponding to **y** in terms of numeraire.

Other variables and functions are as in *The General Theory*, except that χ
and Φ are now vector functions, and D_2 is replaced by Θ, which allows
current investment to vary with the price of capital-goods. Θ takes as
parameters a given state of long-term expectation Ω and a given structure of
interest rates r (see *C.W.* XIII, p. 441). The functions χ, Φ, Θ and the
parameters $\bar{x}$, Ω, r are exogenous, while all of **n, x, y, p^d, p^s** are the
endogenous variables whose equilibrium values are represented by the
solution to the system. Although no time subscripts are shown, this is an
inter-temporal or dynamic system in the sense of Hicks (1939), since all price
and quantity variables are dated; yet it remains static in the usual sense, since
the solution represents the spot and forward values at a point in time of a
'temporary equilibrium' (Arrow and Hahn, 1971, pp. 33–40, 347).[2]
    The money-value variables D and Z are scalar (dot) products of the
relevant vectors (A1.1a, A1.2a), and similarly $N = \mathbf{e'n}$ where $\mathbf{e'}$ is the unit
row vector, the transpose of **e**. The transformation illuminates Keynes's
reasoning for working in aggregates only of money-value and labour,
meaning that his system of scalar equations (A1.1), (A1.2) and (A1.3)
captures the heterogeneity of output quite as correctly as does the vector
system, since the aggregate functions $f(N)$ and $\phi(N)$ are defined if the
vector system has a solution. That is to say, they are defined for $N = N^*$; we
get correspondences rather than functional relations away from the
equilibrium point, with a range of scalar values of D and Z for each value of
N (see Figure 1.3). The implication is that the traditional Post Keynesian Z
(line) diagram should be used only to illustrate the point of equilibrium.
    Equation (A1.1a) represents the money-value of consumption and current
investment demand, while equation (A1.2a) represents the aggregate supply
price of output. Note that both D and Z are aggregates of values at different
dates. Equation (A1.1b) shows the demand for the product of each industry
varying with (the aggregate income arising from) employment and the

ownership of the capital equipment, and on all relative prices, thus allowing for complementarity. Equation (A1.2b) shows the price and quantity offers of the product of each industry varying with employment and the capital equipment.

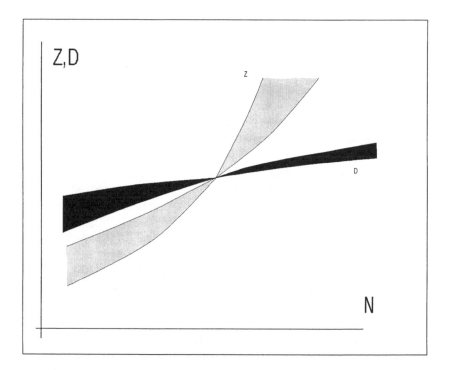

Figure 1.3 The 'true' Z diagram

If each level of effective demand is uniquely distributed (*G.T.* 282, which incidentally implies that an equilibrium solution exists), there is a functional relation, as an exercise in comparative statics, between the equilibrium values of the effective demand D^* in terms of money (or wage-units, without loss of generality) and of the level of aggregate employment N^*, corresponding to different rates of current investment and propensities to consume, in our terms, different values of the parameters Ω and r, and different functional forms χ. As Keynes emphasises (*G.T.* 286), the distribution of employment may differ at two levels of aggregate employment, or in the above terms, an equilibrium employment vector n_1^* need not be a scalar multiple of n_2^*. This functional relation between D^* and N^* (the 'employment function') is the very backbone of *The General Theory*.

A1.3.2 Keynes and Walras

The treatment of effective demand in the previous section starts to look very like a modern Walrasian general equilibrium model, and will look even more so when we reach Section A2.2.2 and have defined the state of expectation as a matrix of equilibrium forward market prices. Yet the Walrasian model differs from Keynes's enhancement of Marshall's system in a number of crucial respects. The first structural difference, apart from the major question of the process of price adjustment, is that the Walrasian demand and supply vectors include the endowment of non-producible factor services, and the future goods producible with the capital-goods producible today. Implicit in the inclusion of factor services is the idea that households have as good access to product markets as do firms, but prefer to sell factor services rather than products. In Keynes's model as expressed above, $\mathbf{x}$ and $\mathbf{y}$ refer only to the *products of industries*, including the stock of producible capital-goods carried forward each day. In the Walrasian model there is no difference between factor services and any other goods, so that $\mathbf{x}$ becomes $\breve{\mathbf{x}}$, a vector including as negative elements the supply of non-producible factor services by households ($\bar{\mathbf{x}}$ defined accordingly) and $\mathbf{y}$ becomes $\breve{\mathbf{y}}$, a vector including as negative elements the demand for factor services by firms. The corresponding price vectors are also denoted by cups. Given optimisation, the scalar products $\breve{\mathbf{x}}'\breve{\mathbf{p}}^a$ and $\breve{\mathbf{y}}'\breve{\mathbf{p}}^a$ are both zero, reflecting respectively the household budget constraint and the zero profit condition. Say's Law is implicit in the equation $\breve{\mathbf{x}}'\breve{\mathbf{p}}^a = 0$. The Walrasian excess demand function is then defined as $\mathbf{z}(\breve{\mathbf{p}}) = \breve{\mathbf{x}} - \bar{\mathbf{x}} - \breve{\mathbf{y}}$, where $\breve{\mathbf{p}} = \breve{\mathbf{p}}^s = \breve{\mathbf{p}}^a$ and various mathematical theorems identify the conditions under which the equilibrium solution $\mathbf{z}(\breve{\mathbf{p}}) = \mathbf{0}$ exists and is unique and stable. Walras' Law requires also that the scalar product $\breve{\mathbf{p}}'\mathbf{z}(\breve{\mathbf{p}}) = 0$. An excess supply of any good (including labour) is compatible with equilibrium only if its price is zero and disposal is free, which tells us nothing helpful about the involuntary unemployment of labour and other factors of production. In Keynes's system, by contrast, both the household budget constraint and the firm's supply decision depend on the amount of labour firms in aggregate decide to hire, as expressed in the employment vector $\mathbf{n}$, as well as on the endowment $\bar{\mathbf{x}}$. The endowment of non-producible factors of production is not part of Keynes's system, because their owners do not make production and employment decisions, which are reserved by definition to entrepreneurs. The existence of a wage-dependent labour force is a sufficient condition for preferring Keynes's treatment over Walras'.

The second structural difference is that in the Walrasian system there is no division between short- and long-term expectation, corresponding to employment and investment decisions; there is only inter-temporal equilibrium in what amounts to a 'fixed and reliable' state of expectation (*G.T.* 293), within stochastic limits. In formal terms this means $\breve{x}$ and $\breve{y}$ include not only the goods currently in production or producible today, but also the future goods producible in turn with the capital-goods in production or producible today. This amounts to making the state of expectation endogenous and money inessential, and postulating some nexus (*G.T.* 21) that brings the propensity to consume χ into harmony with the investment function Θ, such as a complete set of futures and insurance markets to fix the state of long-term expectation and remove the need for liquidity-preference (Arrow and Hahn, 1971, pp. 33–4). The absence of this nexus in practice is precisely the primary concern of *The General Theory*.

NOTES

1.   For a more detailed discussion of this issue see my exchange with De Vroey (Hayes, 2006a). Note that Mankiw follows Lucas in treating job-search as frictional, and Keynes's frictional unemployment as 'structural'; he notes that if labour is homogeneous, there can be no job-search unemployment (2003, p. 159).
2.   This temporary equilibrium is not, of course, the full-employment temporary equilibrium of Hicks (1939): see Hahn (1977, p. 77).

2. Definitions and Ideas

Keynes refers to Book II of *The General Theory* as a digression, since it justifies in detail the method of *G.T.* Chapter 3 rather than advancing the argument. Yet it contains ideas of great importance, which modern theory has neglected or distorted, and essential modifications to Marshall's theory of value. *The General Theory* radically alters the theory of the individual firm and industry in order to introduce a properly grounded theory of the output of industry as a whole. The three main concerns of *G.T.* Book II are the definition of appropriate measures of price and quantity for the analysis of industry as a whole (*G.T.* Chapter 4, considered in Section 2.1); the role of expectation in economic theory, which is closely related to the concept of effective demand and the meaning of the short and long periods (*G.T.* Chapter 5, considered in Section 2.2); and the definition of income, and thus of investment and saving (*G.T.* Chapters 6 and 7, considered in Section 2.3).

Keynes considers in great detail in *G.T.* Chapter 4 the meaning of the price and output of industry as a whole, when output and the existing stock of capital-goods are heterogeneous, and the indispensable need to use valid units of measure; a competitive monetary production economy cannot properly be represented by a 'competitive corn model' that assumes homogeneous output (Dutt, 1987). The six pages of *G.T.* Chapter 5, on 'expectation as determining output and employment', are of pivotal importance to Keynes's entire construction, including the formal relationship between the entrepreneurial expectations of the principle of effective demand and the expenditure decisions of consumers and investors in Books III and IV, and the role of dynamics in the convergence of production from short- to long-period equilibrium in a given state of expectation. A careful reading of *G.T.* Chapters 6 and 7 reveals an investment-saving identity but surprisingly *not* an Old Keynesian income-expenditure identity. Throughout Book II flexible relative prices are central to the argument and the Marshallian theory of value is substantially extended, and far from neglected.

2.1   DEFINING PRICE AND QUANTITY

The great virtue of Marshall's equilibrium analysis is its precision. In equilibrium, a firm fixes its level of production at the point where expected price equals expected marginal cost. Price and cost are money-values, and even if Marshall concentrates on relative rather than absolute prices, they remain money prices, and not quantities of other products. Keynes's concern is to maintain this logical precision when the causal analysis is extended from partial to system equilibrium by the definition of aggregate demand and supply functions (*D* and *Z*), and in the process he needs to plug a major hole in the Marshallian structure, regarding the treatment of the existing capital equipment.

Keynes's colourful discussion of the use of aggregate measures in historical and statistical analysis recognises the usefulness of an index, which is a scalar transformation (into a single number) of a vector (or set) of heterogeneous objects. He merely points out that vector quantities cannot in general be treated as scalars. This is not an error of which sophisticated Classical theorists are guilty, but it rumbles on in the loose but widespread use of the marginal productivity theory of distribution, and still more in modern growth theory based on the aggregate production function of the Swan-Solow model.[1] The Cambridge capital controversy (Cohen and Harcourt, 2003), to which *G.T.* Chapter 4 is a prelude, is still regarded as a minor curiosity by Classical economists.

Since there is no solution to the conundrums created by trying to treat vectors as scalars, Keynes works in only two units of measure, money-value and labour. The aggregate demand and supply functions are designed to overcome the problem that the price and output of industry as a whole, and especially the current output arising from the activity of the current period, cannot be defined as single numbers; the functions are specified in terms of money-income (which can be so defined, with the help of the concept of user cost, the value of capital-goods consumed in production) and labour.

Demand in a monetary production economy arises in terms of money-value, so that the demand for the output of each industry can properly be added together to arrive at the demand for the output of industry as a whole; but an adjustment is required to the aggregate value, to convert demand expenditure into a measure of aggregate expected money-income, by deducting user cost. Thus Keynes's aggregate demand differs from the Old Keynesian aggregate demand on two accounts, firstly because it is a measure of income, not expenditure, and secondly because it is income expected by entrepreneurs, not expenditure planned by consumers and investors.

There is no Marshallian equivalent of the aggregate demand function, but the 'aggregate supply function' can be defined equally well for a firm, an individual industry, or industry as a whole. The aggregate supply price Z_r differs from the Marshallian unit supply price p, because Z_r is a measure of expected income or 'proceeds', net of user cost. The proceeds are the total income of the entrepreneur and the factors of production taken together, which is maximised when marginal proceeds equals marginal factor cost. The aggregate supply function also differs from Marshall's supply function in relating a measure of expected income, not to output, but to employment, which is a close proxy for output and can realistically be treated as homogeneous in the short term where output cannot. ▶ **A2.1.1** The importance of the aggregate supply function is that it can properly be defined for industry as a whole as the sum of its parts: the expected income of each firm being a money-value, which can be added to those of other firms to give aggregate expected income, and the employment of each firm being added together to give aggregate employment. ▶ **A2.1.2**

Keynes's concepts of aggregate demand and supply complement and do not replace Marshall's analysis of industry demand, and supply by individual firms. Keynes's entrepreneurs still set their individual output and employment in Marshallian fashion, in accordance with their expectation of the price in their own industry. The aggregate supply function for a single industry or firm, $Z_r = \phi_r(N_r)$, stands in a formal relation to the ordinary Marshallian supply curve based on a measure of physical output (*G.T.* 44). In this case, a short-period production function $O_r = \psi_r(N_r)$ can be used to express the ordinary supply curve in terms of the aggregate supply function $\phi_r(N_r)$. Since the aggregate supply price Z is the required proceeds, net of user cost, the supply price of homogeneous output equals the value of proceeds plus user cost per unit of output,

$$p = \frac{\phi_r(N_r) + U_r(N_r)}{\psi_r(N_r)}$$

Note that this is not a marginal condition but a transformation mapping Z_r onto p.

The link between the ordinary Marshallian supply curve and Keynes's aggregate supply function, as expressed clearly in this equation, is the much neglected concept of user cost. This is the value of capital-goods that firms physically *consume in production*, although Keynes employs the term 'use' rather than 'consume' when referring to firms and production, in order to reserve 'consumption' for the demand function. User cost is a measure of value and not a physical quantity and, since it relates to the decision to produce, it is voluntary, in contrast with the expected and unexpected involuntary depreciation of capital-goods defined respectively as supplementary cost and windfall losses. User cost is the opportunity cost of using up a capital-good in production, rather than holding it purely as an investment asset. ▶ **A2.1.3** User cost, the value of capital-goods consumed as a result of the physical act of production, is the direct opposite of investment, the value of capital-goods physically produced, and the manner in which user cost enters into the employment decision bears a close relation to the investment decision, since both involve the consideration of the prospective yield of an asset. At the aggregate level, user cost excludes the sale of assets, just as investment excludes the purchase of existing assets. The neglect of user cost has led to the view that income can be defined equally well either as the value of current output (*G.T.* 63), or as the value of expenditure, with serious consequences to be discussed later in this chapter.

The neglect of user cost in Marshallian theory involves the tacit assumption that marginal user cost is zero, or that the deterioration of the capital-goods is made good by immediate replacement. Implicit in this is that metaphysical entity, Capital, which commercial practice requires to be maintained, and which Classical theory treats as possessing an homogeneous existence independent of its embodiment in real assets.[2] Keynes points out that no-one would regard the user cost of a ton of copper as zero, and there is no difference of economic principle between raw materials and machinery which wears out with use. It is therefore of vital importance to develop the theory of value to take account of the consumption of the existing stock of capital-goods. User cost is also necessary to link the microeconomic theory of supply price to a macroeconomic theory of aggregate supply which is independent of the structure of industry and the degree of integration of production. Without such a link, Marshallian theory becomes lost in 'the whole pack of perplexities which attend the definition of income' (*G.T.* 67).

The concept of user cost allows Keynes not only to complete the Marshallian theory of supply price, but to provide the foundation for an unambiguous definition of income. Attempts to define income without a clear conception of user cost founder on the problem of identifying how much of a firm's sales in any given period (*A*) represents newly produced output and how much is in some sense the value of output brought forward from previous periods; in other words, how to define *current* output. Indeed this corresponds directly to the opposite problem, of the status of output which is not sold, but carried forward to the next period. Fisher (1930) goes so far as to exclude investment from the definition of income, so that investment is merely a cost of production of future income (= consumption), and Keynes's separate controversies with Hawtrey and Robertson are referred to in *The General Theory* itself.

Both total and marginal user cost play key roles in Keynes's argument. In daily equilibrium, firms set production and employment at the level where the expected unit price of finished output, for delivery at the end of the production period, equals the expected marginal prime cost, defined as the sum of marginal factor cost and marginal user cost over the production period. User cost involves long-term as well as short-term expectation if the life of the capital-goods extends beyond the period of production. User cost is therefore an aspect of the discussion of the valuation of capital-goods which plays so great a role in *G.T.* Book IV. It is a crucial part of Keynes's integration of macroeconomic and microeconomic analysis, and an important element of the incorporation of expectation into both the principle of effective demand and the theory of the supply price of an individual firm.

User cost, then, is the inverse of investment. The decision to consume a capital-good in production involves the same considerations as the decision to produce a new one, and as the decision of the form in which to store value and relates, as we shall see in Chapter 4 of this book, to the discussion of the nature of money in *G.T.* Chapter 17. There is a remarkable unity in Keynes's conception of the relationship between time and capital-goods; he refers to capital-goods, in the context of all three types of decision, as the bridge between the present and the future.

2.2 EXPECTATION AS DETERMINING OUTPUT AND EMPLOYMENT

The brevity of *G.T.* Chapter 5 has proven to be a major obstacle to the understanding of *The General Theory*, and the source of much confusion. The Chapter contains the elements of Keynes's treatment of time, upon which depends the rest of the theoretical structure, including his concepts of equilibrium, the state of expectation, effective demand and income. This chapter is therefore rather important. The interpretative confusion runs very deep and centres on the 'Swedish' (*ex ante*, *ex post*) concept of equilibrium income in the sense of the fourth criterion of the Prologue of this book, the fulfilment of expectations, as opposed to the idea that income at any time is an equilibrium value in the mechanical sense here ascribed to Keynes. The importance of this difference between Keynes and the 'Swedes' (here including Hicks) will become clear in this and the next section.

In the standard text-book exposition, the point of effective demand is the intersection of the Keynesian cross, the level of aggregate output where entrepreneurial expectations of income (*ex ante*) are fulfilled (*ex post*). On this understanding of the point of effective demand, as a position of equilibrium in the sense of our fourth criterion, there is no difference at the point of equilibrium between income (both expected and realised) and effective demand. Since price changes are abstracted from, effective demand and aggregate demand (in the expenditure sense) are also equivalent in equilibrium. These Old Keynesian propositions are captured by an equilibrium condition

$$Y^* \equiv D^* = D \tag{2.1}$$

where Y^* means equilibrium income (in the sense of the fourth criterion, the fulfilment of expectations), D^* effective demand, and D aggregate demand.

In the Post Keynesian tradition, the point of effective demand D^* and the aggregate demand function D are more clearly distinguished from each other and Keynes's aggregate supply function (Z) is explicitly restored. The effective demand D^* is now given by the intersection of the Z and D curves and once again, in equilibrium, income corresponds to effective demand. So we can now write the equilibrium condition as:

$$Y^* \equiv D^* = D = Z \tag{2.2}$$

The Post Keynesian treatment identifies that at the point of effective demand individual firms are maximising expected profits, since Z is a transformation of the set of Marshallian supply prices on which aggregate output is based. In both Old Keynesian and Post Keynesian treatments, it is possible for entrepreneurial expectations of income to depart from their equilibrium values, so that realised income does not equal expected income, and $Y \neq Y^*$. In a dynamic process involving the multiplier, firms adjust output and employment over time so that expected income converges on its equilibrium value $Y^* \equiv D^*$. It is important to note that in these treatments the levels of expected income and of employment at any time can be *disequilibrium* values.

Chapter 1 of this book has argued, by contrast, that Keynes treats the system as at all times in equilibrium at the point of effective demand. I must emphasise once again that this means equilibrium in the mechanical sense (based on the first two criteria), not in the sense of the fourth criterion (the fulfilment of expectations) that underpins the concept of equilibrium income employed by received Old Keynesian and Post Keynesian economics, let alone the third criterion of Walrasian general equilibrium. As a corollary, I am arguing that the level of employment (but not the labour market) is for theoretical purposes treated by Keynes as at all times in equilibrium in the mechanical sense. The level of employment is determined by the state of expectation through effective demand, and strictly, it is not relevant to employment whether expectations are fulfilled. The level of aggregate income Y, whether realised or expected to arise on any given day, bears no simple relation to the aggregate effective demand on that or any earlier day, and the equilibrium level of income Y^* (defined on the fourth criterion) is conceptually quite different from the point of effective demand D^*, and indeed in my view plays no role in *The General Theory*. In the earlier shorthand this may be written as the proposition

$$Y \neq Y^* \neq D^* = D = Z \qquad (2.3)$$

This means that while it is conceivable, if unlikely, that the income realised from the sale of finished output could equal the expected value that originally prompted its production, such coincidence does not define the equilibrium level of employment. Employment is *always* in equilibrium (in our mechanical sense) corresponding to D^*, and in general the value of D^* need correspond neither to realised income Y nor to a level of income Y^* corresponding in some sense to the fulfilment of expectations. Indeed, the received (fourth criterion) concept of equilibrium income Y^* does not in fact stand up to intense scrutiny. It implies that a comparison is possible between aggregate expected and actual income on a given day leading to a stabilising feedback process. However, actual income reflects decisions to produce finished output at a variety of different dates in the past, as well as windfall profits on work-in-progress at many different stages of completion. Similarly, the expectation of income due to arise on any given day may have been subject to as many revisions as there are days in the production period. Furthermore, even in the absence of changes in the state of expectation, the sale price of today's finished output relates not to effective demand on any single day, but to a series of past values of expected income over the production period. Income and effective demand have, in general, different dimensions in time (see Figure 1.2 on page 58). The concept of equilibrium income can be made meaningful, if output is assumed to be homogeneous and if the day is defined as the production period, but this is clearly not Keynes's method.

The state of short-term expectation that governs decisions to produce consumption- and capital-goods can be represented numerically by the set of equilibrium expected prices or 'rational expectations' corresponding to effective demand. If, as I have argued, Keynes's equilibrium short period is equal to his calendar day, and the day is the quantum unit of time, the state of expectation and its corresponding level of effective demand defines an equilibrium level of employment at any time. Provided that entrepreneurs maximise expected profits, the daily level of employment will always be in short-period equilibrium in the mechanical sense. The state of expectation and effective demand may change from day to day, and the level of employment may change with them but will remain in short-period equilibrium. Nevertheless, a further aspect of production time must be taken into account, that the aggregate capital equipment cannot be adjusted (through the production of new goods or the using up of old goods in production) as quickly as the state of expectation and employment may change. It is necessary to introduce a long period, in the technical sense of the time required to adjust the aggregate stock of capital-goods, as well as aggregate employment, to a new state of expectation.

Keynes denotes as the 'long-period employment' the equilibrium level and distribution of employment corresponding to a given state of expectation once the disequilibrium fluctuations, arising from the change that led to the current state of expectation, have fully worked themselves out (*G.T.* 48). ▶ **A2.2.1** The source of the disequilibrium fluctuations described by Keynes is emphatically not expectational error but production time, which introduces lags into the dynamic process of convergence of employment on its long-period position (*G.T.* 47–51, 122–4, 287–8). Although the state of expectation will most likely change before employment has reached its long-period position (*G.T.* 50), on any given day employment will be both in short-period equilibrium and on a traverse or convergence path towards the long-period position. ▶ **A2.2.2**

Thus the title of *G.T.* Chapter 5 should be taken literally, that the state of expectation determines output and employment. On this reading, it is not relevant to today's decision whether today's state of expectation is correct; if tomorrow's market prices lead to a change in the state of expectation, employment will change accordingly, yet tomorrow's state of expectation is strictly independent of today's and of the day after tomorrow's. Furthermore, although expectational error is one cause for revision in the state of expectation, it is neither the only one, nor necessarily the most important. The state of short-term expectation that determines effective demand depends partly on the state of long-term expectation, itself a function of the state of confidence, on the state of liquidity-preference, and on the propensity to consume. All three of these major psychological independent variables are capable of unpredictable shifts, leading to the disappointment of previous expectations.

In a key passage Keynes writes:

> Express reference to current long-term expectations can seldom be avoided. But it will often be safe to omit express reference to *short-term* expectation, in view of the fact that in practice the process of revision of short-term expectation is a gradual and continuous one, carried on largely in the light of realised results; so that expected and realised results run into and overlap one another in their influence. For, although output and employment are determined by the producer's short-term expectations and not by past results, the most recent results usually play a predominant part in determining what these expectations are. (*G.T.* 50–51)

These statements have usually been read, in line with a definition of employment equilibrium as a point where expectations are fulfilled, as evidence of an assumption in *G.T.* Chapter 3 that short-term expectations are so fulfilled. The present argument takes the passage more literally as meaning, not that current expectations correctly anticipate future results, but that past results heavily influence current expectations; so that if change is at a gradual pace, relative to the shortness of the day, expectations often will be fulfilled, or 'overlap' with realised results. This passage is part of Keynes's concern throughout *The General Theory* to reflect the empirical stability of the price system, and remains consistent with his statement that 'employment is determined *solely* by effective demand' (*C.W.* XIV, p. 180).

This passage also gives explicit notice of Keynes's switch in focus, in discussing aggregate demand, from entrepreneurial expectations in *G.T.* Book II to the expenditure decisions of *G.T.* Books III and IV. This point is of great importance and requires emphasis. The change also corresponds to a switch to discussing income rather than effective demand, which returns to prominence only from *G.T.* Chapter 18 onwards. The coupling between expectations and expenditure, between effective demand and income, cannot be made formally exact; by the time final output is delivered, the state of expectation will almost certainly have changed as a result of changing views about the long-term future. Nevertheless it is realistic to link today's aggregate demand (i.e. dealers' expectations) with today's expenditure (as opposed to employment), because today's consumption depends mainly on the income of the factors of production, which is fixed when they are employed and equals the effective demand for their services (ibid.); while the consumption of entrepreneurs (especially corporations and their shareholders) out of profits is likely to be insensitive to minor differences between expected and realised income. The theoretical link of *G.T.* Chapter 3 between employment (as opposed to income) and aggregate demand is thereby preserved.[3]

Like *G.T.* Chapter 3, this discussion of expectation and effective demand has made no mention of the multiplier, which plays such an important role in the Old Keynesian interpretation. The multiplier quite rightly turns up only in *G.T.* Chapter 10, as a market-period equilibrium relationship between the realised values of consumption and current investment output, a determinant of the level of income, which may thereby affect the state of expectation, but is not itself a causal element of the principle of effective demand. Indeed, as we shall see in the next section, it is realised income *Y* (without the asterisk) which is to be understood as an equilibrium value in itself, without any reference to the concept of expected income. Income and the equilibrium spot prices of current output are determined by expenditure, in which the multiplier relationship plays a role; effective demand and the equilibrium forward prices on which employment is based are determined by expectation, where we have analytically separated the expectations of employers and dealers in order to show how expected forward prices can be regarded as equilibrium prices. These two matters, expenditure and expectation, are conceptually quite different: the link through factor income to the revision of expectations in the light of realised results is a loose coupling, which allows for the revision of expectation for many reasons other than expectational error. Equilibrium of any sort is possible only in a given state of expectation, and Keynes's method both permits the use of equilibrium analysis and allows for a continually shifting state of expectation. ▶ **A2.2.3**

2.3   THE INVESTMENT-SAVING IDENTITY

Keynes's definition of user cost unlocks the 'perplexities which attend' (*G.T.* 67) the definitions of aggregate income, investment and saving as well as completing the Marshallian theory of supply price. It is most ironic, given the importance and amount of attention Keynes gives to the definition of income, that Hansen should state 'The section on Income is of no great importance for an understanding of *The General Theory* and may quite well be omitted if the student so wishes' (1953, p. 54). On the contrary, it is of paramount importance to recognise that Keynes defines *income* as the market value of output and not the value of expenditure, which explains the attention Keynes gives to *user cost*, the value of the capital-goods consumed by firms in the production of output. Keynes approaches income from the supply as well as the demand side, in terms of production, a perspective thoroughly obscured by the income-expenditure model. As Colander (2001) reminds us, following Chick (1983), Keynes could just as well have called *G.T.* Chapter 3 'the principle of effective *supply*'.

In order to appreciate Keynes's definition of income, it may be wise to use *investment* (unqualified) solely to refer to the production of new capital-goods, where a 'capital-good' means any good held by a firm (even if it is held for sale to a consumer, e.g. stocks of finished consumption-goods). What Keynes initially defines as *current investment* (*G.T.* 62), but then immediately for convenience calls simply 'investment', is the value of newly produced capital-goods less user cost, the value of capital-goods used up in production. *Net investment* means the increase in the value of the stock of capital-goods after further deducting supplementary cost, the expected depreciation of capital-goods independent of their use in production. Although the value of *investment* (or gross capital formation) can be aggregated easily since each new capital-good can be identified, both *current* and *net investment* require consolidation, since at the individual level they include purchases of capital-goods (both new and old) less disposals of value whether by sale, use in production or depreciation. Throughout the discussion income and current investment are always money-values, and consumption is defined *ipso facto* as sales other than to entrepreneurs (*G.T.* 62). Keynes deliberately side-steps the problems of defining real income and of consumer durables: when he does refer to *real* income ('in some sense', *G.T.* 91) he means money-income deflated by the wage-unit, not Pigou's concept of the national dividend: he deals in money-income and not the utilities yielded by consumption-goods, because the level of employment in a monetary economy is in the first instance the result of entrepreneurs maximising their money-income and not directly of households choosing a preferred allocation of their productive resources.

Using Keynes's symbols to denote aggregate values, A represents total sales by firms and A_1 total sales between firms, so that the aggregate value of sales to consumers (C) is $A - A_1$. Aggregate current investment (I) is sales between firms less user cost, $A_1 - U$. Entrepreneurial income or profit (P) is total sales less total prime cost, $P = A - F - U$, where factor cost is F; aggregate income (Y) is the total income of factors and entrepreneurs $Y = F + P = A - U$. Therefore income equals consumption plus current investment $Y = C + I = A - A_1 + A_1 - U$. If saving (Keynes uses no symbol, perhaps pointedly, but call it S) is defined as equal to income less consumption, we have $S \equiv A - U - (A - A_1) = A_1 - U = I$. Net income, net investment and net saving present no subtle problem of definition, being arrived at in each case simply by the further deduction of supplementary cost V. Income is the concept relevant to production, and net income the one relevant to consumption.

Aggregate current investment and saving are identically equal, as a matter of double-entry book-keeping: saving is simply the accounting record of investment.[4] Keynes's 'investment-saving identity' is *not* the Old Keynesian 'income-expenditure identity', since current investment reflects both expenditure A_1 and user cost U, which involves no expenditure. There is only an income-expenditure identity on one of two conditions. Either user cost must be excluded by incorrectly including it with supplementary cost and treating the depreciation of capital-goods as relevant only to net income; or alternatively, user cost must be treated as (negative) expenditure even though it involves no sale. There is always of course a sales-expenditure identity $Y + U = A \equiv (A - A_1) + A_1 = C + I + U$. This may seem a fine semantic point – I am not suggesting the national accounts do not balance – but it draws out the difference between the definitions of income by Keynes and by the 'Keynesians': the latter define income as consolidated aggregate sales (treating the consumption of stocks as a sale or negative purchase, but neglecting the user cost of fixed capital equipment) or Gross Domestic Product. ▶ **A2.3.2**

The whole of *G.T.* Chapter 7 addresses the attempts of various authors (including Keynes himself in *A Treatise on Money*, Vol. 1, *C.W.* V) to escape the remorseless book-keeper's logic of the investment-saving identity. The most important problem has proven to be the perception of a relationship between saving and changes in the quantity of money and debts, represented by loanable funds theory, which seeks to maintain the Classical linkage between the rate of interest and the rate of saving. The refusal of this controversy to die reflects its importance to neo-classical theory (in Keynes's strict sense, *G.T.* 177), as the version of Say's Law required if money is to be neutral in the long term. Robertson's version (Hicks has another) holds that saving is a form of cash flow (i.e. income realised in cash but not spent), and since investment at some point requires finance in cash, it seems reasonable to regard saving as part of the problem of finance. The rate of interest then clears the market for the demand and supply of finance, the demand for finance being driven by expected investment returns, the supply of finance being determined mainly by decisions to prefer future to present consumption, in the absence of monetary disturbances.[5]

The problem with Robertson's version of loanable funds theory can be understood in terms of accounting concepts, as the confusion between income and cash flow, and between the two sides of a balance sheet; between a reserve in the sense of a liability, such as a profit and loss account, and a reserve in the sense of an asset, usually a money balance. A cash flow statement reconciles the gross changes between two balance sheets (being statements of assets and liabilities at two different points in time), in terms of the acquisition and disposal of assets and liabilities on both income and capital account. An income or profit and loss statement over a period of time bears no simple relation to the balance sheets at each end of the period.

▶ **A2.3.3**

Aggregate saving is never independent of aggregate current investment, while saving and money (Keynes's 'cash' or 'finance') always appear on opposite sides of a balance sheet (a bank deposit is money only for the creditor, not for the issuing bank). Like chalk and cheese, saving and money look very similar, but cannot legitimately be inter-changed or combined, as implied by the loanable funds equation $S + \Delta M = I + \Delta H$; saving, despite common usage, is not a 'loanable fund' at all. To demonstrate this more clearly requires further consideration of the nature of income.

A sale occurs when an agreement to exchange one good (including a service, by a firm or a factor of production) for another, usually a sum of money, is fulfilled at the agreed price. If the good sold already exists, this is an agreement for sale on capital account and does not create income. If the good sold is to be newly produced, this agreement is directly or indirectly an order for factor services, and a prelude to income. Income itself arises (is 'recognised' in accounting terminology) when the newly produced good or service is *delivered*. Whether on income or capital account, the sale is recorded as taking place on delivery.

The economic value of a good is what it can be sold for, and is independent of whether or not a sale actually takes place. For the purposes of causal analysis of production and employment decisions, income must be treated as arising on the production of a new good (delivery within the firm from one workshop to another, if you like; but delivery is not *per se* a sale, as required if user cost is to be treated in terms of expenditure); although accounting standards recognise income only when the new good is delivered to a third party under a sale agreement. For economic purposes, on the assumption of perfect competition, income arises at current market prices when a good is newly produced, as a matter of temporary market-period equilibrium, whether it is taken into the firm's own stock (negative user cost, or investment) or delivered to a customer (a sale). A sale creates a debt, an obligation of the buyer to pay the sum of money specified in the sale agreement, which the buyer must settle on delivery or at some agreed future date after a period of trade credit. The sale has been made, whether or not the debt has been settled. Indeed if the buyer defaults on the debt, the accountants treat this as a 'bad debt' rather than a cancellation of the sale which created the debt.

Corresponding to the debt from the customer or the newly produced asset held in stock, on one side of the balance sheet, there has to be a balancing increase in liability on the other side of the balance sheet, where liability includes net worth: this increase in liability is saving. In the case of factors, there is no difference of principle: I may receive my salary monthly, but I earn income every day that I go to work (as I soon learn if I leave a job half-way through the month, and find my final pay cheque reduced from the previous monthly amount). Every day that I turn up for work creates a debt from my employer, which is settled every month. At the same time I am incurring expense, perhaps on credit (such as utility bills), and my saving in any period presents the difference between income earned and expense accrued – irrespective of whether it is pay-day or whether I pay my bills. Conversely, many a small business goes broke with expanding sales and a full order-book, not for a lack of retained profit (saving) but because of a lack of cash. You cannot meet a payroll from the profit and loss account.[6]

Aggregate income is the value of newly produced goods delivered by firms (A), less the value of capital-goods lost through use in production (U). Saving is the value of newly produced goods delivered by firms (A), less the value of goods lost through use in production (U) and delivered to consumers (C). Aggregate current investment is the value of newly produced goods delivered to firms $(A-C)$, including their own 'internal deliveries', less the value of goods lost through use in production (U), and amounts to the same as saving $(A-C-U)$. Cash flows arise only on settlement of any debts created by these deliveries, and are in logic an entirely separate matter. The necessary equality between aggregate saving and current investment stems from the physical acts of delivery and use of capital-goods, and there is no means by which a change in the terms on which cash is available to pay debts can alter the balance between saving and investment. Of course, a change in the price of finance may alter decisions to enter as a buyer into particular agreements for sale, or the decisions of firms to carry out production at a certain level. *G.T.* Books III and IV address in detail the influence of the rate of interest on the propensity to consume and the inducement for an investor to commit to the production of a new capital-good. This does not alter the fact that there is quite simply no direct connection between aggregate expenditure, cash flow and income. All three have quite distinct and separate meanings.

As Keynes puts it, far more succinctly,

> [N]o-one can save without acquiring an asset, whether it be cash or a debt or capital-goods; and no one can acquire an asset which he did not previously possess, unless *either* an asset of equal value is newly produced *or* someone else parts with an asset of that value which he previously had. In the first alternative there is a corresponding new investment: in the second alternative someone else must be dis-saving an equal sum. For his loss of wealth must be due to his consumption exceeding his income ... (*G.T.* 81–2)

The significance of the aggregate investment-saving value identity is far-reaching. In *G.T.* Chapter 2 Keynes identified, as central to the Neutral economy of the Classical theory of employment, the idea that the interest rate is a price which keeps aggregate saving from income in equilibrium with the aggregate current investment of income. In *G.T.* Chapter 6 by careful definition of terms he has identified that saving has no independent existence and is always purely a reflection of current investment. Saving and current investment are kept in equilibrium by movements, not of the rate of interest, but in the level of income. If the markets for consumption-goods and capital-goods in each industry are in competitive equilibrium, there is no sense in which saving and current investment can be equal but not in equilibrium: the existence of a market value for output is a sufficient condition for equilibrium at any time (*G.T.* 64).

Hicks developed a more subtle form of the loanable funds doctrine using the Swedish concepts of *ex ante* and *ex post*, based on a Walrasian concept of equilibrium over time, with clearing factor markets and a constant state of expectation. Our previous discussion has already indicated why this is not an appropriate foundation for a theory of the monetary production economy.
▶ A2.3.4

2.4 SUMMARY

Book II of *The General Theory* addresses fundamental issues which modern theorists have continued to debate, apparently without realising that Keynes has already resolved them. Most seriously, the Classical microeconomic foundations of macroeconomics are already there in *The General Theory* itself.

Macroeconomic theory is not valid without recognition of the heterogeneous nature of output, prices and capital-goods. Keynes devises a technique for causal macroeconomic analysis in terms of money-value and labour alone, since this is all that entrepreneurs need in practice to make employment and investment decisions. This allows him to propose a determinate theory of aggregate employment without compromising, and indeed by enhancing, the theory of the supply price of the individual profit-maximising firm.

Far from neglecting the theory of value, Keynes extends Marshall's analysis from partial to system equilibrium, in part through introducing the concepts of user cost and the aggregate supply function. User cost is the inverse of investment, and an integral part of Keynes's conception of durable assets as a bridge between the present and the future. Consumption by firms is integrated into both microeconomic and macroeconomic analysis alongside investment and personal consumption, thus rectifying a major omission from the theory of value. The aggregate supply function is shown to be a more general form of the Marshallian supply curve by dispensing with the requirement to specify output in physical terms, and it provides an analytical tool which can be used equally at the level of the firm, the industry or the economy as a whole.

The rigorous definition of income and current investment as the market value of output, not expenditure, is the foundation stone both of the principle of effective demand and of the refutation of the Loanable Funds version of Say's Law. The aggregate investment-saving identity is a matter of book-keeping logic that leaves no room or need for the rate of interest to clear a market for saving and investment. Saving is a residual in the aggregate income account, and has absolutely nothing to do with finance, which is a matter of balance sheets.

Behind the whole discussion is the recognition that production by any process that takes time must be based on expectations of future prices and so on expected income. The employment decision, the primary concern of *The General Theory*, depends on the short-term expected prices of consumption- and capital-goods. Disappointment of past expectations does not affect output and employment except insofar as it affects current expectations, and is of secondary importance. The state of expectation and effective demand may change from day to day for reasons other than disappointment, and the level of employment may change with them, but will remain in short-period equilibrium. Nevertheless, a further aspect of production time must be taken into account, that the capital equipment cannot be adjusted as quickly as the state of expectation and employment may change. This leads, on the hypothesis of a constant state of expectation over the period of production, to a dynamic process of convergence of employment to a long-period equilibrium position.

Keynes stated that he wrote *G.T.* Book II 'to clear up certain perplexities which have no peculiar or exclusive relevance to the problems which it is our special purpose to examine ... so that I could not express myself conveniently until I had found some solutions for them' (*G.T.* 37). The underpinning of current macroeconomic theory is a simplified dynamic inter-temporal general equilibrium model based on the Swan-Solow model, with a constant state of expectation, homogeneous output and capital, and saving brought into equilibrium with current investment by the rate of interest. The importance of the subtle problems raised by Keynes in these chapters, and of the solutions offered by him, has simply not been recognised.

NOTES

1. See Mankiw (2003), Chapter 3 and the whole of Part III. A recent restatement of the econometric case against the use of 'empirical' aggregate production functions is set out in McCombie (2001a, 2001b). Contra Mankiw (2003, p. 73), the evidence of stable income shares does not provide empirical support for the Cobb-Douglas production function.
2. Pigou uses the analogy of a lake, into which flow streams of new capital-goods, which flow out again as consumption in one form or another (1932, pp. 43–9). Other metaphors have included jelly, putty, ectoplasm and leets.
3. Amadeo (1989) interprets this switch as Keynes almost dropping 'supply' in moving from *A Treatise on Money* to a final 'expenditure' version of the principle of effective demand. On the present reading, the principle of effective demand relates exclusively to 'supply', meaning the production decisions of entrepreneurs in short-period equilibrium, but after Chapter 5 of *The General Theory*, Keynes assumes that the short-term expectations behind those production decisions are based mainly on realised results, as determined by the 'expenditure' decisions of consumers and investors in market-period equilibrium.
4. I owe this turn of phrase to Basil Moore.
5. For a recent critical review of the loanable funds controversy, see Bibow (2000). The continued importance of loanable funds thinking cannot be over-emphasised: the orthodox debate over policies for economic growth, based on the full-employment Solow growth model, concentrates on private and public thrift where it should be addressing the finance of investment (see the Golden Rule argument in Mankiw, 2003, pp. 192–9).
6. Boulding writes 'The income and outgo concepts, which are essentially value aggregates of additions to and subtractions from the total stock of assets, must be distinguished clearly from the receipts and expenditure concepts. Receipts consist of the additions to liquid assets or money. Expenditures consist of the subtractions from liquid assets or money. It is hardly any exaggeration to say that the failure to distinguish clearly between receipts and income on the one hand, and between expenditures and consumption on the other, has been the source of most of the confusion in economics, and, especially in macroeconomics, in the past generation' (quoted in Wray, 1990). If 'outgo' is understood as expense and 'expenditure' as payments, in line with current accounting conventions, this passage makes the point exactly. Boulding also uses the example of the earnings accrued by a worker (Wray, ibid., pp. 3–4).

Appendix to Chapter 2

A2.1 DEFINING PRICE AND QUANTITY

A2.1.1 Homogeneous labour

There can be no dispute that money-value is a scalar measure of a homogeneous quantity, but is Keynes correct to assert that heterogeneous labour can be reduced to units of standard labour, of which the price is the wage-unit? His argument falls into two parts. First, if workers are paid in proportion to their efficiency, workers who command higher wages can be treated as providing proportionally more labour. Secondly, if workers of varying efficiency receive the same wage, provided that workers are hired in descending order of efficiency, their heterogeneity can be treated as part of the diminishing returns associated with working with the capital equipment. He defines a quantity of standard labour as the scalar product of heterogeneous labour and relative wage vectors, with the residual heterogeneity of labour in terms of efficiency subsumed into the capital equipment (*G.T.* 41–2).

Even if labour is treated as homogeneous for an individual firm, there remain possible (as noted in Chapter 1 of this book) different vectors of the distribution of aggregate employment across industries **n** with the same scalar value *N*. Keynes is very much aware of this and addresses the implications in footnotes (*G.T.* 43) and in *G.T.* Chapter 20.

A2.1.2 Keynes and Sraffa

It does not appear to have been recognised that Keynes's aggregate supply function addresses the critique of the ordinary supply curve made by Sraffa (1926), which was a prelude to the developments of the theory of monopolistic competition and of a non-marginalist theory of value (Sraffa, 1960). Sraffa argued that the 'law of diminishing returns', upon which the supply curve is based, arises from an inappropriate extension of the Ricardian theory of rent, from land to factors of production in general. Sraffa noted that diminishing returns could properly be expected in the case of land, and of agriculture as the industry in which most land is employed. Yet in fact there are very few industries other than agriculture, such as the extractive, which employ the whole of a factor of production, and still fewer in which the supply of the factor cannot be increased over time by production ('the production of commodities by means of commodities'). A further implication of diminishing returns is that the independence of supply and demand is undermined, since an increase in the price of a factor used by one industry is transmitted to others using the same factor, and this will in general affect the demand for the product of the first industry.

Keynes overcomes Sraffa's critique by two devices. Firstly, the aggregate supply function is defined at a point in time, Keynes's short-period day, thereby avoiding the problem of changes in the aggregate capital equipment. Secondly, there is one major 'class of commodities in the production of which the whole of a factor of production is employed', namely the output of industry as a whole. It is natural to think of the aggregate supply function being built up, from the bottom up as it were, as the summation of the aggregate supply functions of individual firms: based upon the 'microfoundations' of industry supply and demand. This would be vulnerable to Sraffa's critique, since the supply curve of each firm is not in general independent of the others'. By contrast, Keynes's method runs the other way, from the top down, from the aggregate supply function of industry as a whole to those of individual industries: truly the 'macrofoundation of microeconomics'. The inter-dependence of supply and demand in individual industries is addressed by Keynes under the heading of the employment function, considered further in Chapter 5 of this book.

On any given day, the aggregate capital equipment is given, and its distribution among entrepreneurs depends on their expectations of prospective yield and on the degree of competition. The equilibrium distribution of the capital equipment may be taken as decided simultaneously with the employment of other factors, including labour. In other words, the decision by an individual entrepreneur to employ a particular combination of factors is a single complex decision that takes into account both the expectation of the price of final output in that industry and the state of expectation embodied in the value of the capital equipment as determined in competitive markets. Thus individual entrepreneurs may vary their individual capital equipment as well as their employment of labour and other factors in deciding to vary their output, but for entrepreneurs as a whole, the capital equipment is fixed. A physical aggregate supply function for industry as a whole can thus be arrived at, defining the aggregate expected income required to warrant the aggregate employment of different quantities of labour, based on the given capital equipment (provided that each quantity of aggregate employment is associated with a unique distribution of employment, so that a function can be defined). By analogy with the case of land, the aggregate supply function for industry as a whole will, by Sraffa's argument, be subject to diminishing returns in the application of labour with a given capital equipment, although the empirical evidence for or against this proposition has been the subject of much debate. While Keynes subsequently admitted the force of this evidence in requiring a fundamental reappraisal of the Marshallian theory of value and distribution (*C.W.* VII, p. 411), this does not detract from the fact that, in *The General Theory* itself, he had answered Sraffa's purely logical critique.

Since individual entrepreneurs can vary the quantity of their capital equipment, the aggregate supply function of an individual firm is not independent of the output of industry as a whole. As noted above, this does not vitiate the aggregate supply function of industry as a whole, provided that there exists a unique equilibrium distribution of the equipment for any given level of aggregate employment. The aggregate supply function and the ordinary supply curve of an individual firm are defined only *ceteris paribus* and for a given capital equipment held by the firm itself, and this is the form in which they are, perhaps unfortunately, usually expressed. The value of the concept of an individual differentiable supply function is for expressing the marginal productivity condition of the first Classical postulate, which is an equilibrium condition deemed to hold for infinitesimal changes in output that do not shift the function itself (i.e. *ceteris paribus*). However, as discussed in Section **A2.1.4** below, the marginal productivity condition cannot be generalised to industry as a whole except on special assumptions that fix the capital equipment of each firm.

A2.1.3   More on user cost

The elements of capital consumption that represent capital-goods bought from other firms and wholly used up (e.g. raw materials included in A_1), or rented from investors (included in factor cost F), or which are directly offset by new investment (e.g. oiling the machine), are straightforward from the view-point of the entrepreneur and require no elucidation. The depreciation of capital-goods rented from investors (here meaning, literally, rentiers, who do not undertake production) must be included in supplementary cost (see below), and is deducted in calculating *net* income, rather than income.

The cost of using in production a capital-good, which is already owned by the entrepreneur, is given by the difference $(G' - B') - G$, composed of the value G' that the entrepreneur would expect the asset to have at the end of the production period, if the asset were kept unused, less the optimal costs B' of maintaining and perhaps improving the asset while it is held; compared with its residual expected value G after use. This framework accommodates all types of capital-good, which differ for economic purposes only in the period over which they are used up. In the case of working capital or liquid goods that are to be fully used up in the current production period, the potential loss from an unexpected fall in their spot price is avoided by using the assets. The user cost can therefore be quantified as the current spot price plus the price of a 'call option' to buy replacements at the end of the production period at the original spot price (Kregel, 1998, p. 121). A call option allows the holder to benefit from a rise in the spot price without suffering from a fall.

In the case of liquid goods, the concept of user cost sheds light on the question of the relationship between short-term expectations and realised results, and the long-standing issue of price versus quantity adjustment. In the market period under perfect competition, a firm has a choice between accepting the spot market price or holding on to the goods. Holding makes sense if the firm expects the spot market price to rise over any given period by more than the related carrying costs. This condition can be expressed as the user cost exceeding the spot market value. Equally, selling the goods makes sense even if the firm needs them for future production, but expects the spot market price to fall by more than the carrying costs, so that replacement goods can be bought more cheaply when required. In this case, the spot market value exceeds the user cost.

For these reasons, Keynes considers expected price to be the factor determining employment (*G.T.* 123–4), and does not attribute causal significance to endogenous quantity changes in stocks (inventories) except as symptoms of changes in the expectation, of the price that the firm will receive for finished output on which it decides to employ labour today, at the end of the production period for that output (*G.T.* 51, n1). An unexpected increase in stocks of finished goods will not affect production and employment, except insofar as it affects the price expected at the end of the production period. The case of excess stocks is no different in its effect from the spot market price being below original expectation: spot market prices are not automatically the future expected prices upon which the current production decision is based. To the extent that excess stocks are produced and held off the market, their value at spot market prices is added to the value of the capital equipment and represents additional investment or negative user cost. If the excess stocks are sold at spot market prices below original expectation, this means simply that realised income is less than expected.

Realised income does not affect production and employment unless it affects expected income. Keynes accepts that Hawtrey may be right in believing that changes in stocks of liquid capital affect the production decision, and that Robertson may be right to believe that expected income is determined by realised income. The disagreement is over whether this is necessarily the case, and over Keynes identifying expected income as the exclusive causal factor, which may be influenced by liquid stocks and realised income, but also by all the other ingredients of effective demand.

The user cost of capital-goods whose economic life exceeds the production period is considered further in Section **A4.2.1**. Apart from user cost, the value of capital-goods may also be expected to depreciate for reasons independent of their use in production, through the passage of time and obsolescence, which Keynes defines as supplementary cost. Keynes's definition differs significantly from that of Marshall, who makes the terms 'prime' and 'supplementary' refer to variable and fixed costs, the latter including salaries (1920, p. 299). Supplementary cost is relevant to the long period, since when added to *average* prime (unit) cost, together with the cost of finance, it gives the Normal supply price above which it is worth the firm staying in business rather than selling up (or a new firm starting up with new or existing assets). Under perfect competition, where price equals marginal prime cost, the difference between marginal and average prime cost, reflecting diminishing returns, must cover the supplementary cost and the cost of finance (*G.T.* 68). The *basic* supplementary cost is the supplementary cost expected when the capital-good is first acquired, while the *current* supplementary cost is based on current market value (*G.T.* 59).

Supplementary cost is also the difference between income and *net* income, which is the relevant concept when the propensity to consume is considered in *G.T.* Book III. Windfall losses and gains, i.e. unexpected changes in the value of existing capital-goods as a result of changes in the state of expectation, including unforeseen technological change and simple catastrophe, may also affect consumption. Nevertheless supplementary cost does not enter into the short-period employment decision, since this is governed by expected marginal prime cost, and neither do windfall losses, precisely because they are unexpected.

A2.1.4 The linear Z function

Long-standing confusion has arisen (Hansen, 1953, p. 31; Patinkin, 1976, p. 88; Nevile, 1992, p. 259) from Keynes's desire to show that his aggregate supply function encompasses, without invoking quantities of physical product, the Marshallian supply curve for an individual firm. This confusion has led to the controversy as to whether the Z function is subject to diminishing returns to labour, or linear with constant returns, or indeed can be represented by the 45° line of the Keynesian cross. The main source of the confusion is Keynes's derivation of the conditions necessary if the Classical theorem, that marginal proceeds (i.e. price, net of user cost) equals marginal factor cost, is to hold at the level of industry as a whole as well as of the individual firm. Keynes writes:

> This set of definitions also has the advantage that we can equate the marginal proceeds (or income) to the marginal factor cost; and thus arrive at the same sort of propositions relating marginal proceeds thus defined to marginal factor costs as have been stated by those economists who, by ignoring user cost or assuming it to be zero, have equated supply price to marginal factor cost. (*G.T.* 55)

For example, let us take $Z_w = \phi(N)$, or alternatively $Z = W.\phi(N)$ as the aggregate supply function (where W is the wage-unit and $W.Z_w = Z$). Then, since the proceeds of the marginal product is equal to the marginal factor-cost at every point on the aggregate supply curve, we have

$$\Delta N = \Delta A_w - \Delta U_w = \Delta Z_w = \Delta \phi(N),$$

that is to say $\phi'(N) = 1$; provided that factor cost bears a constant ratio to wage cost, and that the aggregate supply function for each firm (the number of which is assumed to be constant) is independent of the number of men employed in other industries, so that the terms of the above equation, which hold good for each individual entrepreneur, can be summed for the entrepreneurs as a whole. This means that, if wages are constant and other factor costs are a constant proportion of the wages-bill, the aggregate supply function is linear with a slope given by the reciprocal of the money-wage. (*G.T.* 55, n2)

The confusion arises partly from the assumption that in this paragraph and footnote, Keynes is discussing the extensive, rather than the intensive, margin of employment of labour (where extensive and intensive are used here in the sense in which Ricardo applied them to the use of land). The extensive margin denotes the level of employment that is most profitable when the employment and costs of all factors can vary, given the demand-price; the intensive margin identifies the most profitable position when only one factor can vary, and thus here identifies the marginal product of labour. Even for industry as a whole in the short period, the extensive and intensive margins do not coincide because the capital equipment may not be fully employed.

The equation in the footnote $\Delta N = \Delta A_w - \Delta U_w = \Delta Z_w = \Delta\phi(N)$ is the condition for maximum profit at the intensive margin of aggregate employment, where factor input apart from labour is held constant. To see this, note that the expected income of the *individual firm* equals factor cost plus the expected profit of the entrepreneur:

$$Z_r = A_r - U_r = W.\phi_r(N_r) = F_r + P_r = WN_r + \overline{F}_r + P_r \qquad (A2.1)$$

where $\overline{F}$ (Keynes uses no symbol) means the cost of factor services other than labour (i.e. the services of capital-goods of all kinds, including land and money), P means the entrepreneur's profits or income, the subscript r follows Keynes's convention in distinguishing the firm or industry from the aggregate (*G.T.* 44), and other symbols are as in *The General Theory*. Converting to wage units and rearranging gives:

$$N_r = A_{wr} - U_{wr} - \overline{F}_{wr} - P_{wr} \qquad (A2.2)$$

For an individual firm under perfect competition all factor prices are assumed invariant with respect to changes in the employment of the individual firm N_r. In the analysis of the intensive margin, where employment is set to maximise profits so that $\partial P_{wr}/\partial N_r = 0$, the quantity of capital-services is held constant so that the product $\overline{F}_{wr}$ of the quantity and marginal cost of capital-services is constant and drops out upon differentiation with respect to N_r. The conclusion $\phi'_r(N_r) = 1$ is the Classical microeconomic proposition expressed in terms of the aggregate supply function $\phi_r(N_r)$ of an individual firm, without reference to physical output.

This conclusion is valid for an individual firm *ceteris paribus,* but the extension of the Classical marginal productivity theorem to industry as a whole, so that the subscript r can be dropped in equation (A2.2), requires three special assumptions: constant income shares, a constant number of firms, and the independence of each firm's aggregate supply function. The assumption of constant income shares, which Keynes expresses as the constant ratio of (total) factor cost to (total) wage cost, means that the marginal cost of capital-services is constant in terms of wage-units (though not necessarily in money-value), with respect to changes in aggregate employment and not only in the employment of an individual firm. Since the aggregate real wage equals the money-wage divided by marginal (total) factor cost, this amounts to assuming that the real wage is independent of the level of aggregate employment, an assumption that Keynes explicitly does *not* make in general. This first assumption means that $\bar{F}_w$ is constant at the intensive margin as in the case of the individual firm, and again drops out upon differentiation.

Two further assumptions are necessary, that the number of firms is constant and that the aggregate supply function for each firm is independent of employment by other industries. The individual functions $\phi_r(N_r)$ must not themselves shift with changes in N, if they are to be summed together and the aggregate function $\phi(N)$ is to be differentiable. The constancy of individual functions requires that the individual firm's holding of capital-goods remains unchanged as aggregate employment N increases. Capital-goods must not be drawn away from individual firms by competition from new firms, or by a change in the composition of effective demand across industries. Taken together, these three assumptions mean $\Delta \bar{F}_w = 0$ and in equilibrium $\Delta P = 0$ so that from (A2.2) we can derive Keynes's equation at the aggregate level:

$$\Delta N = \Delta A_w - \Delta U_w = \Delta Z_w = \Delta \phi(N) \qquad (A2.3)$$

Ironically, Keynes's concluding statement that the aggregate supply function for industry as a whole (expressed in wage-units) must be linear is a statement, not of his own assumptions, but of the corollary of the three special assumptions required for the Classical marginal productivity theorem to hold at the macroeconomic as well as the microeconomic level. The three special assumptions required, if the marginal product of labour is to be defined for industry as a whole, also require that the Z curve, expressed in wage-units, is linear. In the general case, under standard Marshallian assumptions, the theorem will hold only at the microeconomic level.

There is definitely something wrong with the last sentence of the footnote, and this has usually been taken (e.g. Patinkin, 1976, p. 88, n8) to be the use of the term 'reciprocal', rather odd for a trained mathematician. Although a textual change must be the last resort of any exegesis, our discussion suggests a different conclusion: that 'money-wage' should be replaced by 'real wage', where this means the real cost of labour to entrepreneurs in terms of product (the real product wage) rather than the purchasing power of the money-wage in terms of wage-goods. If this change is incorporated, the last sentence would mean that the conditions required for the validity of the Classical marginal productivity theorem at the aggregate level, together with the assumption of a constant money-wage, imply a linear Z function, not at 45°, but with a slope p/W, where p is the 'price level' implicit in Z (Keynes does allow for such a vague thing in *G.T.* Chapters 20 and 21, pp. 285, 304–5, precisely in a similar discussion of Classical theory, namely the quantity theory of money and prices). For writing equation (A2.1) in aggregate terms and on the assumption of constant income shares, we obtain

$$Z = WN + \overline{F} + P = kWN + P \text{, where } k = \frac{WN + \overline{F}}{WN} > 1 \qquad \text{(A2.4)}$$

from which the profit-maximising first-order condition is

$$\frac{dZ_w}{dN} = k = \frac{W + \overline{F}/N}{W} = \frac{p}{W} \qquad \text{(A2.5)}$$

p is also Keynes's cost-unit, being a 'weighted average of the rewards of the factors entering into marginal prime cost' (*G.T.* 302). Equation (A2.5) is not the same as equation (A2.3) because it is a total derivative, allowing for all factor inputs to adjust (see also *G.T.* 272, n1). It bears some resemblance to the Classical marginal productivity result for an individual firm except that, in a curious paradox, the *aggregate* marginal real product of labour ('real' in the sense of measured in wage-units) is equal to the *reciprocal* of the real product wage, underlining the fact that the real wage is only a ratio derived from money prices (including factor prices), and not itself a causal variable.

A2.2   EXPECTATION AS DETERMINING OUTPUT AND EMPLOYMENT

A2.2.1   Long-period employment

Production and employment decisions are based on short-term expectation, but the short-term expectations of the prices of capital-goods in turn depend on the long-term expectations of investors. The short-term horizon extends to the length of the period of production and Keynes's long period. It is at first puzzling that this definition of the long period relates to short-term expectation, in a given state of long-term expectation, until one recalls that 'long period' is quite different from 'long term'. The long period refers specifically to the process of reaching an equilibrium in which the changes that are optimal in a given state of expectation have been made to the aggregate stock of capital-goods, as well as to the level and distribution of employment. By contrast, the long-term horizon extends over at least one, and likely many more than one, long periods. While Marshall links the long period to a stationary or steady state of production achievable only in the long term, Keynes allows only a link to a given state of expectation, that may at least in theory persist in the short term.

As we have noted, Keynes defines the 'long-period employment' as the equilibrium level and distribution of employment corresponding to a given state of expectation once the fluctuations, arising from the change that led to the current state of expectation, have fully worked themselves out. He notes that the state of expectation may well change again during the transition before employment has reached its long-period level, and furthermore that fluctuations may arise from changes in the equilibrium distribution of employment as well as in its aggregate level. Nevertheless, the concept of long-period employment is central to the theoretical determinacy of Keynes's system, since it takes formal account of the consequences of a change in the state of expectation for the aggregate stock of capital-goods as well as the employment of labour, and also identifies a key point of continuity with, and of departure from, Marshall.

The reference to a steady, rather than stationary, state as part of the given state of expectation arises in a footnote (*G.T.* 48, n1). The long-period employment remains a position of static equilibrium, but one that can move as the population or other parameters change, just as Marshall's long-period position can move over the secular period. Furthermore, since Keynes's long period is short-term, it may involve continuing investment and increase in wealth independently of changes in the Classical parameters, unlike Marshall's long-period position in which aggregate investment is limited to the replacement of consumed capital-goods in the absence of secular change. 'The only condition is that the existing expectations [on any given day in long-period equilibrium] should have been foreseen sufficiently far ahead' (ibid.). This last condition confirms that Keynes's long period is not his long term, since Keynes explicitly denies that future expectations (or outcomes) can be foreseen in this way over the long term.

A2.2.2   Production time and convergence to long-period equilibrium

On *G.T.* pp. 47–50, Keynes devotes considerable attention to the process of transition to a new position of long-period employment equilibrium after a change in the state of expectation. Much ink has been spilt over these disequilibrium dynamics, which in this context means how a series of positions of daily short-period equilibrium converge on a long-period equilibrium. Confusion has arisen from treating this passage (and those at *G.T.* 122–4 and 287–8) as an exposition of the convergence of expectations to their equilibrium values, rather than of the conformance of the structure of production to a new state of expectation. It is important to separate these two processes for the purposes of analysis, particularly as they are hard to disentangle in practice. This section assumes the 'rational expectations' or perfect foresight method of *G.T.* Chapter 3, by which effective demand is determined in short-term forward markets for the output of current employment, supplied by employers to meet demand from wholesale dealers. The following section will consider how the same result may be achieved by trial and error.

In accordance with the logic of the forward market device, the adjustment from one position of long-period equilibrium to another might in theory be made in a single day, if the availability of the capital-goods needed for each stage of production could be neglected; Keynes describes such a possibility when 'there are surplus stocks and surplus capacity at every stage of production' (*G.T.* 288). As always, a change in the forward market prices at the end of each industry's production period determines 'instantaneously' the new short-period employment that firms find it most profitable to offer today. If the forward prices for both sales and costs were to move immediately to their new long-period equilibrium values, then today's employment would move directly to the long-period equilibrium position.

However, Keynes notes that this is not the case in practice because most production takes time. There will be an optimal inter-temporal path of employment towards a new long-period equilibrium, say, higher in one or more industries. It may not be profitable to hire more labour for the later stages of a production process until more capital-goods, particularly the output of the previous stages of production, are available to work with; the prices and therefore the user cost of such capital-goods (both those to be delivered during the long period and those already held at the time of the change in the state of expectation) increase in short-period equilibrium, and this increase in user cost prevents the daily rate of increase in employment exceeding some optimal level. The increases in the forward prices of capital-goods will induce further employment in the production of additional stocks and perhaps fixed equipment. Together with, in turn, the production of additional consumption-goods to meet demand arising from the higher employment associated with this additional investment, the optimal path of aggregate employment may well overshoot the new long-period equilibrium before converging. Conversely, if the new long-period employment in any industry is lower, the prices of capital-goods fall, de-stocking of intermediate goods takes place, and aggregate employment may fall below its new equilibrium level before recovering. One can envisage some asymmetry here: it may take longer to use up fixed capital equipment than to produce it, so that the long period is longer for a fall in employment than a rise.

In the context of this more complex dynamic analysis, the state of short-term expectation must now refer, not only to the short-period equilibrium prices that determine today's employment, nor to the long-period equilibrium prices that will reign once the adjustment process is complete, but to the entire constellation of short-period equilibrium prices for each day of the long period, making a matrix of expected prices or 'expectations matrix' reminiscent of Hicks's 'production plan' (1939, p. 193). Thus, if complete short-term futures markets exist, on any given day the prices for each day of the long period are known by employers.

The rate of convergence from short-period to long-period equilibrium depends entirely on the availability and price of capital-goods. An increase in a given supply price (*mutatis mutandis* for a decrease) will partly reflect, under diminishing returns, a decision to increase employment today in that industry; and partly, a temporary increase in the user cost of capital-goods. The additional user cost will reduce each day as employment converges on the long-period equilibrium and the temporary scarcity of capital-goods is eliminated. The transition to the long-period equilibrium therefore takes place over a number of days, on each of which the forward market for delivery of each product at the end of its production period clears at the supply price corresponding to the employment offered on that day, although this short-period employment will differ from the long-period level. The product with the longest microeconomic production period governs the length of the macroeconomic period of production, which will equal that microeconomic production period plus the number of days that must elapse before the finished output of that product can reach its long-period equilibrium level.

As Keynes points out, as if this were not complicated enough, in practice the state of expectation can change again before the end of the long period. This implies a further shift in the constellation of forward prices representing the state of short-term expectation, corresponding to the new convergence path from today's employment (which yesterday was expected to be on a different convergence path, related to the former state of expectation) towards the new long-period equilibrium vector. If the state of expectation were to change every day, today's employment would always be on a new convergence path tracking towards today's long-period equilibrium, but would never actually reach it (although this does not mean the long period has no physical basis in production time). Nevertheless, provided the convergence path can be assumed to exist, today's long-period employment (and not only today's employment) is determined by today's state of expectation in conjunction with the parameters of Keynes's model.

The preceding argument can be expressed compactly in mathematical terms as follows, for the benefit of those who find it makes things clearer. Continuing to employ the symbols of Section **A1.3.1**, the employment vector on any given day can be expressed as $\mathbf{n}'(t)$ and the long-period employment vector as:

$$\mathbf{n}^{**}\big|\Omega_t, r_t \text{ such that } \mathbf{n}^*(t+\lambda) = \mathbf{n}^{**}\big|\Omega_t, r_t, \text{ if } \Omega_{t+\lambda} = \Omega_t \text{ and } r_{t+\lambda} = r_t$$

In this expression, Ω_t means the state of long-term expectation on day t, r_t represents the structure of interest rates on day t, and λ is the length of the long period in days. This condition holds the valuation of investment opportunities constant while allowing the cost of capital goods to vary. Where the analysis is conducted in a constant state of expectation and liquidity-preference, express reference to Ω_t and r_t can be omitted. λ is finite if the minimum labour unit is a discrete quantum, so that the process of asymptotic convergence comes to an end.

Today's state of short term expectation, conditional on yesterday's employment vector and today's state of long-term expectation, may then be expressed as a matrix

$$\Pi_t\big|\mathbf{n}^*(t-1), \Omega_t, r_t = \big[\mathbf{p}(t), \mathbf{p}(t+1), ...\mathbf{p}(t+\lambda)\big]$$

where $\mathbf{n}'(t-1)$ is yesterday's employment and $\mathbf{p}(t)$ is the equilibrium price vector corresponding to the point of effective demand on a given day. $\mathbf{p}(t)$ depends on the aggregate demand function $\chi(\mathbf{n}(t), \overline{\mathbf{x}}(t), \mathbf{p}^d(t))$ and the aggregate supply function $\Phi(\mathbf{n}(t), \overline{\mathbf{x}}(t))$, with $\mathbf{p}(t) = \mathbf{p}'(t) = \mathbf{p}'(t)$ in equilibrium. The propensity to consume χ, investment Θ and aggregate supply Φ functions are held constant during the long period. When a given state of long-term expectation and initial employment vector are assumed, the short-term price matrix will be the same for each day of the long period and can for convenience simply be written Π, a numerical expression of the state of short-term expectation. The path of employment over the long period from any given initial position in a given state of long-term expectation is then expressed by the process $\mathbf{n}^{*}(t|\Pi) \to \mathbf{n}^{**}$.

This raises the question of the conditions under which such a solution path exists, such that the long-period equilibrium is stable and the process convergent in disequilibrium. Keynes's description of the equilibrium solution path on *G.T.* 49 can be expressed as the solution to three equations:

$$n_I^{*}(t) = \alpha \dot{n}_C^{*}(t) + n_I^{**} \tag{A2.6}$$

$$\dot{n}_C^{*}(t) = \beta \left(n_C^{**} - n_C^{*}(t) \right) \tag{A2.7}$$

$$n_C^{*}(t) = \gamma \left(n_C^{*}(t) + n_I^{*}(t) \right) \tag{A2.8}$$

$n_I^{*}(t)$ and $n_c^{*}(t)$ are the sums of the elements of the daily employment vector $\mathbf{n}^{*}(t)$ corresponding to the capital- and consumption-goods industries respectively (*i.e.* the levels of employment in each sector). These are all short-period equilibrium values, corresponding to the point of effective demand each day. n_I^{**} and n_c^{**} are the long-period equilibrium values determined by supply and demand in forward markets; we leave for the following section the different question whether, if expectations are not fulfilled, a Marshallian process of price adjustment will lead to such a long-period equilibrium. Neither do we consider what determines the long-period position, or the relationship between the long-period employment vectors corresponding to different states of expectation, which will be the subject of Chapter 3 of this book.

Equation (A2.6) then expresses the level of employment in the capital-goods industries $n_I^{*}(t)$ as the sum of an exogenously given long-period level n_I^{**} together with a dynamic term $\alpha \dot{n}_c^{*}(t)$, making it a function of the rate of change of employment in the consumption-goods industries. This represents the employment in the capital-goods industries to produce the additional capital equipment required by the consumption-goods industries to support their increased employment.

Equation (A2.7) is an expositional device: it merely states that, if there is a long-period equilibrium, the level of employment in the consumption-goods industries will tend towards it at a rate β proportional to the level of disequilibrium. We will consider later why this should be the case. Similarly, equation (A2.8) establishes a relation between the level of employment in the consumption-goods industries and total employment. The proportion γ is a variant of the employment multiplier, to be considered in Chapter 3 of this book.

Reducing the system of equations (dropping the time subscripts for convenience) gives

$$\dddot{n}_C + \frac{1}{\alpha}\ddot{n}_C + \frac{\beta}{\alpha\gamma}\dot{n}_C = \frac{\beta}{\alpha\gamma}\ddot{n}_C \qquad\qquad (A2.9)$$

This process is convergent since $\alpha, \beta, \gamma > 0$. The condition for the damped simple harmonic motion described by Keynes is $\gamma < 4\alpha\beta$. Since $\gamma < 1$, oscillation takes place unless the capital intensity of the new employment in consumption-goods production (α), and/or the rate of response to disequilibrium (β) are sufficiently low. Equation (A2.9) does not capture the whole of Keynes's argument, since it cannot describe the cyclical effects of a change in the composition of a given level of total employment: to do this with mathematics would require a higher order system of partial differential equations, with one equation for each industry. Since not much can be said *a priori* about the value or behaviour of the parameters α and β, a technical exercise of this sort would add little.

The rate of response to disequilibrium (β) and the length of the long period depend on the supply and demand elasticities in each industry, taking into account the user cost of existing stocks of capital-goods. By assumption, the long-period employment vector is known, determined in the markets for the final day of the long period by the aggregate supply functions of employers and the aggregate demand functions of wholesale dealers. On a particular day, the demand for a consumption-good relative to its long-period value will reflect the level of employment expected by the wholesalers, the relative price on that day, and the consequent degree of substitution in favour of other products, or deferral of purchase until a later day. Conversely the supply price of a product will reflect not only the diminishing returns associated with increased output, but also the opportunity cost of using existing stocks now rather than later. If the new long-period employment represents an increase, the level of output in the early days of the long period will be constrained by a shortage of capital-goods and a limitation of demand by both the high price and the shortfall in the level of employment from its new long-period value. If today's market price is too low in relation to a later day within the long period, it may pay to hold the capital equipment in stock rather than use it in production, thus increasing the spot price. Inter-temporal arbitrage on both the demand and supply sides, between the forward markets for different days of the long period, determines an equilibrium convergence path. Whether the equilibrium convergence path involves overshooting oscillations depends mainly on the physical supply and demand elasticities.

A2.2.3 Expectations and realised results

In the above exposition, the expectations of the employers, which govern each day's employment decision, are fulfilled by forward contracts with dealers in the wholesale markets. The assumption of the necessary forward markets is equivalent to assuming accurate or so-called 'rational' short-term expectations on the part of employers. How then are the expectations of the dealers arrived at, and what are the implications of disappointment? What if there are no dealers or forward markets and the only market prices are current spot prices? It is best to address these questions in stages, considering first the implications of a change in the state of expectation, given forward markets; secondly, the sources of change in the state of expectation, distinguishing between disappointment and error in expectations; and thirdly, the implications of basing expectations on realised results rather than forward markets.

The previous section has considered the implications of a change in the state of expectation for the dynamics of production and the process of convergence on the long-period equilibrium. While this adjustment process is taking place, dealers awaiting delivery of production orders, in progress when the state of expectation and its associated expectations matrix change, can expect to command spot market prices on delivery different from the original supply prices. These gains or losses are windfalls, unexpected differences between the income now expected or realised at the end of the production period for these goods and the income or effective demand originally expected at the beginning. Holders of stocks of capital-goods (employers, wholesalers and rentiers) at the time of the change in the state of expectation also reap windfall gains or losses. Yet the production decisions for each day of the long period remain governed by the forward prices in the new state of expectation for delivery at the end of the next production period, and not by the differences in price represented by windfalls (*G.T.* 288).

Keynes's exposition assumes, in places, that changes in aggregate demand are foreseen or that 'sufficient notice' has been given (*G.T.* 122, 288), where sufficient notice means that forward orders are placed for delivery not earlier than the end of the period of production, defining a new state of expectation but without 'more disturbance to the price of consumption-goods than is consequential, in conditions of decreasing returns, on an increase in the quantity which is produced' (*G.T.* 122). In our terms, this means that when, as it were, 'notice is given', the extreme right-hand column of today's expectations matrix differs from that of yesterday's, implying a difference in today's long-period employment from yesterday's and a new convergence path towards it. Any change in the state of expectation and employment involves windfalls, but the expected price of consumption-goods at the end of the long period will nevertheless reflect their normal supply price at the new level of employment.

So far we have assumed that employers' expectations of income are fulfilled by contract, and their windfalls are limited to stocks of capital-goods used in production. Dealers can experience windfalls both on existing stocks and on goods in production under contract. Orders are placed with employers by entrepreneurs, here including other employers, wholesale dealers, and rentiers. It is convenient to assume that most capital-goods are ordered directly by firms or rentiers, and that consumption-goods are ordered by wholesale dealers, and sold by them, directly or indirectly, in retail markets. The expectations of wholesale dealers of the demand from the final consumers are expressed in the aggregate demand for consumption-goods D_1, which is not the same as the actual retail demand they (or the retail dealers to whom the wholesalers sell) encounter on any given day. The retail trade is all about the management of short-term uncertainty so that fluctuations within a certain range will not affect wholesale aggregate demand and the state of expectation. Furthermore, fluctuations in consumer demand arise for many reasons, including changes in the weather or in fashion, and a failure to sell a particular good at a particular price on a particular day should not be regarded simply as an error of expectation. Expectations are as often disappointed by changes in the uncertain determinants of consumer demand as by misjudgements of a fixed demand. Retail expectations are never exactly fulfilled, as may be judged by frequent 'sales', 'special offers' and the extensive trade in 'end of line' and 'clearance' goods, with recycling at the very end of the dealer chain.

The disappointment of retail expectations, at least in part, is inevitable, and what is significant for employment is the wholesale demand which results in production orders. It is no accident that Keynes specifies aggregate demand as 'the proceeds which the entrepreneurs expect to receive from the employment' (*G.T.* 25). If the state of expectation is defined in terms of wholesale demand and represents the price expectations of employers, it is possible to define a level of daily and long-period employment which is independent of the fulfilment of retail expectations. Keynes recognises fully that this state of expectation may change from day to day, but expectational error is only one source of such change among many, alongside unanticipated changes in the independent variables and parameters of the equilibrium system. The disappointment of (dealer) expectations plays no direct causal role in relation to the determination of equilibrium employment, but exerts its influence through changing the state of expectation. Keynes writes:

> ... the importance [of the difference between expected and actual income resulting to an entrepreneur from a particular decision, due to a mistake in the short-period expectation] ... lies in the fact that this difference will be one of the relevant factors in determining subsequent effective demand. I began, as I have said, by regarding this difference as important. But eventually I felt it to be of secondary importance, emphasis on it obscuring the real argument. For the theory of effective demand is substantially the same if we assume that short-period expectations are always fulfilled ... For other economists, I find, lay the whole emphasis, and find the whole explanation in the differences between effective demand and income; and they are so convinced that this is the right course that they do not notice that in my treatment this is *not* so. (*C.W.* XIV, p. 181)

In our terms, the dynamic passages of *The General Theory* relate to the convergence of employment to its long-period equilibrium after a change in the state of expectation which then persists. Any windfalls, arising from the initial change being unforeseen, have no effect on employment. The theory of employment is the same if the change was fully anticipated and the state of expectation persists. Keynes then writes:

> Entrepreneurs have to endeavour to forecast demand. They do not, as a rule, make wildly wrong forecasts of the equilibrium position. But, as the matter is very complex, they do not get it just right; and they endeavour to approximate to the true position by a method of trial and error. Contracting where they find that they are overshooting their market, expanding where the opposite occurs. It corresponds precisely to the higgling of the market by means of which buyers and sellers endeavour to discover the true equilibrium position of supply and demand ... The main point is to distinguish the forces determining the position of equilibrium from the technique of trial and error by means of which the entrepreneur discovers where the position is ...

Let us suppose identity of *ex ante* and *ex post*, my theory remains. *Ex ante* decisions may be decided by trial and error or by judicious foresight, or (as in fact) by both. I should have distinguished more sharply between a theory based on *ex ante* effective demand, however arrived at, and a psychological chapter indicating how the business world reaches its *ex ante* decisions. It is only in this chapter that income, investment and saving, which are *ex post* concepts, come in. (*C.W.* XIV, pp. 182–3)

This passage, taken in isolation, certainly invites confusion between the point of effective demand and the 'true equilibrium position' where expectations are fulfilled, which is only dispelled in the final paragraph quoted. Here Keynes acknowledges that the equilibrium employment determined by the principle of effective demand may not be a 'true equilibrium' in the sense of our fourth criterion, but this admission and latter concept of equilibrium do *not* appear in *The General Theory* itself. It is a mistake to identify this 'higgling' with the equilibrium process of *G.T.* 25, rather than with the revision of short-term expectation of *G.T.* 50; trial and error or higgling is an *alternative* to that process (*C.W.* XIII, p. 603). As Keynes makes clear, effective demand is an entirely *ex ante* concept relating solely to expectations, but open to revision in line with *ex post* income. From his reference to the 'psychological' nature of the missing chapter on the formation of (dealer) expectations, we may infer a reluctance to model this process in formal terms.

At this point we have considered the effects of a change in the state of expectation, given short-term forward markets; and secondly, the sources of change in the state of expectation, distinguishing between mere disappointment and 'error' in expectations; there remains to consider the implications of basing expectations on realised results rather than forward markets. Keynes suggests that 'although output and employment are determined by the producer's short-term expectations and not by past results, the most recent results usually play a predominant part in determining what these expectations are' (*G.T.* 50–51). We should consider in particular whether the assumption of short-term forward markets extending over the long period is essential, or as Keynes suggests, a useful abstraction to identify the forces determining the position of equilibrium, to be distinguished from the technique of trial and error by means of which, at least in some cases, the entrepreneur discovers where the position is.

The question may be framed as whether employment will converge to long-period equilibrium in a given state of long-term expectation, if short-term expectations are based on current spot prices rather than forward market prices. Today's spot prices are determined by expenditure decisions based on the offer prices of available stocks of finished output, including today's deliveries of new goods. These spot market prices are not conceptually the same as the expected or forward market prices for the heterogeneous output expected to result from today's employment at the end of their various production periods. Nevertheless today's aggregate demand (i.e. Keynes's *ex ante* entrepreneurial expectations) can be linked as a first approximation to today's expenditure (the *ex post* aggregate demand of Old Keynesian economics). Current investment expenditure is determined directly by entrepreneurial expectations, and consumption expenditure depends mainly on the income of factors of production, which is identical to the effective demand for their services; while the consumption of entrepreneurs is likely to be insensitive to minor differences between expected and realised income. Thus in the absence of changes in the propensity to consume or other major disturbances, expectations based on spot prices will determine a level of employment and consumption consistent with those spot prices.

An unanticipated change in consumption demand, arising (say) as at *G.T.* 122–4 from an increase in employment in the capital-goods industries, will lead to an increase in the spot prices of consumption-goods to clear the market, and so in the prices of existing capital-goods, certainly in the consumption-good industries and perhaps across industry as a whole. If expectations are based on spot prices, these increased prices will encourage production, not only of additional consumption-goods, but of additional capital-goods in the form of work-in-progress and other stocks of materials and finished goods; by assumption, long-term expectations and the demand for new durable plant are unaffected. The process is similar to that set out above in Section **A2.2.2** except that, depending on the elasticity of expectations with respect to changes in spot prices, expectations will differ from the values they would take if they were determined by supply and demand in a forward market. On the one hand, spot prices reflect current demand, given the current and not the future supply; on the other hand, current demand reflects current employment, rather than employment at the time that the output from current employment is delivered to the spot market. The process of convergence to long-period equilibrium will thus depend on the elasticity of price expectations as well as on the physical supply and demand elasticities. Keynes assumes that 'the process of revision of short-term expectation is a gradual and continuous one' (recall '*natura non facit saltum*'), suggesting that the combination of the values of all these elasticities is such as to avoid major oscillations in production.

Thus it is possible to describe Keynes's system in terms of expectations based solely on realised results and the discovery of the long-period position by trial and error, rather than by the equilibrium of supply and demand in forward markets. This does not alter the fact that effective demand and employment are based on expectation and not directly on realised results. The convergence of employment to long-period equilibrium over time must not be confused with the determination of effective demand, which Keynes treats as in continuous equilibrium whether expectations are based on forward markets or realised results. Furthermore, the state of expectation may well change from day to day, more rapidly than employment can converge to long-period equilibrium.

In Keynes, as in Marshall, there is some ambiguity as to whether at any point the discussion involves forward markets or realised results. Marshall is simultaneously explicit that Normal prices are 'determined at the position of stable equilibrium of normal demand and normal supply' (1920, p. 282) and that they are expectations in the minds of entrepreneurs (1920, pp. 309–10). These statements can only be reconciled by the assumption either of forward markets or of a stationary or steady state, which Marshall interprets physically and Keynes as a state of expectation. The assumption of a steady state with expectations based on trial and error gives rise to a process of convergence from one position of equilibrium to another that is very similar, although not strictly identical, to that of a process based on forward markets, the difference lying in the formation of expectations. From the economist's point of view the assumption of forward markets is to be preferred, since 'the main point is to distinguish the forces determining the position of equilibrium from the technique of trial and error by means of which the entrepreneur discovers where the position is'.

A2.3   THE INVESTMENT-SAVING IDENTITY

A2.3.1   The Keynesian cross

The Hicks–Hansen income-expenditure model has defined Old Keynesian economics and so warrants a review. The Hicks IS-LM model will be addressed in Section **A5.1.1**; here we consider the Hansen–Samuelson 'Keynesian cross'. As most of us have been taught, this diagram (Hansen, 1953, p. 34; Mankiw, 2003, pp. 259–62) shows real income (Y) determined by expenditure ($C+I$) and equilibrium real income Y^* as the point of 'goods market' equilibrium. Y^* is the point of intersection of the sum of investment expenditure (constant with respect to income) and consumption expenditure (an increasing function of income) with the 45° line representing the equilibrium condition $Y = C + I$.

There are several problems with this exposition of the principle of effective demand. The aggregate supply function has disappeared and been replaced by the line where income equals expenditure. This substitution was no doubt encouraged by the confusion over Keynes's reference to a linear aggregate supply function (with a slope of 45° if proceeds are expressed in wage-units) as a condition for the Classical marginal productivity theorem to hold at the aggregate level (see Section **A2.1.4**). In employing an income-expenditure identity Hansen specifically misquotes Keynes as defining income as arising from ('spring[ing] from') sales (1953, p. 28) when Keynes in fact defines income as the *value* of output (*G.T.* 20, original emphasis). Hansen's emphasis on spending rather than employment corresponds to the neglect of supply in favour of demand and a definition of income gross of the user cost of fixed equipment. Real income has replaced employment in Hansen's diagram, breaking the explicit link between effective demand and the hiring decision, and encouraging the idea that income is created by spending rather than employment decisions. Income and money demand are expressed in real terms, tacitly assuming fixed prices (Hansen, 1953, pp. 30–35). The 45° line represents both the income-expenditure identity (*ex post*) and the equilibrium condition for realised income to equal expected income (*ex ante*) over time. The equilibrium is reached between *aggregate* demand and supply (again tacitly assuming homogeneous output for which an aggregate *excess* demand function can be defined) so that the microeconomic mechanism by which aggregate demand is linked to the supply decisions of individual firms is lost.

It should be clear to the reader from this brief critique and Chapter 1 above that Hansen makes a large number of implicit assumptions and definitions that are not in *The General Theory* and substantially change the meaning and scope of the principle of effective demand. Davidson and Smolensky, following Weintraub (1957), took steps towards recovering the original meaning, by re-introducing the aggregate supply function and drawing the Z diagram in terms of money-value and labour (Davidson and Smolensky, 1964, pp. 4, 145). However, their treatments omit user cost and do not follow Keynes the whole way in his recognition of the need to replace the Marshallian supply curve with the aggregate supply function at the level of the firm as well as the industry, since relative prices include an element representing marginal user cost as well as marginal factor cost.

A2.3.2   Keynes's income vs. Gross National Product

The definition of income is a headache for accountants as well as economists. By assuming perfect competition, Keynes the economist is able to determine the opportunity cost of an existing capital-good $G' - B'$ as the highest net present value of its prospective yield placed upon it by any investor, and this is sufficient for causal analysis. For the accountancy profession, the policies for the valuation of inventories, work-in-progress and fixed assets are perennial meat and drink, since market prices are not readily available for most existing capital-goods, and both shareholders and tax inspectors require an alternative and verifiable measure. The preference for historic cost (backed up by invoices) is understandable, even if sometimes it leads to measures of reported income which differ substantially from economic income.

Keynes's aggregate income Y lies somewhere between GNP (gross national product at factor cost) and NNP (net national product), and his aggregate net income $(Y - V)$ does not correspond to NNP. GNP is calculated without deducting the user cost of fixed capital equipment. NNP deducts all three forms of capital consumption, including windfall losses that Keynes deducts from capital and not income, since capital consumption is calculated by a comparison of the estimated values of the opening and closing capital equipment. National income accountants have become increasingly sophisticated in bringing their valuations of fixed capital and stocks (inventories) closer to economic values, and to derive better 'real' measures (e.g. by chain-linked indices) but their work remains an art and not an exact science.

The above reference to national rather than domestic income is deliberate, partly because *The General Theory* does not, as generally thought, describe only a closed economy (see Chapter 3 of this book). Keynes's definition of income as the value of output rather than expenditure avoids the concentration on the 'circular flow' of income and expenditure characteristic of Old Keynesian economics, into which fits awkwardly the net factor income from foreign sources that is the difference between GDP and GNP.

A2.3.3   Saving and finance

The confusion over accounting concepts in Robertson's version of loanable funds theory can be illustrated by a worked example. Table 2.1 has nine columns, representing five points in time (T0–4) and the four periods between them. At each point in time balance sheets are shown, an unconsolidated aggregate balance sheet and three separate sectoral balance sheets for firms, households and banks. For the period between each pair of balance sheets is shown an aggregate income statement. The opening balance sheet (T0) shows that all capital-assets (value 500) are owned by firms, which also hold bank deposits as active/transactions balances (20), and are financed partly by debts to households and banks (270) and partly by retained earnings (250). Households hold part of these non-bank debts (80) and also hold bank deposits (140), which are identified as idle/speculative balances (60) and active/transactions balances (80). Together these equal the households' net worth (220), excluding the net worth of the firms and banks. Banks hold part of the debts issued by firms (190) and by other banks (150), the latter as idle/speculative balances, and are financed by debts (310) and retained earnings (30); we assume banks do not need active/transactions balances.

Having set the scene, the action unfolds as follows: we assume that income is initially 100 per period and increases over two periods to 120 where it remains for the fourth period. 80% of income arises in the production of consumption-goods and 20% in the production less use of capital-goods, and accrues as to 10% in the form of earnings retained by firms and as to 90% directly to households; we abstract from supplementary cost and bank profits. We follow Robertson in assuming that the active/transactions balances at the beginning of the period equal planned consumption and current investment by households and firms respectively. 50% of the current investment by firms in each period is financed by firms from their own resources and the balance by the issue of non-bank debts to households, while the increase in firms' active/transactions balances is financed by issuing non-bank debt to banks, for which the banks are assumed to pay from their idle/speculative balances with other banks, thus holding the total bank debt or money supply constant. Thus current investment is matched by the saving of firms and households, the latter purchasing non-bank debts in an amount equal to their saving (so that current investment is 'fully funded', Davidson 1986; Chick 1997) while the increased demand for active/transactions balances is met from the idle/speculative balances, of banks in the case of firms, and directly in the case of households.

This example is only one of any number of combinations of financing arrangements that are possible for a given pattern of income and current investment over time: firms may finance their investment entirely from their own resources or by issuing debt to banks; households may prefer to hold a different mix of non-bank debt and bank deposits in either category; the total of bank debt may increase or decrease; or the sectors may be defined otherwise and income distributed differently. In every case the growth in the value of aggregate capital-assets is necessarily matched by the growth of aggregate net worth. The point of presenting this particular case (despite its artificial assumption that the banks subscribe for non-bank debt from balances held with other banks) is that it describes the case of 'fully funded' investment, where in each period current investment is matched by an increase in the retained earnings of firms together with the issue of non-bank debt equal to the saving of households, without any increase in the money supply. Even though there is a match between current investment and 'funding', there is nevertheless pressure on liquidity because of the increased transactions (or finance) demand for money to finance planned output. This is an interesting twist on the usual loanable funds story.

Comparing T2 with T0 we see that households must shift the balance of their holdings of bank deposits (total 140) from 60/80 to 44/96, transferring idle/speculative balances to active/transactions. Similarly banks must shift from 190/150 to 194/146, transferring idle/speculative balances into loans to firms. If households are concerned about the proportion of idle/speculative balances as well as the absolute amount, there is pressure from the reduction in the ratio of these balances to total net worth, from 60/220 to 44/241, as their holdings of non-bank debt increase. So we can see how an increase in investment may tend to raise interest rates, through the transactions demand for money, including the finance motive. Yet as Keynes points out (*C.W.* XIV, pp. 220–21; see also Davidson, 1965), such an increase in the demand for money arises from any plan to increase income; it is easy to produce an example where income and consumption increase for constant current investment, with precisely the same effect on cash balances.

Table 2.1 also shows Robertson's definition of disposable income and planned saving and investment, indicating an excess demand for loanable funds at dates T1 and T2. In this example, this excess corresponds directly to the increased demand for active/transactions balances and is met from 'dishoarding' by households and banks, given the constant money supply. Yet this is entirely a result of the definition of disposable income as the income of the previous period and of the transactions demand as the planned expenditure of the current period now beginning. The loanable funds analysis must relate to supply and demand at a point in time, the balance sheet date, so that the flows of past income and planned expenditure can be translated to supply and demand for cash balances at a point in time: the figures are thus shown in the balance sheet, rather than the income, column. Yet if income is understood in terms of production rather than expenditure, income cannot arise at a point in time, even though financial provision for future expenditure can be made at any time. Thus the flows of disposable income and of planned expenditure implicit in the *ex ante* loanable funds equation $S + \Delta M = I + \Delta H$ not only relate to different periods of time, they cannot exist at all, since

$$\int I dt = \int S dt = 0$$

at any *point* in time, whether *ex ante* or *ex post*.

This point is fundamental. There is a world of difference between a point in time and the infinitesimal interval or 'slice of time'. However short the accounting period, an income or profit and loss statement can never become a balance sheet. We are thus necessarily left with the supply and demand for a stock of money at a point in time and the need for a correspondingly appropriate theory of the rate of interest.

Table 2.1   Saving and finance: an accounting example

	T0 ⇨	T1 ⇨	T2 ⇨	T3 ⇨	T4
Aggregate income statements					
Consumption	80	88	96	96	
Current investment	20	22	24	24	
Keynes's income	100	110	120	120	
Firms' retained earnings	10	11	12	12	
Household saving	10	11	12	12	
Aggregate saving	20	22	24	24	
Unconsolidated aggregate balance sheets					
Capital-assets	500	520	542	566	590
Non-bank debts	270	282	295	307	319
Bank deposits - idle/speculative	210	200	190	190	190
Bank deposits - active/transactions	100	110	120	120	120
	1,080	1,112	1,147	1,183	1,219
Net worth b/f	500	500	520	542	566
Saving in current period	-	20	22	24	24
Non-bank debts	270	282	295	307	319
Bank debts	310	310	310	310	310
	1,080	1,112	1,147	1,183	1,219
Robertson's analysis					
Robertson's disposable income	100	100	110	120	
Planned consumption	80	88	96	96	
Planned saving	20	12	14	24	
Planned investment	20	22	24	24	
Excess demand for loanable funds	-	(10)	(10)	-	
Unconsolidated sector balance sheets					
Firms					
Capital-assets	500	520	542	566	590
Bank deposits - active/transactions	20	22	24	24	24
Non-bank debts	(270)	(282)	(295)	(307)	(319)
Retained earnings	250	260	271	283	295
Households					
Non-bank debts	80	90	101	113	125
Bank deposits - idle/speculative	60	52	44	44	44
Bank deposits - active/transactions	80	88	96	96	96
Net worth	220	230	241	253	265
Banks					
Non-bank debts	190	192	194	194	194
Bank deposits - idle/speculative	150	148	146	146	146
Bank debts	(310)	(310)	(310)	(310)	(310)
Retained earnings	30	30	30	30	30

A2.3.4 Equilibrium income vs. income as an equilibrium value

The common element of all versions of loanable funds theory is the Swedish distinction between *ex ante* and *ex post*, between plans and outcomes. There is no dispute that the investment-saving identity holds *ex post*; the nub of the debate is captured by Hansen's claim that Keynes did not see clearly that 'saving and investment, while always *equal*, are not always or necessarily in *equilibrium*' (1953, p. 60, original emphasis). The dispute hinges upon the tacit use of the different criteria for equilibrium discussed in our Prologue: Keynes adopts the mechanical sense of the first two criteria, Hansen in this quotation refers to the fourth criterion (fulfilment of expectations), while Hicks goes on to include all four criteria in distinguishing different types of equilibrium and disequilibrium from a Classical perspective. None of the writers are wholly explicit about their use of terms, and are often accordingly at cross purposes.

The matter is not helped by the fact that the terms *ex ante* and *ex post* are also open to different interpretation, and indeed have different meanings in relation to different concepts of equilibrium. Keynes writes, in the short hand of his 1937 lecture notes:

> *Ex ante* saving and *ex ante* investment *not* equal. But *ex post* dittos [saving and investment] are equal. *Ex ante* decisions in their influence on effective demand relate solely to entrepreneurs' decisions. *Ex ante* saving a very dubious concept – the decisions don't have to be made. *Ex ante* investment and *ex post* investment would differ even though widespread fluctuations in stocks did not occur and the disappointment of expectation influences the next *ex ante* decisions. I'm more Classical than the Swedes, for I am still discussing the conditions of short-period equilibrium. ... [I]ncome, investment and saving ... are *ex post* concepts ... Multiplier is *ex post* ... Marginal efficiency and interest are *ex ante* ... there is a law relating *ex post* investment and consumption. (*C.W.* XIV, pp. 182–3)

In this lecture, Keynes was attempting to explain the relationship between *The General Theory* and the Swedish concepts, an enterprise that he did not, unfortunately, complete (*C.W.* XIV, p. 216). Keynes's use of *ex ante* and *ex post* in this passage is subtly different from Hansen's and Hicks's, reflecting a different understanding of equilibrium. Although there must surely be general agreement that *ex ante* means plans or expectations, and that *ex post* mean outcomes or realisations, these meanings change slightly in different contexts. For Hansen, *ex post* can mean disequilibrium (e.g. unexpected changes in inventories), and usually does, except in a state of expectation that persists long enough for the equilibrium income to be discovered. For Hicks, *ex post* means temporary (market-period) equilibrium on the first criterion (market clearing), but not equilibrium on the fourth criterion (fulfilment of expectations). For Keynes, *ex post* means temporary market-period equilibrium on the first two criteria (the mechanical sense): unlike Hansen, there is never any question for Keynes of market-period disequilibrium (non-clearing goods markets).

Similarly, the use of the term *ex ante* in relation to income, saving and investment is explicitly rejected by Keynes (ibid.). The Swedish concepts are central to the Old Keynesian conception of the point of effective demand as equilibrium income Y^*, such that income *ex ante* and *ex post* are equal. As discussed earlier ▶ **A2.3.1**, the convergence between expected and actual income, depicted by Hansen using the Keynesian cross, does not in fact involve effective demand as Keynes defines it: Keynes explicitly repudiated this type of interpretation (*C.W.* XIV, p. 181). Hicks is more subtle; for example, his concept of the production plan resembles in certain respects Keynes's effective demand and allows for heterogeneous output. He argues that 'during the week, savings *ex ante* equal investment *ex ante*; but this is a property of the week, and not of any longer period. The *ex post* magnitudes will be equal whatever period we take, but the *ex ante* magnitudes will only be necessarily equal if plans are consistent. Equality between savings *ex ante* and investment *ex ante* is then one of the conditions of equilibrium over time' (1939, p. 183). Here, Hicks strikes a contrast between the first (market clearing) and the fourth (fulfilment of expectations) criteria of equilibrium as respectively *ex post* and *ex ante*.

From Keynes's perspective, the concept of *ex ante* saving is very dubious. Even at the individual level, it is preferable to speak of plans to spend, or not, rather than to save (*G.T.* 65). Saving can be planned only in relation to a given income and set of (spot) market consumption-goods prices; yet the level of income (especially in the aggregate) is itself endogenous, a function of consumption and investment expenditures (this does not mean that income is the value of expenditure). Thus saving, income, consumption, and current investment are co-determined simultaneously on a given day, and there can be no difference between *ex ante* and *ex post* saving. The concept of *ex ante* saving is empty, unless it is defined in relation to a different concept of income from Keynes's, such as yesterday's income (Robertson) or full employment income (Hicks, implicitly, as we shall see), or to a different concept of equilibrium (Hicks and Hansen).

The concept of *ex ante* investment fares little better under scrutiny, especially as part of a conception of equilibrium income. On Keynes's terms, *ex ante* current investment can only mean the net addition to the value of the capital equipment planned for any given *future* day during the period of production that, when added to the value of consumption-goods delivered, equals effective demand on that day. *Ex post* current investment can only mean the value of *today's* current investment, as determined in market-period equilibrium: current investment is therefore both planned and actual on any given day, although it need not correspond to previous plans. Market-period equilibrium can be reached by changes in the value and quantity of stocks of working and liquid capital-goods or in the value and use of fixed capital-goods. In fact, the comparison of *ex ante* and *ex post* investment presents the same dimensional problems (*C.W.* XIV, p. 210, n1) as the comparison of income and effective demand for a given day (Figure 1.2), with fatal consequences for the concept of equilibrium income, except on the special assumptions of homogeneous output and the equation of the day and the production period. That there is otherwise a lack of rigour in the *ex ante* concept is shown by the question, which *ex ante* value? Does it mean the value on the day when a production process (which one?) is first commenced, or on the day before the day when the *ex post* value is measured, or on some other day in between? *Ex ante* value is only uniquely defined in a given state of expectation.

For Keynes, both income Y (*ex post*, actual or realised) and effective demand D^* (*ex ante*, planned or expected) are each separately equilibrium values in the mechanical sense, between which no direct comparison is possible. The important idea here is 'income as an equilibrium value', rather than 'equilibrium income' Y^*. Chapter 1 of this book has looked in some detail at the determination of effective demand as an equilibrium value. Having identified Keynes's definition of income as 'the value of output', emphasising the difference between output and expenditure, we must now consider in more depth the meaning of the term 'value'. In Marshall's system the only observable prices are market prices, established by the temporary equilibrium of competitive supply and demand in the market period; value means equilibrium market price or 'market value', based on the market-period supply and demand schedules, which differ from the short-period schedules. Marshall defines the market period in terms of a fixed stock of goods – 'supply is taken to mean the stock of the commodity in question which is on hand or at all events "in sight"' (Marshall, 1920, p. 314). Keynes's 'day' corresponds, not only to the short period, but to the market period, since it is the maximum interval for which the supply of finished output is limited to the stock on hand or producible on demand (e.g. electricity). Market-period supply is not quite the same as the available stock, if the reservation demand of its holders is understood to be deducted from supply, rather than added to demand: the holders of the stock are free not to sell it to consumers or use it in production, and their choice will depend on the relationship between the spot market price and their expectations of future prices. Unsold finished goods, whether brought forward or newly delivered, are valued at market prices on the assumption of perfect competition, as are additions to the capital equipment including work-in-progress. Thus the quantum of income is the money-value at market prices of the output produced on a given day, by way of consumption or current investment, and income for longer periods can properly be calculated by summing the income of each day.

We are not here discussing a process over time but the conditions of price and quantity equilibrium on a given day, essentially at a point in time: the relationship between money-income and consumption demand must be such that equilibrium is maintained in the spot markets for consumption- and capital-goods, reflecting the particular slopes of the market-period supply and demand curves, which embody the 'habits of psychological response which allow of an equilibrium being reached at which the readiness to buy is equal to the readiness to sell ... the aggregate amount which saving individuals decide to save [must] be equal to the aggregate amount which investing individuals decide to invest' (*G.T.* 64). The equilibrium relation between consumption and current investment represents, of course, the 'logical theory of the multiplier which holds good, continuously, without time-lag, at all moments of time' (*G.T.* 122): the multiplier is therefore, in the first instance, an *ex post* relationship (*C.W.* XIV, p. 183). The next chapter of this book considers this in further detail.

If no equilibrium in the mechanical sense were reached, 'output would no longer have a definite market value' (*G.T.* 64) and income would not be defined. Given the axiom that goods markets clear, there is no escaping the conclusion that the values of consumption and current investment at any time are equilibrium values, since we always observe a market value for output as whole. Equilibrium between current investment and saving is reached principally by changes in the market prices of consumption- and capital-goods. The question is whether this amounts to any more than a truism (Hicks, 1939, p. 182), or arithmetic tautology (Hansen, 1953, p. 111). Each author demands more because, I believe, neither has fully grasped the nature of the principle of effective demand.

Hicks's understanding of temporary equilibrium (which also combines Marshall's market and short periods, but in quite a different fashion from Keynes) is entirely Walrasian, in the sense of our third criterion (a state in which all parties make their preferred choices, meaning that factor markets clear, as well as goods markets). He writes that in a given state of expectation 'the demand for securities can be taken as formally equivalent to a demand for given quantities of physical commodities to be supplied in the future; the price of these commodities (the only part of their price which can vary) being the rate of interest ... the individual behaves as if he were buying the commodities now' (ibid., 249), thereby directly contradicting Keynes (*G.T.* 210).[1] Hicks explicitly assumes full employment in equilibrium (ibid., 266–9), so that in equilibrium an increase in investment (future consumption) requires a reduction in (present) consumption and the interest rate is the price which balances the rate of substitution between them. Hicks is truly neo-classical (in Keynes's strict sense, *G.T.* 177) in allowing for temporary disequilibrium as a result of inelastic price expectations, including interest-rate expectations: thus equilibrium (on the third criterion) may be reached only over time if expectations adjust appropriately, yet without rigid wages (and consequent unemployment) the system tends towards instability. There is no recognition by Hicks that Keynes's principle of effective demand defines equilibrium in quite different terms, which allow for non-clearing factor markets despite flexible prices.

Hicks's version of the loanable funds doctrine is based on the Classical idea that full-employment *ex ante* saving and *ex ante* current investment are brought into equilibrium over time by changes in the rate of interest. He therefore invokes the third and fourth criteria of equilibrium (preferred allocation and fulfilment of expectations) as well as the first two accepted by Keynes. In using the third criterion, Hicks ignores the fact that employers and workers cannot as a whole bargain over real wages to clear the labour market. In using the fourth criterion, Hicks ignores the problem of a shifting state of expectation. In both cases, Hicks has abstracted from the key problems of a monetary economy that Keynes sought to address in *The General Theory*.

There is no warrant, theoretically or empirically, for using the third and fourth criteria of equilibrium in the analysis of a monetary economy. Equilibrium in Hicks's sense cannot be observed and lacks empirical rigour (as he readily admits, ibid., 133), whereas Keynes's mechanical concept is both formally and empirically more exact, since the point of effective demand is a position of equilibrium, not disequilibrium, and determines the observed level of employment. There is no market mechanism to bring the propensity to consume into balance with the inducement to invest at full employment as Hicks requires (*G.T.* 21).

NOTE

1. Mankiw (2003), pp. 58–65, follows Hicks. The equilibrium (real) interest rate for Mankiw and Hicks is therefore Wicksell's full-employment natural rate, to which Keynes refers as the neutral or optimum rate (*G.T.* 243).

3. The Propensity to Consume

After the 'digression' of *G.T.* Book II, in *G.T.* Books III and IV Keynes continues the process of detailed articulation of the principle of effective demand outlined in *G.T.* Chapter 3, by addressing the two components of the aggregate demand function, the demand for the production of consumption- and capital-goods respectively. Recall that the aggregate supply function Z provides a direct relation between the level of employment N and the money-income required by entrepreneurs to warrant that level of employment: the causation runs from required income to employment. The other blade of the Marshallian scissors is the aggregate demand function, the relationship between the level of employment N and the value of aggregate demand D, where the causation runs from employment to the income expected by entrepreneurs. It is vital to bear in mind the point made in the last chapter, that in this part of *The General Theory* Keynes switches from the study of entrepreneurial expectations to the expenditure decisions of consumers and investors, which are linked only loosely through factor income and the state of expectation. Keynes might helpfully have been more explicit about this, although he does distinguish at the outset of his discussion between the '"proceeds" which that level of employment is expected to realise' and the 'proceeds' themselves (*G.T.* 89), and makes his working assumption a little clearer in section IV of *G.T.* Chapter 10 (*G.T.* 122).

The separation of the discussions of consumption and investment into *G.T.* Books III and IV corresponds to the division between short-term and long-term expectation made in *G.T.* Chapter 5. While discussing consumption, Keynes takes as given the views about the future demand conditions for the services of individual capital-goods whose life extends beyond the period of production, which are expressed as the state of long-term expectation. Making long-term expectation exogenous, i.e. temporarily given, is legitimate because of the brevity of the short and long periods, which correspond to the day and the period of production. The state of long-term expectation is a complex affair involving many elements of both supply and demand (*G.T.* 147), but it is certain that long-term demand conditions will be unaffected by changes in the capacity of the capital equipment during the single day while the new capital-goods are being produced but have not yet been installed, and it is at least plausible, for the theoretical purposes of Keynes's long period, that the state of long-term expectation is unaffected by changes in capacity in the short term.

G.T. Book IV and Chapter 4 of this book accordingly address the determinants of the demand for capital-goods, and the level of employment in each of the capital-goods industries (together making what Keynes calls the 'primary' employment) follows directly from their aggregate supply functions. The purpose of the present chapter and *G.T.* Book III is to provide the required relation between the rate of current investment and the level of total employment, in both capital- and consumption-goods industries, using the concept of the propensity to consume. *G.T.* Book III therefore closes the model and completes the theory of employment, for a *given* state of expectation and liquidity-preference.

The aim of this chapter is to clarify and explain *G.T.* Book III (*G.T.* Chapters 8–10) in terms of three main themes: the distinction between the average and marginal propensity to consume (Section 3.1); the relation between consumption and employment (Section 3.2); and the definition of the multiplier (Section 3.3). These themes respond, not directly to the three *G.T.* chapters, but to difficulties that have arisen in their interpretation.

We reach the interesting conclusions that Keynes offered no formal theory (meaning, in this context, an equilibrium theory in the mechanical sense) of the *level* of consumption out of income; did not assume a closed economy without foreign trade, government or corporations; and that the 'sequence' multiplier of Old Keynesian economics cannot be found in *The General Theory*. The empirical basis of the claim that the marginal propensity to consume is less than unity proves to be, quite simply, the observation of a market value for aggregate output, and the multiplier is a corollary of market-period equilibrium.

3.1   AVERAGE AND MARGINAL

G.T. Book III presents Keynes's case for assuming a stable functional relation between the aggregate values of consumption and money-income, a relation he defines as 'the propensity to consume'. The relation is functional since Keynes proceeds to differentiate it in order to arrive at the marginal propensity to consume. The question of its stability raises important issues that have occupied much of the literature.

Stability must be defined always in relation to something, and a failure to recognise the point of reference leads to much confusion. In particular, stability in relation to income does not mean stability over time, or in relation to anything else. Once again, Keynes's use of periods and the distinction between the short and the long term are of paramount importance, if his meaning is to be grasped. The principle of effective demand operates in Keynes's short period, the day, and the calendar length of Keynes's long period is within the horizon of short-term expectation. As will be shown below, the propensity to consume must be considered stable for the duration of the (short-term) long period if the 'normal' value of the multiplier is to be observed. The need to concentrate on the short term explains Keynes's division (*G.T.* 91) between the short-term objective influences on the propensity to consume considered in *G.T.* Chapter 8 and the long-term subjective influences considered in *G.T.* Chapter 9.

The propensity to consume is defined as a function χ relating the aggregate money-values of consumption (C_w) and income (Y_w), both measured in terms of wage-units (*G.T.* 90), such that $C_w = \chi(Y_w)$. Note that Keynes uses the same symbol χ here as when defining aggregate consumption demand in terms of entrepreneurial expectations $D_1 = \chi(N)$ in *G.T.* Chapter 3, in line with his assumption that factor income is a sufficient proxy for effective demand and employment for the purposes of consumption (this is part of the 'switch' discussed above). ▶ **A3.2.1** We shall see shortly that this switch from employment to income is a necessary element of the definition of the multiplier as a 'market-period' equilibrium relationship. As with the corresponding measures of D_w and Z_w, this definition in terms of wage-units eliminates changes in the money-wage from the outset as a direct influence on effective demand.

Although Keynes places most emphasis on the effect of various factors in *changing* the propensity to consume, he is also concerned about its *level*. The term 'average' rather than 'level' must be used with care, since it suggests a stability of the propensity to consume, beyond the short term and with respect to influences other than income, which Keynes is quite careful not to assume. Strictly, 'average' should be interpreted in relation to a *given* propensity to consume function, as when Keynes refers to the 'average marginal propensity to consume' (*G.T.* 121). ▶ **A3.1.1**

In enumerating the possible sources of short-term changes in the level of consumption, he rules out influences other than 'real' income (i.e. money-income expressed in wage-units) as being either too slow to change (all the subjective factors), too unpredictable or exogenous (windfall changes, changes in income prospects, changes in fiscal policy) or second order (changes in the distribution of income, in the difference between income and net income, and in the rate of interest). Nevertheless in settling upon the marginal propensity to consume $\partial C_w/\partial Y_w$ as the key partial derivative for theoretical purposes, he emphasises that the other influences must be kept 'at the back of our heads' even if explicit account cannot be taken of them in the form of 'partial differentials' (*cf G.T.* 275, 297).

By contrast with its second-order influence on *changes* in the propensity to consume, the difference between income and net income is, in Keynes's opinion, a major determinant of the *level* of the propensity to consume. The whole of section IV of *G.T.* Chapter 8 (*G.T.* 98–106) is devoted to the contemporary empirical evidence in support of this contention: to the difference between financial and physical provision for the future, and the suggestion of a widening gap between the two as a community accumulates wealth.

On the other hand Keynes makes no mention at all in *The General Theory* of the 'real balance' or 'Pigou' effect which plays so large a role in modern AD/AS macroeconomics, which might be written $\partial C_w/\partial M_w$. Partly this is because he discusses changes in the price-level at length in *G.T.* Chapter 19, but even there he makes no allowance for a direct influence on the propensity to consume. We can only speculate why he did not consider it worth even a mention, after making a fairly exhaustive inventory of the other possible influences on the propensity to consume. A number of possible reasons are consistent with the rest of *The General Theory*. Firstly, although *The General Theory* does not discuss 'technical monetary detail' (*G.T.* xxii), the author of *A Treatise on Money* may be taken to assume that in a modern economy the bulk of money is in the form of bank deposits, so that a falling price-level harms bank debtors as much as it benefits bank depositors: so there is no significant aggregate real balance effect to discuss. If money is assumed to take the form only of state paper or a commodity, the windfall gain to its holders must still have set against it the distributional effects of windfall transfers from non-bank debtors to creditors, including the increased real value of government debt service. If by a heroic assumption, easily hidden by the Classical method of treating money as otherwise neutral, we go still further to abstract from all debt or at least the related distributional effects, any positive *short-term* influence of the real balance effect on consumption (through windfall gains) is likely to require such a rapid change in the price-level as to amount to a 'hyper-deflation', something neither observed in practice nor conducive to confidence and employment. Finally, any *long-term* real balance effect, even in such a debt-free and bank-free economy, implies that the propensity to consume rises with an increase in real income and wealth, while Keynes explicitly assumes the opposite case as a rule (*G.T.* 31,

97). Taken together, these reasons suggest that his omission of the real balance effect is entirely deliberate.[1]

Nevertheless there is nothing in the formal analysis of *The General Theory* to suggest that the average propensity to consume must fall as the real income of the community increases over time (as Keynes acknowledges, *G.T.* 97), nor is any such tendency its main conclusion. Although the average propensity to consume must fall for a change in income at a given point in time, if the marginal propensity to consume is less than the average, this statement says nothing about shifts in the level of the propensity to consume over time. Keynes can make no allowance in an equilibrium model for innovations in technology and consumption. The crucial element of his analysis of consumption is that the marginal propensity to consume must be less than unity, for reasons of stability discussed further below. Conversely his analysis of the influence of the rate of interest suggests no significant or unambiguous effect on the propensity to consume in either the short or long term, while maintaining the Classical inverse relationship between the rate of interest and the rate of current investment. The development of consumer credit in its various forms merely strengthens Keynes's case: a rise in the rate of interest will deter not only current investment but also debt-financed consumption, reducing the propensity to consume but doing nothing to increase saving, which must reduce in line with current investment. Higher interest rates thus lead only to reduced current investment *and* consumption at a lower level of income and employment. The more sensitive are current investment and the propensity to consume to the rate of interest, the more the level of income will have to fall. The equilibrium propensity to spend on new goods (in either form) may be sensitive to the rate of interest, but saving is determined solely by current investment and is accordingly *inversely* related to the rate of interest, the opposite to the postulate of Classical theory. Only at full employment is there a trade-off between current investment and consumption, and even then it is not clear that the rate of interest is an important influence on the balance between them.

Unlike Classical theory, Keynes does not claim to offer a theory of the *level* of the propensity to consume, which is largely determined by a complex psychological response to the unknown future, made up of motives such as 'Precaution, Foresight, Calculation, Improvement, Independence, Enterprise, Pride and Avarice', no more suitable as 'material for the differential calculus' than the merits of Queens (*G.T.* 40), and certainly not a simple matter of the rate of interest.[2]

3.2 CONSUMPTION AND EMPLOYMENT

Keynes's exogenous, psychological, short-term propensity to consume replaces the Classical, long-term, long-period equilibrium between consumption and investment. The definition of income and the investment-saving identity discussed above in Chapter 2 refute *a priori* the idea that saving is brought into equilibrium with current investment by the rate of interest. *G.T.* Book III provides instead an explanation of the relationship between the equilibrium levels of consumption and current investment and their corresponding levels of employment in a competitive monetary production economy where the level of employment is not determined simply by the supply of available labour. It is a vital part of the story, since it demonstrates formally the 'fallacy of composition' and shows precisely how an individual decision to abstain, from either consumption or investment of income, reduces the level of aggregate income rather than increasing aggregate current investment.

Consumption takes place when an entrepreneur makes a sale to a consumer. If goods are sold from stock and not replaced, this consumption represents user cost, the consumption of capital, and not income: consumption of goods (unlike services) does not necessarily create income. Income arises from production and employment, and is the value of the output produced, so Keynes's interest in consumption and investment derives ultimately from the employment created by each activity. The relevance of the propensity to consume is thus in the end about the decisions of entrepreneurs to hire labour and other factors to produce consumption goods and services, and it is the expectations of entrepreneurs (including dealers), rather than the intentions of consumers, which directly determine employment; even though those expectations ultimately depend upon the expenditure decisions of consumers and investors. ▶ **A3.2.1**

Since Keynes's concern, therefore, is with the employment consequences of decisions to consume and invest, the identity of the consumers and investors is not of fundamental importance. Contrary to received wisdom, *The General Theory* allows for government, foreign trade and the corporate sector, and it is not a model which describes only a closed economy. Keynes clearly regards differences in behaviour between these sectors and the personal sector as important for applied economics, and indeed devotes a large section (*G.T.* 98–104) to the empirical significance of corporate depreciation allowances. He also explicitly considers fiscal policy (*G.T.* 94-5) and foreign trade in his discussion of the likely value of the multiplier (*G.T.* 120–22). Yet his main object in *The General Theory* is not to place specific values on variables, but to establish general principles of causation that are independent of the degree to which an economy is open. For this purpose it is sufficient to consider the propensity to consume of the community as a whole, where a community means the population of any given geographical area with its associated stock of capital-goods, and to abstract from the particular institutions by which the community is organised, other than those of the market. The demand of the foreign sector for consumption-goods is largely independent of domestic employment, but so indeed is the demand of domestic rentiers, and both can be accommodated within the aggregate propensity to consume. Similarly, the demand for imports is not for this purpose fundamentally different from domestic saving, since both represent decisions not to consume domestically produced consumption-goods. Government, like the rentier, is in a position to spend on consumption- or capital-goods an amount in excess of its income funded by deficit financing or asset sales, but this raises no issue of fundamental principle in the present context. The implications of trade policy are briefly considered in *G.T.* Book VI.

3.3 INCOME, EFFECTIVE DEMAND AND THE MULTIPLIER

Keynes's ultimate objective is to show how the equilibrium of a competitive monetary production economy is determined, not by the supply of available labour, but by the point of effective demand. In the Classical system the division of output between investment and consumption is determined by the rate of interest (strictly, by the rate of time-discounting), while output itself is determined in the labour market by the second postulate, by the equilibrium between the marginal revenue product and marginal disutility of labour. In Keynes's system, consumption is determined by current investment without reference to the supply of available labour, through the level of income; the equilibrium between current investment and consumption is reflected in the 'multiplier' relationship between current investment and income.

Keynes's *investment* multiplier must be understood as in the first instance a relation between aggregate income, current investment and consumption, that follows directly from the definition of aggregate income as the sum of the values of current investment and consumption. Income is a matter of price as well as quantity, and prices may change to clear each industry's product market each day. The multiplier is a corollary of the existence of a market value for aggregate output, in other words, of the temporary equilibrium of the daily market period. The Appendix to this Chapter contains a mathematical proof that if equilibrium market prices can be observed, the marginal propensity to consume must be less than unity. This 'fundamental psychological law' follows directly from the observation of a set of market prices for output and is therefore, as Keynes states, a matter of logic, not an *ad hoc* assumption. The marginal propensity to consume, as we have seen above, is a separate matter from the level of the propensity to consume, of which Keynes offers no equilibrium analysis because of its dependence on the long-term future, and which the short term of his long period allows him to take as largely independent of influences other than 'real' money-income. The existence of a market value for aggregate output corresponds both to a value of the marginal propensity to consume below unity and to the traditional Marshallian conditions for the stability of equilibrium in each industry. ▶ **A3.3.1**

However, as we have seen in Chapter 1, employment is determined by effective demand, while income and effective demand are not the same thing. Old Keynesian economics simplifies matters by assuming they coincide in equilibrium, thus allowing current investment and the multiplier to determine employment directly through expenditure and income. The main problem with 'the neo-classical synthesis' is that it is not as Classical as Keynes. Aggregate demand substitutes for effective demand and is interpreted as expenditure rather than income at various different future dates; homogeneous output replaces deflated money-income and ignores the problems addressed by user cost; the multiplier becomes a sequence of rounds of expenditure, income and leakages; while investment and the price-level are exogenous. Competition, relative prices, expectation, and aggregate supply disappear from the model completely. The contribution of modern Classical economists in insisting on the resurrection of these key elements of economic theory must be acknowledged.

The Old Keynesian interpretation was, no doubt, encouraged by the fact that there is no mention of effective demand in *G.T.* Book III, and Keynes here does indeed for the most part treat income and effective demand as equivalent, for the reasons already given. *G.T.* Book III, shorn of most of the rest of *The General Theory*, is the core of Old Keynesian economics. Only section IV of *G.T.* Chapter 10 reminds the reader of the importance of expectation and supply, yet this section, intended by Keynes to reduce confusion over the nature of the multiplier, seems mainly to have increased it.

The multiplier is first and foremost a marginal condition at a *point* of equilibrium, as expressed by Keynes in his definition of the marginal propensity to consume as the formal derivative dC/dY (*G.T.* 115), a concept from the *infinitesimal* calculus. In that context it is appropriate to describe the multiplier as establishing 'a precise relationship, given the propensity to consume, between aggregate employment and income and the rate of investment' (*G.T.* 113, *C.W.* XIV, p. 121), rather than between *changes* in these variables. This represents the 'logical theory of the multiplier, which holds good, continuously, without time lag, at all moments of time' (*G.T.* 122). Secondly, if (and only if) it can be assumed that the propensity to consume is a stable function over time, the multiplier can be calculated as the ratio between the observed changes in income and current investment over a period of time (e.g. *G.T.* 127). Thirdly, if in addition the change in current investment is fully anticipated, those observed changes will reflect the 'normal' or long-period equilibrium value of the multiplier (*G.T.* 123, 125). These three multipliers, and others, are explored further in Section **A3.3.2**.

3.4 SUMMARY

Keynes offers no equilibrium theory of the level of consumption, and his claim that the marginal propensity to consume is less than unity is a simple corollary of the existence of a market value for output (i.e. of the existence of money-income). The Pigou effect does not appear in *The General Theory*, not because Keynes overlooked it, but mainly because it is inconsistent with an economy based largely on bank-money, and because Keynes was of the informal view that increases in real income and wealth would reduce the propensity to consume rather than increase it. The long-term Pigou effect has in any case no place in a short-term theory of employment.

Keynes presents employment as determined by entrepreneurial expectations in the first instance, but those expectations ultimately depend on the expenditure decisions of consumers and investors. The identity of the consumers and investors is not of fundamental theoretical importance, so that *The General Theory* is not a model of a closed economy without government or corporations. The multiplier is a condition of equilibrium that follows directly from the observation of a market value for output and holds good continuously at any time; it may be measured by comparing two positions of equilibrium over time only if the propensity to consume is assumed to be constant. It is a matter entirely of income and market prices, rather than effective demand and expected prices.

NOTES

1. Tobin records the Kalecki and Fisher critiques of the Pigou effect and of Leontief's quip that if the price-level fell sufficiently, the entire national income could be purchased 'with a dime'. He concludes that the long-term Pigou effect has no place in a world of historical time, but argues that Keynes 'did not show the existence of an excess-supply equilibrium, at least not in the meaning of the magic word equilibrium in the Classical, or neo-Classical, economics he was criticizing. In that meaning, equilibrium is a stationary state, and *a state in which expectations are fulfilled*' (1980, emphasis added).
2. Bunting (2001) offers an important methodological critique of the empirical analysis cited in support of Friedman's permanent income hypothesis, similar to McCombie's critique of the 'empirical' aggregate production function (McCombie, 2001a, 2001b).

Appendix to Chapter 3

A3.1   AVERAGE AND MARGINAL

A3.1.1   Patinkin and the proportional multiplier

Footnote 2 of *G.T.* 126 presents a general formula of the relation between the average and marginal propensity to consume and a short description of its meaning, that Patinkin (1978) has discovered to be imprecise. The 'proportional multiplier' or 'investment-elasticity of income' can be written

$$\varepsilon_{Y,I} = \frac{dY}{Y} \bigg/ \frac{dI}{I} = \frac{1 - \dfrac{C}{Y}}{1 - \dfrac{dC}{dY}} = \frac{APS}{MPS}$$

where APS and MPS refer to the average and marginal 'propensity to save' (this is merely short-hand for the mathematical expressions and not a useful economic concept). Keynes states 'As wealth increases dC/dY diminishes, but C/Y also diminishes. Thus the fraction [$\varepsilon_{Y,I}$ above] increases or diminishes according as consumption increases or diminishes in a smaller or greater proportion than income.'

This final statement is correct if the marginal propensity to consume is constant and the change in the average propensity to consume results solely from the difference between the average and marginal propensity to consume, since $dAPS/dY > 0$ if $MPS > APS$. However, if the marginal propensity to consume changes with income (as it does in the worked example on the same page) the condition for $\varepsilon_{Y,I}$ to increase with income becomes

$$\varepsilon_{APS,Y} > \varepsilon_{MPS,Y}$$

where this expression means that the income-elasticity of the average propensity to save exceeds the income-elasticity of the marginal propensity to save. This need not always be the case, although it is so in Keynes's example.

The reader as meticulous as Patinkin will also find that the figure of 6,900,000 in the example on the same page should be 7,300,000, if Keynes is working to the nearest 100,000, as he does on the next page (*G.T.* 127).

A3.2   CONSUMPTION AND EMPLOYMENT

A3.2.1   Factor income and effective demand

Keynes is careful to point out (*G.T.* 90) that 'real' income (in the sense of money-income measured in wage-units) is merely a proxy for employment and that the correspondence is not necessarily unique.[1] In terms of our earlier notation, there may be a set of different distributions of employment, of vectors $\{n\}$ with the same scalar value N, but different levels of effective demand D^* and of current income Y. There is no suggestion of Hansen's assumption that employment can properly be proxied by a measure of homogeneous output (truly real, as opposed to 'real', income), which contradicts *G.T.* Chapter 4. The difference between distributions of the same aggregate employment is not important provided that it is reasonable to assume that 'there is a unique distribution of [aggregate *effective* demand] between different industries' (*G.T.* 282, emphasis added) so that a functional relation (the employment function) can be derived in equilibrium between the two scalar values of employment N^* and effective demand D^* (see Section **A1.3.1**). Keynes's use of the term *effective* demand when he might appear to mean *aggregate* demand is not accidental. ▶ **A5.3.4**

However, there is a further step, which Keynes does not here make explicit. The aggregate demand function $D_1 = D_1(N) = \chi(N)$ of *G.T.* Chapter 3 is a relation between expected proceeds and employment, and not a relation between income and expenditure. The treatment of income and expected proceeds (effective demand) as equivalent partly reflects their equivalence for factors of production; it also follows from Keynes's decision 'to omit express reference to short-term expectation' (*G.T.* 50) and to treat the effect on consumption of the disappointment of entrepreneur's expectations, as reflected in windfall losses, as a matter of practical importance but impossible to express by a mathematical function (*G.T.* 95–6).

The effective demand for consumption-goods refers to the expected value of the output of consumption-goods in production today; meaning the value expected, not today, but at the end of their production periods. There is no automatic equivalence of income and effective demand, which correspond respectively to the value of today's deliveries and the expected value of the future deliveries in which today's employment will result. Today's aggregate demand for consumption-goods does not mean today's expenditure on goods by consumers; and today's income is not the same concept as today's effective demand.

Nevertheless, while effective demand represents the future income expected by entrepreneurs, its value includes factor income, which accrues as the factors are employed. The monetary nature of production is important, since factors must be credited with money-income at today's market prices as they deliver their services, quite independently of the future market value of their output. For the purpose of the propensity to consume, this is convenient, since it means that the bulk of the value of effective demand translates into immediate income, both for workers and rentiers. It is only entrepreneurs (or indeed, dealers) who must wait for future spot market prices to determine their income. If the state of expectation remains constant, income and effective demand will coincide for them too (although only over time as deliveries are made, and not on the same day); if the state of expectation changes today, entrepreneurs will make windfall gains or losses on work-in-progress (and other capital-goods), which may affect the propensity to consume today, irrespective of the date of delivery of the work-in-progress.

In the notes for his 1937 lectures Keynes writes:

> Propensity to consume is determined solely by a psychological composite of actual and expected income and is determined neither by effective demand at a definite date nor by income at a definite date. Income, ie realised results as distinct from effective demand, only exists for entrepreneurs and for them is relevant only because it reacts on their subsequent determination of effective demand and on their personal consumption. Thus it was that I came to lay all stress on effective demand as operative factor ... I found I could get all that was required by the conceptions of effective demand and income which were identical for factors but income of entrepreneurs at any time depended on outcome of prediction undertaken at various previous periods under influence of effective demand. (*C.W.* XIV, p. 180)

A3.3   INCOME, EFFECTIVE DEMAND AND THE MULTIPLIER

A3.3.1   The multiplier as a condition of market-period equilibrium

A marginal propensity to consume less than unity can be shown to be the macroeconomic equivalent of the Marshallian conditions of market-period equilibrium. The 'logical' multiplier corresponds directly to the existence of a 'market value for output as a whole [which] is, at the same time, a necessary condition for money-income to possess a definite value and a sufficient condition for the aggregate amount which saving individuals decide to save to be equal to the aggregate amount which investing individuals decide to invest' (*G.T.* 64).

This can be demonstrated in mathematical terms using the notation of Section **A1.3.1**, where:

Y aggregate value of income $\equiv \mathbf{y'p^s} = \left(\mathbf{x}-\overline{\mathbf{x}}\right)' \mathbf{p^d}$ in price equilibrium

C aggregate value of consumption $\equiv \mathbf{x'_c p^d_c} = \mathbf{y'_c p^s_c}$ in price equilibrium, where the subscript C denotes that the vectors include only the consumer goods industries

I aggregate value of current investment (exogenous)

The postulated functional relations are

$$\mathbf{x} = \mathbf{x(p^d},Y) \qquad\qquad (A3.1)$$
$$\mathbf{y} = \mathbf{y(p^s)} \qquad\qquad (A3.2)$$
$$\mathbf{p^d} = \mathbf{p^d}(Y) \qquad\qquad (A3.3)$$
$$\mathbf{p^s} = \mathbf{p^s}(Y) \qquad\qquad (A3.4)$$

and without relative prices, the aggregate functions are

$$C = C(Y) \qquad\qquad (A3.5)$$
$$Y \equiv C + I \qquad\qquad (A3.6)$$

Note that the demand and supply functions (A3.1) and (A3.2) are those for the daily market period. Some variation in supply is possible, through the depletion of stocks, the finishing of work-in-progress and the provision of services on demand, so that **y** need not be assumed constant. All variables are undated, i.e. simultaneous, so this is a static equilibrium problem.

The traditional (point) multiplier can be obtained by differentiating the national income identity (A3.6), giving

$$\frac{dY}{dI} = \frac{1}{1 - \frac{dC}{dY}} \tag{A3.7}$$

which for stability requires $\frac{dC}{dY} < 1$.

We can instead include the relative prices of consumer goods and write

$$Y \equiv C + I \equiv \mathbf{x}'_c \mathbf{p}^d_c + I \equiv \mathbf{y}'_c \mathbf{p}^s_c + I \tag{A3.8}$$

Dropping the subscript, the multiplier can now be written in two forms corresponding to demand and supply:

$$\frac{dY}{dI} = \frac{1}{1 - \left[\left(\frac{\partial \mathbf{x}}{\partial \mathbf{p}^d} \frac{d\mathbf{p}^d}{dY} + \frac{\partial \mathbf{x}}{\partial Y} \right)' \mathbf{p}^d + \mathbf{x}' \frac{d\mathbf{p}^d}{dY} \right]} \tag{A3.9}$$

$$\frac{dY}{dI} = \frac{1}{1 - \left[\left(\frac{d\mathbf{y}}{d\mathbf{p}^s} \frac{d\mathbf{p}^s}{dY} \right)' \mathbf{p}^s + \mathbf{y}' \frac{d\mathbf{p}^s}{dY} \right]} \tag{A3.10}$$

Note the extra term in the demand version (A3.9), reflecting the direct influence of aggregate income on demand independent of its influence through the demand price. In the case of supply, the quantity is determined solely by the supply price, which is thus the only channel through which aggregate income can affect supply.

The condition of market-period equilibrium is that expressions (A3.9) and (A3.10) for the multiplier are equal. In each industry this means (abstracting from complementarity between industries)

$$\left(x + p^d \frac{\partial x}{\partial p^d}\right)\frac{dp^d}{dY} + p^d \frac{\partial x}{\partial Y} = \left(y + p^s \frac{dy}{dp^s}\right)\frac{dp^s}{dY} \qquad (A3.11)$$

In equilibrium $x = y$, $p^s = p^d$ so we can write:

$$\left[\frac{dp^d}{dY}\frac{Y}{p^d} + \frac{\partial x}{\partial p^d}\frac{p^d}{x}\frac{dp^d}{dY}\frac{Y}{p^d} + \frac{\partial x}{\partial Y}\frac{Y}{x}\right]\frac{p^d x}{Y} = \left[\frac{dp^s}{dY}\frac{Y}{p^s} + \frac{dy}{dp^s}\frac{p^s}{y}\frac{dp^s}{dY}\frac{Y}{p^s}\right]\frac{p^s y}{Y} \quad (A3.12)$$

which can be restated as

$$\varepsilon_{p^d Y}\left(1 + \varepsilon_{xp^d}\right) + \varepsilon_{xY} = \varepsilon_{p^s Y}\left(1 + \varepsilon_{yp^s}\right) \qquad (A3.13)$$

where ε_{xY} denotes the aggregate income elasticity of demand

$$\frac{\partial x}{\partial Y}\frac{Y}{x},$$

$\varepsilon_{p^s Y}$ the aggregate income elasticity of the supply price

$$\frac{dp^s}{dY}\frac{Y}{p^s}$$

and the other elasticities are written accordingly.

For normal goods, $\varepsilon_{xY} > 0$, so that

$$\frac{\left(1 + \varepsilon_{xp^d}\right)}{\left(1 + \varepsilon_{yp^s}\right)} < \frac{\varepsilon_{p^s Y}}{\varepsilon_{p^d Y}} \text{ and therefore } \varepsilon_{xp^d} < \varepsilon_{yp^s}, \text{ if } \varepsilon_{p^s Y} \le \varepsilon_{p^d Y} \quad (A3.14)$$

Putting (A3.14) into words, the condition for aggregate money-income to be defined is equivalent to the standard Marshallian condition that in each industry the market-period price elasticity of demand is less than the market-period price elasticity of supply for normal goods, provided that the aggregate income elasticity of the supply price is less than or equal to the aggregate income elasticity of the demand price. The latter pair of 'aggregate' elasticities do not appear explicitly in Marshall.

In the market period, the price elasticity of demand is negative for normal goods, and the price elasticity of supply is either zero, or positive mainly through the depletion of stocks. *A priori* one would expect the second half of the condition to hold as an inequality for normal goods below full employment, and the strict equality to hold at full employment. The definition of a normal good is that the quantity consumed increases with total consumption. Although all supply prices will increase as aggregate output increases, through diminishing returns in market-period production and increasing demand for a given quantity of capital-goods, an increase in the quantity consumed implies that the demand price increases with aggregate income by more than the supply price. Only at full employment, when no increase in the quantity produced is possible except by substitution of other goods, can one expect supply prices to increase *pari passu* with aggregate income and demand prices.

It is interesting to compare this approach to that of Samuelson (1947, pp. 278–80) who reaches a similar conclusion that a marginal propensity to consume less than unity is a stability condition, but based on a completely different principle. Samuelson specifies 'the rate of change of income as proportional to the difference between intended savings-investment and actual savings-investment' (ibid., 278).

A3.3.2 Hansen's versions of the multiplier

The three versions of the multiplier referred to in this chapter can be written, using the notation of Sections **A1.3.1** and **A2.2.2**, as follows:

logical, instantaneous
$$\frac{1}{1 - dC/dY} \tag{A3.15}$$

logical, over discrete time
$$\frac{Y_t - Y_{t-j}}{I_t - I_{t-j}} \tag{A3.16}$$

normal
$$\frac{D^{**}\big|\Omega', r' - D^{**}\big|\Omega, r}{I^{**}\big|\Omega', r' - I^{**}\big|\Omega, r} \tag{A3.17}$$

Expression (A3.15) is the familiar result of differentiating the income identity $Y \equiv C + I$. Expression (A3.16) expresses the ratio of the difference between *income* on any two days separated by an interval j (irrespective of any changes in the state of expectation) and the corresponding difference in current investment. This is the observable discrete form of the multiplier, which is equivalent to (A3.15) if the propensity to consume is stable over time and linear, giving a constant marginal propensity to consume. The numerator of expression (A3.17) is the difference in the values of long-period aggregate *effective demand* corresponding to two states of long-term expectation Ω and Ω' and their corresponding interest rates, while the denominator is the corresponding difference in the values of long-period effective demand for current investment. D^{**} is the aggregate effective demand associated with the long-period employment $n''|\Omega, r$, and I^{**} the related effective demand for capital-goods. Expression (A3.17) represents the normal value of the multiplier (*G.T.* 123, 125); all three are exercises in comparative statics, since both income and long-period effective demand are equilibrium values. In a steady state, the values of expressions (A3.16) and (A3.17) will coincide, even though one refers to income and the other to effective demand.

Hansen's interpretation of the multiplier (and of Keynes's use of it) is rooted in the idea that the multiplier establishes equilibrium between *ex ante* and *ex post* consumption at the point of effective demand. This represents a quite different account of the nature of effective demand from the present one. The definition of the multiplier in expressions (A3.15) and (A3.16) is regarded by Hansen as a 'mere *arithmetic* multiplier (i.e. a truism) and not a true *behaviour* multiplier based on a *behaviour* pattern which establishes a verifiable relation between consumption and income' (1953, p. 111, original emphasis), a tautology devoid of behavioural content. In reaching this conclusion, he neglects the behaviour represented by the competitive process of determination of prices in individual markets. Instead he invokes a 'definite expenditure-lag behaviour pattern' (1953, p. 112), but presents no microeconomic explanation of this pattern in terms of the competitive equilibrium of supply and demand.

Hansen distinguishes between a 'moving equilibrium' and a 'period analysis' multiplier (1953, p. 108). He links Keynes's 'logical multiplier' to his own 'moving equilibrium' and relates both to the case where 'a change in aggregate investment ... has been foreseen sufficiently in advance for the consumption industries to advance *pari passu* with the capital-goods industries without more disturbance to the price of consumption-goods than is consequential, in conditions of decreasing returns, on an increase in the quantity which is produced' (*G.T.* 122). On the present account this quotation refers, not to the logical multiplier, but to expression (A3.17), which represents not only a comparison between two positions of static long-period equilibrium, but also an implicit convergence path of employment between the two positions where sufficient notice of change is given (Section **A2.2.3**). Expression (A3.17) provides the behavioural relation sought by Hansen. On the present reading, Keynes's logical multiplier has nothing to do with normal behaviour as Hansen suggests, but relates simply to the change in the (equilibrium) values of income and investment over any period of time, no less behavioural for not being 'normal'. Hansen's 'moving equilibrium' relates to an equilibrium of *ex ante* and *ex post* (1953, p. 59) which is absent from *The General Theory*.

Hansen's second concept of the multiplier in terms of 'period analysis' involves time-lags and the unforeseen change in investment of section IV of *G.T.* Chapter 10. Our account has no room for an unexplained expenditure-lag, but there is a difference between the convergence path of employment in a case where the change in the state of expectation has been wholly foreseen, and where it is wholly or partly unforeseen. As already described in Section **A2.2.3**, a change in the state of expectation will, in the latter case, affect the value of work-in-progress and stocks of finished consumption-goods, so that Keynes's Marshallian 'temporary equilibrium' will be struck so as to clear the markets for consumption-goods at prices above the normal supply prices, until such time as production can increase to eliminate the temporary scarcity. The variations in the multiplier during this process are captured by expression (A3.16).

NOTE

1. It is this inexact correspondence to which 'Okun's Law' refers (Mankiw, 2003, pp. 35–6).

4.   The Inducement to Invest

This chapter corresponds to *G.T.* Book IV, with the exception of *G.T.* Chapter 18 (Keynes's summary chapter), which is taken here under Chapter 5. Having considered consumption and its relation to income and current investment in *G.T.* Book III, Keynes now turns to address the determinants of the aggregate demand for new capital-goods, which in his initial exposition of the Principle in *G.T.* Chapter 3 he presented as exogenous. *G.T.* Book IV (*G.T.* Chapters 11–17) takes us from the short-term world of *G.T.* Books II and III, where expectations can usually reliably be based upon present results, into the world of decisions about the long-term future, where no such assurance can be given. *G.T.* Book IV demonstrates how 'changing views about the future are capable of influencing the quantity of employment' (*G.T.* xxii) by the use of two analytical tools, the schedules of the marginal efficiency of capital and of liquidity-preference, to connect changes in the rate of current investment with changes in the state of long-term expectation.

The marginal efficiency of capital (*G.T.* Chapter 11) has an affinity with user cost through their shared dependence on the state of long-term expectation (*G.T.* Chapter 12), and these complementary concepts reflect the two aspects of capital-goods, as instruments of production and as stores of value. ▶ **A4.2.1** The marginal efficiency of capital draws an analytical line between long-term debts and capital-goods as stores of value, while the preference for liquidity, in the face of the uncertainty of the state of long-term expectation, draws a similar line between money and long-term debts. Keynes's own theory of the rate of interest is developed in *G.T.* Chapters 13 and 15, while *G.T.* Chapter 16 on the nature of capital explains the deliberate choice of 'efficiency' over 'productivity'. *G.T.* Chapter 14 applies the method of *reductio ad absurdum* to the Classical theory of interest, very much as does *G.T.* Chapter 2 to the Classical theory of employment.

This chapter emphasises that liquidity-preference is derived from the state of long-term expectation and is relevant to all kinds of capital-asset, in contrast with the more usual treatment, limiting liquidity-preference to the theory of the rate of interest. Thus the chapter reverses Keynes's order of approach, starting with ideas expressed in their most general form in *G.T.*

Chapter 17, and working towards their more concrete expression in the investment-demand and liquidity-preference functions. The core proposition is that the demand for capital-goods is a function both of the actual state of long-term expectation (expressed through the marginal efficiency of capital) and of the uncertain prospect of indefinite change in that state (expressed through liquidity-preference).

4.1 A HIERARCHY OF LIQUIDITY

One of the axioms of Classical economics is 'gross substitution', meaning that under perfect competition every good or service is, to some degree and at the right price, a substitute for every other, either directly in exchange or indirectly through production. In *The General Theory*, by contrast, goods and services are divided up into the categories of money (including some short-term debts), bonds (long-term debts), labour, natural resources, consumption-goods, and capital-goods. Keynes's rate of interest is the differential between the interest rates on long-term (bond) and short-term (money) debts, in both cases the secure liabilities of either the banking system or the State. Apart from money and labour, these categories do not represent homogeneous aggregates and the classification does not imply any assumption of particular relative prices of natural resources, bonds, consumption-goods and capital-assets, within and between their categories. The three partitions between four of these categories correspond to Keynes's macroeconomic functions, the propensity to consume and the schedules of the marginal efficiency of capital and of liquidity-preference, which do not replace but complement Marshall's microeconomic supply and demand functions. The compartments can be illustrated as follows, where each class of goods is a separate compartment, although the three categories of asset also share a larger compartment:

Figure 4.1 Keynes's compartmentalisation of goods

Thus the propensity to consume determines the level of consumption and aggregate income for a given level of current investment, which in turn changes the stock of wealth held in the form of capital-assets. For the individual, if not for the community as a whole (leaving aside commodity money and foreign lending), money and bonds represent alternative forms in which wealth can be held. Labour and natural resources do not appear explicitly in the diagram but are either consumed directly or employed in the production of consumption-goods or capital-assets. There is a causal sequence (down the page) so that an individual takes two steps: the decision to consume income or wealth; and the decision as to the form in which to hold wealth, old and new. The causal sequence also operates, as we shall see, within the 'wealth box', so that money dominates bonds, and bonds dominate capital-assets.

It is of the greatest importance to realise that in *The General Theory* individuals do not choose between (say) consumption-goods on the one hand and bonds or capital-assets on the other (Fisher and Hicks); nor between money and consumption-goods (Pigou and Friedman), or money and capital-assets (Minsky); nor do employers as a whole substitute between labour and capital-goods in choosing how to produce a given output (the Classical aggregate production function). Each of these missing choices has played a role in the interpretative controversy, but they are ruled out by Keynes's treatment of time. The common foundation of Keynes's three macroeconomic functions and his system of classification is our uncertainty about the future, and it is this which interferes with the 'gross substitution' of Classical theory.

These compartments have nothing to do with obstacles to competition. In *G.T.* Chapter 17, Keynes assumes that the price of each asset is held under perfect competition at the equilibrium point where the net advantage or total prospective return from holding any asset is the same (*G.T.* 227–8). Our discussion of the multiplier in Chapter 3 of this book has made it clear that the balance between consumption and current investment may be affected by movements in relative prices, and that a marginal propensity to consume less than unity is in fact a condition of temporary market-period equilibrium and the existence of a market value for output (i.e. income) under perfect competition. The compartments are not about imperfect competition or *ad hoc* behavioural restrictions, but about the propensity to consume today when the future is unknown, and about differences in the effect of changing views about the future on each class of asset.

With regard to the propensity to consume, the Classical theory holds that the rate of interest (in some 'real' sense) regulates the division of income between consumption and saving/investment, balancing the preference for consumption today against the greater consumption tomorrow arising from the 'productivity' of capital. There is thus no partition between consumption and investment as in *The General Theory*, but an optimum equilibrium allocation of consumption over time based on relative prices. Keynes's critique of the Classical theory of interest begins in *G.T.* Chapters 6 and 7 with the definition of income as the value of output and the investment-saving identity, and Chapter 2 of this book has explained why the familiar Old Keynesian concepts of equilibrium income and the equilibrium of *ex ante* and *ex post* saving, reminiscent of the Classical approach, were rejected by Keynes. The prices and outputs of consumption- and capital-goods are always in competitive equilibrium, provided that output has a market value, and there is nothing left for the rate of interest or the quantity of money to do in bringing about equilibrium between these two aggregates. *G.T.* Chapter 14 approaches the same question from a different angle, emphasising that the investment and saving schedules implicit in contemporary Classical thought are not independent of each other or of money-income.

Keynes's partition between consumption and investment, embodied in the propensity to consume, is not an endogenous outcome but an independent variable of his equilibrium theory of employment. *G.T.* Chapter 9 succinctly summarises the complex long-term subjective influences on the propensity to consume, most of which are not amenable to equilibrium analysis and depend greatly on psychological attitudes towards the future. Certainly the propensity to consume bears no simple functional relation to the rate of interest in the short term, and as for the long term, Keynes is agnostic. On the one hand, he acknowledges that a fall in the rate of interest may increase the propensity to consume (*G.T.* 218); but on the other, he regards it as likely that the accumulation of wealth reduces the propensity to consume (*G.T.* 31, 97). He is quite clear that competition alone provides no 'self-regulatory process of adjustment which takes place without the necessity for any special intervention or grandmotherly care on the part of the monetary authority' (*G.T.* 177).

In moving from the consideration of consumption decisions to investment, Keynes's choice of compartments and partitions within the 'wealth box' is pregnant. He accepts that the total prospective return from holding any asset, new or old, is equalised under perfect competition, and without the compartments, he would have no basis for causal analysis, in particular for picking out the money rate of interest as the significant variable. If there were an asset other than money whose total prospective return (whether measured in terms of money or itself does not matter) were fixed exogenously, the total prospective return from all other assets, including money, would also be held at the same level in equilibrium. If the money rate of interest were below this level, holders of bonds would be better off selling and buying other assets, thus reducing the price of bonds and raising the money rate of interest. In such a case, the causal analysis would need to explain why the prospective return on the 'dominant asset' should be exogenous and impervious to the forces of competition and substitution.

The question, therefore, is how do market forces operate to determine the total prospective return on all types of asset? The sophisticated Classical answer (avoiding the attribution of physical productivity to some homogeneous measure of capital), as set out by Marshall and accepted by Keynes, is that the prospective return on capital-assets in general reflects their relative scarcity in exactly the same way as the return on land and other natural resources in more or less fixed supply. The scarcity of producible capital-assets can in principle be eliminated by increasing their supply, hence Marshall's distinction between their 'quasi-rents' and the true rents of land, etc. Where Keynes and the Classics part company is that the latter invoke the notion of 'waiting' (Pigou adds 'uncertainty-bearing', an interesting half-way house between Marshall and Keynes, 1932, p. 771) as the independent element of 'capital in general' which is in scarce supply. Since output is determined by full employment in this Classical system, capital-assets can be accumulated only if people are willing to postpone consumption in favour of investment, and because they are reluctant to do so without the inducement of a real rate of return, capital-assets remain scarce and continue to earn quasi-rents (see the quotation from Marshall at *G.T.* 242).

Since 'waiting' is 'not consuming', Keynes's identification of the investment-saving identity and its direction of causation (that current investment determines saving) deprives the increment of waiting of any independent causal influence upon the rate of investment and therefore the scarcity of capital-assets. So, if it is not the reluctance to wait, what is it that keeps capital-assets scarce and their total return above zero? Keynes's answer is ultimately the same as that of Aristotle and St Thomas Aquinas, that the love of money is the root of all evil (*G.T.* 351–2), although this phrase needs considerable elaboration and clarification. There is something about money which makes the money rate of interest fall more slowly than the total prospective returns on other assets as they accumulate. This 'something' turns out to be related to the changing views about the future to which a monetary economy is sensitive (*G.T.* xxii), and which he formalises as changes in the state of long-term expectation. Furthermore, this 'something' attaches more strongly to money than to bonds, and to bonds more than to real capital-assets, so that on this dimension bonds are always preferred to real capital-assets, and money is always preferred to bonds. We thus arrive at Keynes's three categories of asset and the two partitions between them, the marginal efficiency of capital and the state of liquidity-preference.

Keynes's objective is to establish a relation between investment and the state of long-term expectation, through the combined mechanism of the functional schedules of the marginal efficiency of capital and of liquidity-preference. The state of long-term expectation cannot itself be captured by a quantitative variable that can be put directly into a function, unlike the rates of interest and of current investment and the quantity of money, yet it is the substrate of the two asset functions themselves. The action in Keynes's system comes, not primarily through movements 'along the curves' caused by changes in the quantity of money, but through shifts in the state of long-term expectation and the related state of liquidity-preference, and in the corresponding functions and positions of equilibrium. His technical achievement is to incorporate something as elusive as changing views about the future into a formal equilibrium framework.

The reason why two functions are necessary emerges in *G.T.* Chapter 17 of which, astonishingly, Hansen writes 'not much would have been lost if it had never been written' (1953, p. 159). The total prospective return can be divided between prospective yield (q), carrying costs (c), and liquidity-premium (l), all measured in terms of the asset in question, so that total prospective return in terms of money equals $a + q - c + l$, where a is the expected appreciation in the money price of the asset. Keynes then divides assets into two groups, one comprising real assets and bonds which offer a return in the form of a prospective money yield less carrying costs ($a + q - c$), and money as the other, offering a return in the form of a liquidity-premium (l). This segregation is a simplification, since Keynes allows that real assets and bonds may offer some liquidity, and that money may offer some prospective yield (when in the form of bank deposits or treasury bills) and incur carrying costs (for safe custody). The prospective yield, carrying costs and liquidity-premium are thus to be understood as defined net, relative to the corresponding forms of return, on money or other assets respectively. Furthermore, for reasons that will become clear, bonds always have a higher (gross) liquidity-premium than real assets, so that liquidity-preference can properly be discussed in terms of the choice between money and bonds alone.

The purpose of this segregation of money from other assets is to isolate the liquidity-premium on money as the rate which 'rules the roost' and holds up the rate of return on capital-assets in general. Keynes's argument requires that he identifies separately the essential properties of money as distinct from other assets, and connects these to the rate of current investment in capital-assets which, unlike money and bonds, can be produced by labour. This is achieved by the separate definition of the two functions, of liquidity-preference and of the marginal efficiency of capital, a distinction which is absent or at least of no causal significance in Classical theory.

Keynes's choice of compartments and of the partitions between them is far from arbitrary, and the lack of substitutability between each compartment, except through the partitioning functions, has nothing to do with obstacles to competition. The Classical axiom of gross substitution, which would dissolve the partitions between the compartments, abstracts from the uncertainty about the future which is the common foundation of Keynes's three macroeconomic functions.

4.2   STOCKS AND FLOWS

The investment-saving identity and Keynes's use of time and equilibrium periods are important to a full appreciation of his two asset functions, of the marginal efficiency of capital and liquidity-preference. In particular, these elements of Keynes's thought shed light on two major interpretative controversies, over the logical consistency of Keynes's use of the marginal efficiency of capital, and over the relationship between Keynes's liquidity-preference and the neo-classical loanable funds theories of the rate of interest.

The difficulty over the marginal efficiency of capital arises from Keynes's statement that the schedule of the marginal efficiency of capital or investment-demand schedule has a downward slope (*G.T.* 136). Critics such as Eatwell (1983) have taken this as evidence that Keynes's marginal efficiency of capital is in fact nothing more than the Classical marginal (revenue) 'productivity' of capital, and indeed Keynes appears to confirm this in his subsequent statement that '[There is no] material difference, relevant in this context, between my schedule of the marginal efficiency of capital or investment-demand schedule and the demand curve for capital contemplated by some of the classical writers who have been quoted above' (*G.T.* 178), where these writers include none other than Walras (*G.T.* 177). Since the Classical theory is based on full employment, there appears to be logical inconsistency in using the marginal efficiency of capital to determine a position of under-employment equilibrium.

The controversy dissolves if the argument of Chapter 1 of this book is accepted, that Keynes's theory of employment is, within the quantum limits of the 'daily' unit of time, one of continuous short-period equilibrium at any time. By recognising Keynes's distinctions between *period* and *term*, we can identify three versions of his investment-demand schedule in different contexts, for the short period, for the short-term long period, and for the long term. Only the third requires the assumption of full employment, as a result of intervention by the authorities (*G.T.* 220), and is used in that context only, not as a description of unaided market outcomes.

Full employment is a sufficient, but not a necessary, condition for a downward slope in the investment-demand schedule; all that is *necessary* is a constant state of long-term expectation, in which the conditions of demand for the output derived from any given type of asset are taken as given.[1] Given inelastic demand, increased supply will reduce the expected market price, or if demand is elastic, the marginal efficiency of capital will reduce as the supply price of the capital-good rises, as more is produced under diminishing returns. The state of expectation may always be treated as constant at a point in time, even if it changes from day to day. Furthermore, as discussed in Chapter 2 of this book, Keynes is ready to admit, at least in theory, that the state of expectation may be constant in the short *term*, allowing employment to reach a corresponding long-period position as the aggregate capital equipment adjusts to the given state of expectation. However, the changing and unpredictable nature of the state of long-term expectation beyond the short term, if not necessarily from day to day, is part of the non-negotiable core of *The General Theory*.

Given the perspective that Keynes's daily short period is instantaneous, there is no significance in Keynes's use of the term 'marginal efficiency of capital' rather than 'marginal efficiency of investment' (the stock/flow distinction, Lerner, 1952), and Keynes's separation of the demand and supply effects of new investment is legitimate. Today's investment represents the production of new capital-goods, which are not themselves available for use in production, but add to the stock of capital equipment upon which tomorrow's effective demand will be based. On any given day, production of new capital-goods will be limited mainly by diminishing returns in production with the existing capital equipment, so that price equilibrium is achieved by an increase in supply price; although to the extent that capital-goods are produced in order to be held as a store of value rather than for use in production, price equilibrium may be reached partly through a rise in carrying costs (*G.T.* 233–4) and the corresponding reduction in the net prospective yield ($a + q - c$). Together these factors give a 'short-period schedule' of the marginal efficiency of capital, based solely on today's state of expectation, which may change tomorrow, and not upon the constant state of expectation necessarily associated with the full employment of the Classical investment-demand schedule.

If the state of expectation remains constant for the duration of the period of production that defines the short term and the length of Keynes's long period, the prospective yield of assets, which were initially in short supply as a result of a previous change in the state of expectation (e.g. shortages of particular components or machines), falls over the long period with an increase in their availability, without any implication that this represents substitution of capital for labour or other factors at the Classical margin of full employment. The marginal efficiency of each type of capital-asset falls in turn more slowly than the prospective yield, since its supply price falls as the rate of investment reduces and the supply curve of this type of capital-asset itself shifts as capital accumulates. The diminishing returns of this 'long-period schedule' reflect the increase in capital equipment relative to the constant state of long-term expectation, rather than relative to the availability of other factors of production.

By further contrast, *G.T.* Chapter 16 considers the case where the period of time is long enough for the marginal efficiency of capital to reach zero in a 'quasi-stationary' state (*G.T.* 220) leading to 'the euthanasia of the rentier' (*G.T.* 376). This 'long-term schedule' of the marginal efficiency of capital depends not only on a constant state of long-term expectation, but explicitly upon the maintenance of full employment by government intervention. The downward slope of the schedule here corresponds exactly to the Classical full-employment investment-demand schedule based on factor substitution.

G.T. Chapter 17 also takes as its hypothetical benchmark this 'long-term schedule' and the position of full employment and capital satiation to which, Keynes accepts, perfect competition would move the system in the absence of 'money-ness' (*G.T.* 235). Yet given less than full employment and a positive marginal efficiency of capital on any day, he returns to the short period when he states the problem as the decline of the rate of interest 'more slowly, as output increases' than the marginal efficiency of capital-assets (*G.T.* 236, note misprint in *C.W.* VII). The reference to output rather than capital equipment means that Keynes here refers to investment (the flow), not capital equipment (the stock), and to the 'short-period investment-demand schedule' for a given day in a given state of expectation. The 'short-period schedule' depends only on the state of expectation on any given day, as does employment as a whole, and not upon the assumption of full employment. The short-period obstacle to investment means we never reach the Classical long-term long-period equilibrium position.

Our understanding of Keynes's treatment of time also sheds further light on a second controversy, over the relationship between Keynes's liquidity-preference and the neo-classical loanable funds theories of the rate of interest. The controversy has been perpetuated by the Old Keynesian idea that the multiplier brings about equilibrium between intended (*ex ante*) and actual (*ex post*) saving, which necessarily takes place as a process over time, and thus inevitably leads to a continuation of the 'muddle' over 'flows of saving' and flows of loanable funds, which Keynes lampoons (*G.T.* 183) and Hansen defends (1953, p. 152). ▶ **A2.3.3** This controversy, too, dissolves once we recognise that effective demand (Chapter 1 of this book), the investment-saving identity (Chapter 2), and the multiplier (Chapter 3) all refer to positions of continuous short-period competitive equilibrium in the mechanical sense at any time; and that Hicks's different concept of equilibrium, over time, invokes a constant state of expectation and is defined to include the clearing of factor markets, in accordance with our third and fourth criteria of equilibrium. ▶ **A2.3.4** There is accordingly no room for investment to take the form of hoarding (new commodity money apart), or for saving to be supplemented by dis-hoarding or money creation. All that is left is the portfolio decision to determine the values of a given stock of each class of asset at any time. All we need for this are the concepts of the marginal efficiency of capital and of liquidity-preference.

4.3   THE STATE OF LONG-TERM EXPECTATION

In earlier chapters we have noted the analytical importance of Keynes's division between the state of short- and long-term expectation, corresponding to the expectations of producers and investors respectively. The state of short-term expectation depends upon the state of long-term expectation, since the latter is a major determinant of the prices and outputs of new capital-goods (the rate of investment) and, through the multiplier, the prices and outputs of consumption-goods also, and it has often been convenient to refer simply to the state of expectation as a whole. The state of short-term expectation can be represented by the set of expectations or expected prices for producible goods, both consumption- and capital-goods, for each day of Keynes's long period. The level of employment on any given day corresponds to the state of expectation, which may change from day to day. We have argued that short-term expectations can properly be regarded for analytical purposes as 'rational expectations' based on the daily equilibrium of forward markets for the product of each industry, and that this is in fact the method of *G.T.* Chapter 3. This section will now consider why it is not legitimate to deal with long-term expectations in the same fashion, and also offer an interpretation of Keynes's concept of 'conventional valuation' in terms of his understanding of probability as summarised in the Prologue.

Keynes defines the state of long-term expectation as 'the state of psychological expectation which covers ... future changes in the type and quantity of the stock of capital-assets and in the tastes of the consumer, the strength of effective demand from time to time during the life of the investment under consideration, and the changes in the wage-unit in terms of money which may occur during its life' (*G.T.* 147–8). The marginal efficiency of capital is the numerical device which translates this complex entity, via the prospective yield over the life of the capital-asset, into a single-valued expectation of a rate of return of the same dimension as the money-rate of interest. As we have already noted, the relationship between the marginal efficiencies of different types of capital-asset plays the central role in Keynes's discussion of the essential properties of money. When considering the influence of the state of long-term expectation on the valuation of capital-assets, it is helpful to follow Keynes in recognising that the marginal efficiency of capital is a corollary of the market price of any capital-asset (*G.T.* 137). The rest of this section will accordingly concentrate on the prices of capital-assets rather than their efficiency.

It is convenient, and does no great violence to reality, to postulate the existence of short-term forward markets, either in fact or as a representation of a process of convergence by trial and error. Thus the uncertainty about the value of today's output at the end of its production period is, in our terms, transferred from employer to wholesale dealer, and the effective demand on any given day is determinate. However, when it comes to the state of long-term expectation, it is self-evident that, in general, long-term forward markets for the output of capital-assets over their economic life do not exist. Examples of considerable practical importance, in which the investor can transfer the risk of a capital-asset to the consumer of its output, from landlord to tenant in the case of buildings, and through monopoly privileges which allow prices to be fixed in relation to cost (*G.T.* 163), are the exceptions which prove the rule.

The modern 'efficient markets hypothesis' (EMH) holds that asset prices reflect fundamental value, meaning that within the limits of random error, long-term expectations do indeed on average reflect the eventual outcome over the life of the asset. To sustain this hypothesis requires one of two assumptions, either

EMH-A   *the world behaves as if complete futures and insurance markets*
             extend to the horizon of long-term expectation; or
EMH-B   *a process of trial and error leads to a convergence of*
             expectations on their equilibrium values.

EMH-B implies EMH-A; while EMH-A is sufficient on its own, if no more than an assertion, given the absence of the required markets. Now Keynes would arguably be quite prepared to accept the two EMH assumptions as complements in the case of short-term expectation: in practice, entrepreneurs correct their expectations by trial and error in circumstances which are usually stable over short production periods (EMH-B); thus, for analytical purposes, it is acceptable to assume 'rational expectations' in the short term (EMH-A). By contrast, 'it is of the nature of long-term expectations that they cannot be checked at short intervals in the light of realised results' (*G.T.* 51). The long-term durable nature of capital-assets is precisely the problem; if the expectations upon which the investment was based prove mistaken, it is not possible, either to reverse the investment today, or to go back in time, adjust the original investment decision, and then check the revised results in the present, in order to find the equilibrium position. It is only in a stationary or steady state that adjustments made today might (given stable dynamics) be expected to have the same effect in the future as the same adjustments, made in the past, would have had today. So, the convergent feedback mechanism, which would be necessary to generate in practice a set of long-term equilibrium prices as the basis of prospective yield, is absent in any economy subject to unforeseen change, such as the one we inhabit. It cannot be emphasised enough that it is simply not legitimate to model the real world in terms of long-term equilibrium over time, because of the historical nature of time.

The efficient markets hypothesis replaces the assumption of perfect foresight with the only slightly weaker assumption of knowledge of an objective frequency distribution governing events.[2] If we follow EMH-B, that this knowledge can be acquired by discovery, every addition to the evidence will improve confidence in the expected value, in the sense of reducing its standard error as the sample size increases. In the more general Keynesian case, an addition to the evidence need not conform to the distribution of previous information in the well-behaved manner of drawings from an urn, so that the expectation may fluctuate dramatically. Even if there is considerable weight behind a given expectation, confidence may be shaken by the arrival of unexpected bad news; the knowledge that we know so little about the future always haunts us.

In the presence of such fundamental or intractable uncertainty, and in the context of highly 'liquid' investment markets, it is only *rational* to pay more attention to tomorrow's market price than to tentative and unreliable expectations of fundamental value. What matters is the expectation of tomorrow's price which, on the balance of Keynesian probabilities, is judged as likely to exceed as to fall short of today's price plus interest; or putting it another way, that today's price balances the bullish tendency against the bearish (where these tendencies may exist together in the mind of the same investor or separately among different investors). Evidence which would not be relevant for the purposes of calculating fundamental value, such as the intentions of other investors, must now take prominence. Indeed, the *only* thing that matters (ignoring transactions costs, etc) is the intentions of other investors, so that individual opinions matter only insofar as they contribute to 'average' opinion. If particular investors ('bears') believe the market is over-priced, they should sell today and buy back tomorrow, even if their long-term intention is to hold the asset for its economic life. There may be serious-minded investors in the market whose intentions reflect a model of fundamental value, yet it is still their intentions in the form of arbitrage operations that matter, and not the accuracy of their model, which can only be established long after the event. As Keynes points out in detail in *G.T.* Chapter 12, the real business of the professional investor must, perforce, be the study of market sentiment, in which the study of fundamental value is at best a minority option. The balance of Keynesian probabilities thus indicates a 'conventional valuation', the price today that balances the bullish and the bearish tendencies in the market as a whole and represents the average opinion or conventional wisdom as to the correct price. ▶ **A4.3.1**

The eloquence of Keynes's description of speculative excess in *G.T.* Chapter 12 has, for the modern Classical reader on the one hand, tended to obscure the fact that conventional valuation is not an aberration or temporary departure from fundamental value, but inevitable in the real-time world of organised asset markets: no forward market or convergence mechanism exists to bring long-term asset prices into line with their fundamental value. On the other hand, much Post Keynesian theory tends to treat investment as entirely exogenous, determined solely by 'animal spirits' or other institutional forces not open to competitive equilibrium analysis. Nevertheless, Keynes himself is explicit that

We should not conclude that everything depends on waves of irrational psychology. On the contrary, the state of long-term expectation is often steady. Thus after giving full weight to the importance of the influence of short-period changes in the state of long-term expectation as distinct from changes in the rate of interest, we are still entitled to return to the latter as exercising, at any rate, in normal circumstances, a great, though not a decisive, influence on the rate of investment. (*G.T.* 162)

The next section argues that in considering long-term accumulation, consistently with this statement, Keynes places his main emphasis on the indirect influence of the possibility of unforeseen changes in the state of long-term expectation upon the money-rate of interest through liquidity-preference, rather than on the direct effect of actual changes (and the speculative anticipation of such changes) in the state of long-term expectation upon the prospective yield. Liquidity-preference, like the propensity to consume, is a psychological response to the uncertainty of the future.

4.4 THE NATURE OF LIQUIDITY

It is common ground among writers on Keynes that the degree of liquidity of an asset is the degree to which a decision to use the asset as a store of wealth can be reversed at short notice and without loss. Liquidity allows investors to cut their losses if their expectations have to be revised. There is less clarity about the nature of liquidity itself, as discussed in the Prologue, and most writers equate liquidity with convertibility or marketability, the ability to exchange an asset for cash at a well-defined market price. This is not a satisfactory interpretation of the meaning of liquidity, at least in *The General Theory*, in which all assets are (as I have argued above) equally convertible in perfectly competitive markets, nor does it make sense of Keynes's reference to the liquidity of land.

Liquidity means more than convertibility and includes the degree to which the value of an asset, measured in any given standard, is independent of changes in the state of long-term expectation. Liquidity risk is then the possible (*not* probable or expected) loss of value as a result of a change in the state of long-term expectation. Keynes's liquidity premium is the margin required by investors between the marginal efficiencies of the asset and the standard in order to overcome preference for the standard. The size of this margin will depend upon the difference in the degree of confidence with which investors view the marginal efficiencies of the asset and the standard respectively.

Keynes comes closest to defining liquidity from first principles in his discussion of a situation where the standard of value (perhaps the goat to which he refers in *A Treatise on Money*, but certainly not land) does not have the normal character of money:

> In [a non-monetary] economy capital equipments will differ from one another (a) in the variety of the consumables in the production of which they are capable of assisting, (b) in the stability of value of their output (in the sense in which the value of bread is more stable through time than the value of fashionable novelties), and (c) in the rapidity with which the wealth embodied in them can become 'liquid', in the sense of producing output, the proceeds of which can be re-embodied if desired in quite a different form. (*G.T.* 240)

Liquidity is firstly a function of the degree to which a capital-asset can be used in the production of different consumables, so that a change in prospective yield based on production in one line can be met by switching to another line. The prospective yield on the second line is lower than originally expected from the first, but higher than now expected from the first after the change in expectations, reducing the impact of the change on the value of the asset. Keynes then refers to the importance of the stability of the value of the consumables produced. Stability in this context means independence from changes in the state of long-term expectation (*e.g.* bread is not a fashion item). The third element of his definition is the 'turnover period', the period over which the asset can be converted through production into consumable output. The shorter the period, the less likely is it that a change in the state of long-term expectation will arise during the life of the asset. Clearly Keynes is here thinking in aggregate terms: although an individual investor can always exchange an asset for money under perfect competition, its convertibility for the community as a whole depends on its conversion into consumption-goods through production and not just exchange. ▶ **A4.4.1**

For the various rather complex reasons set out in *G.T.* Chapter 17, the standard of value tends to be the asset whose value in terms of consumable output is the most stable with respect to changes in the state of long-term expectation. ▶ **A4.4.2** Thus when Keynes refers to liquidity he really does mean money, including short-term bank and state debts whose value is not sensitive to changes in the rate of interest because of the short period to redemption. Keynes treats capital-assets as fully convertible but not liquid, and mentions, almost as a footnote to the above definition (*G.T.* 240), the need for a premium to compensate for their liquidity risk relative to bonds. The rate of interest on bonds, where there is no 'risk proper', is entirely compensation for liquidity risk from unexpected changes in interest rates.

From this it is clear that Keynes regards capital-assets as less liquid than bonds, in the sense that their value is more sensitive to changes in the state of long-term expectation, since the value of capital-assets depends on expectations of both the interest rate and the prospective yield. On this definition of liquidity, money and bonds dominate capital-assets in terms of both 'risk proper' and liquidity risk. The first step in the portfolio decision is to choose between money and the next most liquid and safe class of assets, i.e. bonds; only then does the choice arise between capital-assets and bonds. Thus liquidity risk is the criterion for placing different categories of asset in separate compartments, and the demand for liquidity cannot be satisfied by assets other than money (i.e. the set of assets convertible on demand into means of payment at a fixed price in terms of the standard of value).

In the discussion of *G.T.* Chapters 11 and 12 Keynes takes the rate of interest as given and considers how expectations of prospective yield are affected by changes in both the balance and the weight of evidence. Market prices are determined by the balance of opinion, not so much in the minds of individual investors, but of all investors as expressed through supply and demand in a conventional valuation. Prices reflect not only what Keynes refers to as the 'actuarial' value, corresponding to the balance of evidence, but also the state of confidence, which is related to the weight of evidence. This distinction corresponds to 'the difference between the best estimates we can make of probabilities and the confidence with which we make them' (*G.T.* 240). The celebrated 'animal spirits' or spontaneous optimism relate to the state of confidence and have their counter-poise in liquidity-preference, 'the degree of our distrust of our own calculations and conventions concerning the future' (*C.W.* XIV, p. 116). The state of confidence is not something separate from the state of long-term expectation, but part of it. Confidence is weak when we know that our expectations are likely to change substantially, but we have no precise idea as to their future state: our present expectations already represent the best we can do on the available evidence.

▶ **A4.4.3**

Having held the rate of interest constant while discussing the marginal efficiency of capital, Keynes continues to draw upon his understanding of probability and the state of long-term expectation when he turns to his liquidity-preference theory of interest. Bonds differ from capital-assets in that their prospective yield is fixed from the outset, so that secure bonds carry no actuarial risk or 'risk proper'. By the same token, the state of confidence in this prospective yield (unlike those of capital-goods) is high, if not always absolute, and is not to be confused with the state of confidence in expectations of the future rate at which this prospective yield will be discounted (i.e. the expected future rate of interest). The current rate of discount of the prospective yield on bonds thus reflects only the liquidity risk from holding bonds, so that conversely the bond rate is a measure of the premium required to overcome liquidity-preference, i.e. the lack of confidence that future interest rates will not differ from current expectations and that bond prices will not fall in consequence. The price of bonds is, as with all long-term convertible assets, struck as a conventional valuation based on the expression in terms of supply and demand of the balance of the bullish and bearish tendencies of investors as a whole.

Keynes's liquidity-preference theory of interest has been the subject of many detailed criticisms, and perhaps the most telling is one of the oldest, namely that the conventional 'safe' rate of interest is left 'hanging by its own bootstraps'. Yet this criticism loses its force when full account is taken of the historical nature of time and of the state of long-term expectation. Keynes recognises that the 'safe' rate can be managed down (*G.T.* 204), but that by an inverse square law reminiscent of Newton's (*G.T.* 202) a rate below John Bull's 2% (*G.T.* 309) compensates only to a vanishing extent for the risk from a future upward change in expectations of future interest rates. The future will always be unknown, and any sense of history makes unreasonable the belief that any given state of expectation will persist indefinitely.

Thus, according to Keynes, the rate of interest has a life of its own, based on our well-founded distrust of forecasts of the long-term future and on the security offered by money, as the store of value least affected by changes in such forecasts. There is no market mechanism for bringing the rate of interest into equilibrium with the propensity to consume at full employment, nor do market forces operate to reduce the liquidity-premium in the same manner as they tend to reduce the prospective yield of capital-assets. Behind Keynes's analysis lies an acceptance of the historical nature of time and of the world we inhabit as one 'in which our previous expectations are liable to disappointment and expectations concerning the future affect what we do today'.

4.5 SUMMARY

The demand for new capital-goods is a function of the actual state of long-term expectation (expressed through the marginal efficiency of capital) and of the uncertain prospect of indefinite change in that state (expressed through liquidity-preference). The common foundation of Keynes's three macroeconomic functions (including the propensity to consume) and his classification of goods into four compartments is our uncertainty about the future, and it is this which interferes with the gross substitution axiom of Classical theory. The division of assets into capital-assets, bonds and money and the choice of the two partitioning functions between them reflects different orders of liquidity risk and permits the isolation of the essential properties of money.

The confusion between stocks and flows associated with some discussions of the marginal efficiency of capital and the theory of interest is resolved once the investment-saving identity and Keynes's use of time and equilibrium periods are fully appreciated. Unlike short-term expectations, long-term expectations cannot even for analytical purposes properly be treated as 'rational' in the modern Classical sense; it is only rational (or better, reasonable) to pay more attention to tomorrow's market price than to tentative and unreliable expectations of fundamental value. Yet Keynes places more emphasis, for the purposes of the long term, on the indirect influence upon current investment of the state of confidence through the rate of interest, than he does on the direct effect upon the prospective yield of investment from actual changes (and the speculative anticipation of such changes) in the state of long-term expectation. Liquidity-preference and animal spirits are opposite aspects of the state of confidence, which is a matter of the weight of evidence behind our forecasts of the future. Thus the rate of interest has a life of its own, based on our well-founded distrust of forecasts of the long-term future and on the security offered by money, as the store of value least affected by changes in such forecasts.

NOTES

1. Behind the full-employment investment-demand schedule lies a collection of heterogeneous capital-goods; there is no suggestion here of homogeneous capital with the problems of reswitching and reversing identified by Wicksell and Sraffa. The downward slope only assumes diminishing returns to each type of capital-good, on the assumption that full employment is maintained by intervention.
2. See Glickman (1994), Hayes (2006b). The necessary assumption of direct or indirect knowledge of the frequency distribution applies even to the more sophisticated Classical treatments of uncertainty and capital irreversibility such as real options theory (Dixit and Pindyck, 1994). See also Crotty (1996) on the relationship between asymmetric information and fundamental uncertainty.

Appendix to Chapter 4

A4.2.1 The marginal efficiency of capital and user cost

There is a remarkable unity in Keynes's conception of the relationship between capital-goods and time, of durable capital as the bridge between the present and the future. This can partly be illustrated by applying the concept of the marginal efficiency of capital to the short period, so that the employment decision can be seen as a form of the investment decision. The equilibrium employment offered by an entrepreneur is determined by the equality of expected price with marginal prime cost, which makes no obvious reference to time, nor to processes of production which occupy time. However, in section II of *G.T.* Chapter 16 (*G.T.* 213–17), Keynes discusses in some detail the efficiency of production processes of different duration, and the influence of the rate of interest in determining efficiency, in terms of value as opposed to physical productivity. In production, a series of inputs over time creates an output at a future date, while the prospective yield on the purchase of a new investment is, in general, a series of future outputs. Yet the same considerations apply to both cases, that the marginal efficiency of either stream must equal the rate of interest in equilibrium. This is implicit in the usual description of the equilibrium production decision, because the interest charge on the working capital accumulating during the process of production is treated as an element of factor cost, included in prime cost (Pigou, 1933, pp. 57–8). Production over time by definition means investment in working capital, which is subject to the same requirement to match the rate of interest as any other form of investment. The decision to offer any given level of employment (represented so deceptively simply by the ordinary supply curve) is, on this principle, a complex inter-temporal equilibrium, in which the entrepreneur must decide on the most efficient method of production and combination of capital-goods and labour, in response to the expected price of output, the rental cost (actual or imputed) of each factor of production including the use of money, and the user cost of each capital-good owned or purchased by the entrepreneur.[1]

The value of any capital-good is the present value of its prospective yield discounted at the rate of interest; the only difference between liquid goods and durable equipment is that 'the return to liquid capital consists of a single term', the current spot price (*G.T.* 73). Every capital-good has a certain efficiency as a method of converting present value into future value; the difference between new and old capital-goods is that the price of old goods can fall below their replacement cost, so that their efficiency is always equal to the rate of interest, as in the portfolio equilibrium of *G.T.* Chapter 17 (*G.T.* 227–8). Only new capital-goods can have an efficiency (relative to their normal supply price, *G.T.* 228) greater than the rate of interest, which may be reflected in the demand-prices, or market prices, of goods of that type (*G.T.* 151, n1); although, in short-period equilibrium, the efficiency of the marginal newly produced capital-good equals the rate of interest. Hence it is the marginal, not the average, efficiency of capital (including money) that sets the pace of investment, i.e. the production of new capital-goods. A point which emerges explicitly in the Appendix to *G.T.* Chapter 6 on user cost (although it is implicit from the very outset, *G.T.* 4) is that capital-goods of any particular type, and not only labour, can be involuntarily unemployed, 'redundant' or 'surplus' (*G.T.* 70–72). The implication of redundancy is that the price of this type of capital-good falls below replacement cost, so that no new goods of this type are produced, although the reverse implication does not necessarily hold; capital-goods may not be worth producing in certain circumstances (notably changes in technology), even though the existing goods of this type are not redundant.

The consumption of capital-goods in production is no more than the mirror image of the production of capital-goods for investment. All production is for the purpose of ultimately satisfying a consumer, which means that all capital-goods must ultimately be consumed, yet capital-goods are also a store of value while consumption is deferred. There is always a tension between the perspectives of the entrepreneur (or producer) and the investor (or rentier), which Keynes makes explicit through user cost. A capital-good may either be consumed through use in production; or held in stock as a store of value; or itself become a form of working capital, when the decision is made to enhance its value by modification or renewal. Thus a machine-tool has its primary use in production, but it may be moth-balled, or taken out of service for renewal of its components and upgrading of its control systems. A factory building may be redeveloped as an apartment block. In making such decisions, the entrepreneur is taken to weigh up the prospective yield from using the asset in these different ways. For the purposes of the production decision, the cost of using the asset is not simply an apportionment of its historic cost, as the financial accounts might suggest; the entrepreneur must consider the market value gained by not using the asset, or by investing in the asset as a piece of finished output in itself. Thus, in the definition of user cost, B' refers not only to the carrying costs of an asset held in stock, but also to the cost of improving it, if this gives a better unused value G'.

The calculation of the user cost and marginal user cost of assets whose economic life extends beyond the production period is analytically complex (*G.T.* 70–71), but it provides a justification of the rules of thumb, arrived at through trial and error or by following convention, by which entrepreneurs are deemed in practice to mark up their marginal factor cost in order to calculate their supply price. As with the principle of effective demand, Keynes seeks to 'distinguish the forces determining the position of equilibrium from the technique of trial and error by means of which the entrepreneur discovers where the position is' (*C.W.* XIV, pp. 182–3). In the first instance, the marginal user cost is given by the present value of the additional prospective yield gained by not using the equipment to produce the marginal output. Tarshis (1939) emphasises that user cost is not entirely physical, since the risk of 'spoiling the market' also adds to user cost.

In the simplest case, marginal user cost is equal to the gain from delaying the date of replacement with new equipment; the estimated future replacement cost and the cost per machine-hour, mile or other physical measure of economic life, can be calculated. The matter is more complex when a future temporary surge in demand for the services of the equipment is expected, for which it is not either worthwhile or possible to produce new equipment in order to satisfy the demand at normal prices (*G.T.* 70, n1). The distinction between Keynes's long and short period is involved here, together with the temporary departures of expected prices from normal short-period supply price during the traverse to long-period equilibrium. ▶ **A2.2.2** Conversely, when equipment of a particular type is redundant, the value of all such equipment (in use and otherwise) is discounted below its replacement cost, at a rate determined by the cost of holding the redundant equipment in stock, namely the sum of the interest cost and the current supplementary cost. The redundant equipment must be held until such time as the total equipment of that type has been physically depleted, sufficiently that there is no longer a surplus. So it is that partial scrapping schemes and improvements in the state of expectation directly increase marginal user cost, and therefore prices and profits (although not, directly, employment), by bringing forward the date when the redundancy is expected to be eliminated.

Following Kregel (1998), the calculation of user cost for long-term equipment may also be understood in terms of the pricing of futures and options, assuming perfect markets for capital-goods of all types and ages. We noted earlier that the user cost of short-term capital-goods is their current spot value plus the price of a call option to buy replacements at the end of the production period at the original spot price. In the long-term case, user cost may be calculated as the difference between, on the one hand, the sum of the current spot price and the value of a call option on equipment of the current vintage before the proposed use, and on the other hand, the forward price of comparable equipment after the proposed use. The option may be thought of as covering the value of the portion of the life-span of the equipment to be used up, while the forward contract covers the value of the portion that will remain, whether the equipment is held or used, and is thus open to loss from an unexpected fall in spot prices.

A4.3   THE STATE OF LONG-TERM EXPECTATION

A4.3.1   Fundamental value and conventional value

The concept of fundamental value is central to Classical theory, and it is important to clarify what it means and how it relates to Keynes's concept of conventional valuation. This section draws on Keynes's theory of probability ▶ AP.4.2 to provide formal definitions and a relation between these very different concepts.

Clarity is best arrived at by distinguishing the market price of an investment or financial claim q_t from its fundamental value in prospect (*ex ante*) q_t^* and its fundamental value in retrospect (*ex post*) q_t^{**}; q_t^* is an expectation of the outcome q_t^{**}. Note that both the market price q_t and the *ex post* fundamental value q_t^{**} are observable. It is in the nature of financial assets that they are traded on well-organised markets with well-defined competitive prices, so that q_t can easily be observed. *Ex post* fundamental value q_t^{**} can also in principle be observed, although it is a subject for accountants, and even then, only for those with a peculiarly academic and historical bent. For it is in principle possible, if of little or no commercial importance, to identify the market interest rates and the money yield of an asset over the course of its economic life, and so to identify the price q_t^{**} that would have warranted the holding of the asset at any time as an alternative to a debt, given perfect foresight. By contrast, the *ex ante* fundamental value q_t^* is intrinsically unobservable, except in the case of fixed annuities, and we shall find in due course that this unobservability presents an insuperable problem.

We start from common ground, the case in which $q_t = q_t^* = q_t^{**}$. The market price in equilibrium of a secure claim to a series of fixed future money receipts (what we shall call a 'fixed annuity' – Keynes uses the term slightly differently, *G.T.* 135) is the net present value of the series, which can be expressed as

$$q_t = q_t^* = q_t^{**} = \sum_1^N d_{t+i} \frac{1}{(1+R_{t+i})} \qquad \text{(A4.1)}$$

where N is the number of discrete time periods over which the series extends, d_{t+i} is the receipt due at time $t+i$, and R_{t+i} is the interest on a loan of a unit of money at time t for i periods. The three q's, with and without asterisks, are equivalent because both d_{t+i} and R_{t+i} are known at any time, given a market for secure fixed-rate debts of comparable maturities. Equation (A4.1) can be simplified by the assumptions that the stream of future receipts is a perpetual annuity growing in each period at a constant rate g and that the rate of interest in each period is a constant r, to give

$$q_t = \frac{d_{t+1}}{(r-g)}, \text{ such that } (r > g) \qquad \text{(A4.2)}$$

which looks very much like the standard dividend discount model for the valuation of equity securities. However, it is a considerable leap from the equilibrium price of fixed annuities to the market prices of financial assets in general, and the various assumptions required to make such a leap represent the heart of the controversy.

If, as an alternative to holding the claim to maturity, an investor can transfer the claim at an earlier date (including the next period), the relation between the present and future market prices q_t and q_{t+1} is, in equilibrium, given by the 'no arbitrage opportunity' condition

$$q_t = \frac{d_{t+1} + q_{t+1}}{(1+R_{t+1})} \qquad \text{(A4.3)}$$

where today's asset price equals the net present value of the sum of tomorrow's dividend and tomorrow's asset price. It is a small but significant step from equation (A4.3) to the 'rational expectations hypothesis' and the claim that rational, well-informed agents do not make systematic errors in forming their expectations. This is expressed by incorporating into (A4.3) an 'expected value' operator

$$q_t = E_t \left[\frac{d_{t+1} + q_{t+1}}{(1 + R_{t+1})} \right] \qquad (A4.4)$$

By substitution and the use of the 'law of iterated expectations',

$$E_t \left[E_{t+1} [q_{t+2}] \right] = E_t [q_{t+2}]$$

one solution of the first order difference equation (A4.4) in q_t looks very like equation (A4.1) with the addition of the expected value operator:

$$q_t = q_t^* = E_t \left[\sum_1^N d_{t+i} \frac{1}{(1 + R_{t+i})} \right] = E_t \left[q_t^{**} \right] \qquad (A4.5)$$

Equation (A4.5) states that q_t^* is the expected value of the prospective yield, in turn assumed to be a stochastic variable with a random disturbance term. This crucial assumption takes the only source of uncertainty to be the disturbance term, of which the expected value is zero, so that equations (A4.1) and (A4.5) are otherwise equivalent. If the disturbance term is normally distributed, uncertainty becomes synonymous with variance or 'volatility'. Equations (A4.1) and (A4.5) are indeed equivalent in the case of a fixed annuity, where $E_t[d_{t+i}] \equiv d_{t+i}$ and $q_t^* = q_t^{**}$.

According to Fama (1970, p. 389), the efficient markets hypothesis (EMH) emerged as a theoretical response to the empirical evidence that stock market prices follow a 'random walk'. A random walk (which also describes Brownian motion) can be expressed as

$$q_{t+1} = q_t + \varepsilon_{t+1} \qquad (A4.6)$$

where ε is a random disturbance with zero expected value. This must be carefully distinguished from a stationary stochastic process which represents a disturbance about the equilibrium value (note the asterisk):

$$q_{t+1} = q_t^* + \varepsilon_{t+1} \tag{A4.7}$$

If the EMH is to be based on the discovery of the equilibrium position by trial and error (condition EMH-B in the main text), equation (A4.7) alone is the appropriate description, and this can be relevant only where q_t^* is constant or predictable within an ergodic system. ▶ **AP.5.1** The consistency of the EMH with the random walk of equation (A4.6) requires perfect foresight of future equilibrium prices, not as a complement or analytical representation of trial and error, but as an independent condition (EMH-A). For if market prices always represent *ex ante* fundamental equilibrium values i.e. $q_t = q_t^*$ under EMH-A, then a random walk may be generated as a result of unpredictable shocks to the endowment, technology and tastes which are the parameters taken to determine future general equilibrium prices. However, the possibility of unpredictable shocks to the *parameters* of the system (and thus to q_t^* rather than q_t) conflicts with the assumption of a stationary (ergodic) state required by EMH-B, where expectations and therefore prices can be wrong in the short term, but the underlying equilibrium price stays put (or follows a deterministic trend) and can be discovered by trial and error. The world required by EMH-B does not generate a random walk, but a stationary stochastic process; the futures markets required, if EMH-A is to be more than an assertion, do not exist. Thus although the EMH purports to explain the empirical evidence of a random walk in prices, it can only do so by asserting EMH-A. The random walk cannot itself be offered as evidence in support of EMH-A.

To summarise the argument so far, it is plausible that in competitive equilibrium the market prices of fixed annuities (q_t) represent *ex ante* their fundamental values (q_t^*). Equally, the fundamental value of any past investment can be determined *ex post* at the end of its economic life (q_t^{**}), permitting an historical judgement of the profitability of the initial investment decision. However, the historical nature of time in a world subject to unforeseen change presents insoluble ontological obstacles to the extension of the concept of *ex ante* fundamental value (q_t^*) beyond fixed annuities to financial assets in general.

In terms of Keynesian probability, the *ex ante* expectation q_t^* of the *ex post* fundamental value q_t^{**} is the value of q_t^* which satisfies:

$$\left(q_t^{**} \geq q_t^*\right)\big|\Omega_t = \left(q_t^{**} \leq q_t^*\right)\big|\Omega_t \qquad \text{(A4.8)}$$

where this expression means that the probability (in Keynes's sense) that the outcome q_t^{**} lies at or above the expectation q_t^* equals the probability that the outcome lies at or below the expectation, given the available evidence Ω_t.

A comparison of the Classical equation (A4.5) with the Keynesian equation (A4.8) indicates their foundation in different theories of probability. If we can discover, by repeated sampling of a Classical ergodic system, the population relative frequency density function

$$\varphi\left(q_t^{**}\right),$$

then in Keynes's terms $q_t^* \big| \varphi\left(q_t^{**}\right) = 1$; the expected value and *ex ante* fundamental value

$$\mathrm{E}_t\left[q_t^{**}\right]$$

(although not the actual fundamental value q_t^{**} itself) is *known* rather than merely *probable* in Keynes's sense.

By contrast, in equation (A4.8), the information set Ω_t does not permit conclusive determination of the expectation q_t^* (let alone, *a fortiori*, the actual value q_t^{**}). Ω_t cannot equal the complete information set $\bar{\Omega}$ except in retrospect, and is in practice very scant and unreliable. Its unreliability stems partly from its being composed of a number of propositions that cannot be reduced to indivisible atomistic events in the manner of balls in an urn. As the number of balls drawn from an urn increases, the estimate of the proportions of different colours in the population becomes more reliable. By contrast, the value of an Atlantic liner does not become more reliable with news of the outbreak of war or the invention of the jet engine.

In the presence of fundamental or intractable uncertainty, and in the context of highly liquid investment markets, it is only *rational* to pay more attention to tomorrow's market price q_{t+1} than to tentative and unreliable expectations of fundamental value q_t^*. This can be expressed by the probability equation

$$\left(q_{t+1} \geq \hat{q}_t \left(1+R_{t+1}\right)\right)\big|\Omega_t = \left(q_{t+1} \leq \hat{q}_t \left(1+R_{t+1}\right)\right)\big|\Omega_t \qquad \text{(A4.9)}$$

which expresses in terms of Keynesian probabilities that tomorrow's price is judged as likely to exceed as to fall short of today's price plus interest; or putting it another way, that the bullish tendency is balanced by the bearish (where these tendencies may exist together in the mind of the same investor or separately among different investors). Information in Ω_t which would not be relevant evidence for the purposes of (A4.8), such as the intentions of other investors, must now dominate consideration of fundamentals. Indeed, the *only* thing that matters (ignoring transactions costs, etc) is the intentions of other investors, so that individual opinions matter only insofar as they contribute to 'average' opinion. The solution $\hat{q}_t$ of equation (A4.9) thus provides us with a formal expression of a 'conventional valuation', the price today that balances the bullish and the bearish tendencies in the market as a whole and represents the average opinion or conventional wisdom as to the correct price, given the current information. This price should therefore continue to prevail until there is change in the information – or, of course, in average opinion.

A4.4   THE NATURE OF LIQUIDITY

A4.4.1   Liquidity and the 'liquidity' of organised investment markets

Throughout his discussion of organised investment markets from *G.T.* 153–60 Keynes puts the words 'liquid' or 'liquidity' in inverted commas on no less than five occasions. The connection between the definition of Keynes's liquidity offered here and the 'liquidity' of organised investment markets is indirect, perhaps even obscure. The 'liquidity' of such markets is for Keynes a separate and rather different concept, which depends on the willing suspension of disbelief in the reliability of the conventional basis of valuation, and contrasts with the liquidity of money, which is unaffected by changes in the state of expectation.

The point is illustrated by Keynes's statement 'that each individual investor flatters himself that his commitment is "liquid" (though this cannot be true for all investors collectively)' (*G.T.* 160). Since as noted above

Keynes in general treats real assets and securities as equivalent, this 'liquidity' does not refer to the division of claims on physical assets into standard shares, transferable with low transaction costs: a necessary condition for any organised investment market. Keynes has already assumed perfect transferability and convertibility at the current market price. The benefit of 'true' liquidity in Keynes's sense lies in the ability to reverse an investment decision without loss *after* any future change in the state of long-term expectation. Specifically, an initial decision to hold money can be reversed, and the original value of the sum of money preserved to purchase bonds or real assets if the state of long-term expectation changes so as to favour the latter in the mind of the investor. Unlike Keynes's liquidity, 'liquidity' depends on the maintenance of the current state of long-term expectation long enough for the investor to 'beat the gun' and reverse the investment *before* the state of long-term expectation changes.

Keynes's liquidity is objective, since for the community as a whole the value of money in terms of consumable output is invariant to short-term changes in the state of long-term expectation. The illiquidity of a capital-asset reflects its durability and the period over which its present value can be converted through production into consumable output at uncertain future prices. The transfer of an asset between individuals does not alter its prospective yield for the community as a whole. 'Liquidity' is an illusion fostered by convertibility, and differs from liquidity. 'Liquidity' depends on the 'average' state of long-term expectation of the community as a whole remaining unchanged. To benefit from 'liquidity' requires 'foreseeing changes in the conventional basis of valuation a short time ahead of the general public' (*G.T.* 154), and therefore necessarily involves a speculative element.

The 'liquidity' of investment markets is not strictly an example of the fallacy of composition: 'average opinion' does not have a functional relationship with individual opinion in the same way that aggregate income is directly affected by individual expenditure. It is possible for average opinion to be maintained even if a large number of investors dissent from it; the expression for conventional valuation given by equation (A4.9) of the previous section can reflect the balance of evidence in the minds of individual investors, as well as the supply and demand of the market as a whole. The maintenance of a particular asset valuation requires only that there are sufficient bids from investors (including market-makers) who continue to follow average opinion to meet the offers from dissenting investors, and to clear the market at the current price. By contrast, the liquidity, in Keynes's sense, of money exists for one and all.

A4.4.2   The meaning of the stability of value

Keynes is ambiguous in his use of the term 'stability of value' of an asset. Does he mean stability over time; stability in terms of consumable output or the wage-unit; or stability with respect to changes in the output of the asset itself or in total output? The distinction between stability 'in terms of' and 'with respect to changes in' is important and corresponds in mathematical terms to the difference between a denominator and a derivative. If indeed he does mean stability in terms of consumable output, with respect to changes in what is the value stable? If changes in value over time (i.e. with respect to changes in time) and with respect to changes in output are possible, stable value cannot mean simply constant value. This suggests there is an unstated factor with respect to changes in which Keynes considers value to be stable in terms of consumable output.

This is a case where mathematical notation may once again help to clarify the argument. Let

$$V \equiv m \big/ p_c = V\left(N, q_m, t, x\right)$$

where V is the value of a unit m of the liquid asset divided by the expected general price-level of consumable output p_c in terms of the liquid asset (*C.W.* V, p. 48); N is total employment; q_m is the output of the liquid asset; t is time and x is another unspecified argument. Then does stability of value mean $\partial V / \partial N \approx 0$, or $\partial V / \partial q_m \approx 0$, or $\partial V / \partial t \approx 0$, or $\partial V / \partial x \approx 0$?

Keynes readily accepts that the value of money is not invariant to total output or employment, as discussed at length in *G.T.* Chapter 21, so he explicitly does not mean $\partial V / \partial N \approx 0$. His discussion of an alternative commodity wage-good refers to stability of value both as stability in terms of consumable output with respect to changes in the unspecified factor $\partial V / \partial x$ and as stability with respect to changes in its own output $\partial V / \partial q_m$:

> The expectation of relative stability in the future money-cost of *output* might not be entertained with much confidence if the standard of value were a commodity with a high elasticity of production … Such an expectation requires … that the costs of the commodity in question are expected to be relatively constant in terms of the wage-unit for a greater or smaller scale of *output* both in the short and in the long period (*G.T.* 237–8, emphasis added).

'Output' has a different meaning in these two sentences (*cf* Davidson, 1972, p. 233, n4), the first referring to consumable output as a whole (proxied by *N*) and the second to the output of the liquid commodity q_m. Here there are briefly two concepts of stability in use simultaneously, but Keynes quickly discounts the practical relevance of $\partial V / \partial q_m$. Instead he emphasises the 'zero, or at any rate very small, elasticity of production' of money (*G.T.* 230), so that changes of value with respect to changes in own output are no longer possible to any material extent.

The third possibility, that stability refers to changes in value over time $\partial V / \partial t$, is not so easily set aside. Chick (1983) interprets the perfect liquidity of money in terms of a particular good as meaning that the money price of that good is *certain* to be stable. Uncertainty about the future price reduces the liquidity of money, so that liquidity premium and expected change in price are not independent. This means the choice of numeraire is not neutral, since the degree of liquidity of an asset depends on the relative price of the standard against which it is measured. However, transaction costs and the general acceptability of money as the medium of exchange against which prices are set together limit the liquidity of non-money assets, 'except when inflation is widely expected' (1983, pp. 304–5).

In *G.T.* Chapter 17, Keynes explains the dominance of the money rate of interest using his $q - c + l + a$ analysis of the relationship between spot and forward market prices. The analysis is an exercise in comparative statics, forward looking but conducted at a point in time, as are all portfolio decisions. All assets are assumed fully convertible at the spot and forward market prices ruling at that instant. A forward market gives a price today for delivery tomorrow; there is no uncertainty about the forward price, which is quite different from the spot price that may rule tomorrow. The equilibrium relationship between today's spot and forward prices already includes an allowance for anticipated changes in the value of money, although clearly not for unexpected changes. Anticipated inflation does not directly affect Keynes's argument, as he points out in his critique of Fisher's ascription of a causal role to the real rate of interest (*G.T.* 142).[2]

Since Keynes's liquidity relates to future purchasing power, it may be that the liquidity premium should include an explicit allowance for expected inflation so that

$$l \equiv \dot{p}_c^e + l',$$

where $\dot{p}_c^e$ is expected inflation and l' is the 'real' liquidity premium. a becomes the expected price appreciation of a particular asset in excess of the expected rate of general inflation. A hyper- or 'unstable' inflationary economy may then be one in which $l > 0$ and $l' < c$, similar to Keynes's 'non-monetary' economy in which the standard of value is no longer the asset with the highest l'. There is a hint that Keynes accepts the possibility of $l' \leq 0$ if the money supply is too elastic (*G.T.* 241, n1). On this reading, inflation can destroy liquidity if it reaches catastrophic proportions, but it is not the primary source of liquidity under conditions of 'stable' inflation (such that $l' > c$).

If, following (and simplifying) Chick, liquidity were defined in terms of convertibility tempered by uncertainty about future prices, Keynes's liquidity premium l could no longer be considered independent of the price appreciation term a and indeed the carrying cost term c. Uncertainty about a reduces l relative to the particular asset. Carrying costs affect the attractiveness of using an asset as a medium of exchange for optimising the timing and composition of a flow of heterogeneous purchases, so that the lower is c, the higher is l. Yet Keynes clearly does treat l as an independent variable in the sense that its value cannot be inferred from a and c, and there is evidence from the paragraph inserted in response to criticism by Robinson (*C.W.* XIII, p. 649; *C.W.* XIV, pp. 499, 351) that he considers uncertainty about future prices to be a separate matter. When discussing money becoming a 'bottomless sink for purchasing power', he qualifies this tendency 'when the rise in the value of money leads to uncertainty as to the future maintenance of this rise; in which event a_1 and a_2 are increased, which is tantamount to an increase in the commodity rates of money-interest and is, therefore, stimulating to the output of other assets' (*G.T.* 231). The term 'value of money' means general purchasing power over consumable output, so that here Keynes addresses uncertainty only about the general price-level rather than about relative prices between heterogeneous goods. His inference that uncertainty leads to a rise in the equilibrium values of a_1 and a_2 (rather than a reduction in l) can be understood to mean that the possibility that the value of money may fall, and so the prices of other assets may rise, creates additional demand in the forward market for assets. Hedging buyers are prepared to pay a premium to insure against that possibility and speculative buyers also are prepared to buy forward, to the extent they believe that the future spot price will exceed the current forward price.

The demand for a store of 'value' relates to value as general purchasing power, although the basket of consumable goods in terms of which this is defined may change from time to time and depends on social practices and institutions. Keynes does not consider the possibility of arbitrage over time between the elements of this basket since he does not treat consumables as assets possessing exchange value. He also abstracts from the possibility of arbitrage between individual elements of the basket, or the basket as a whole, against assets, because he takes the propensity to consume as given for the purpose of this analysis (*G.T.* 236). Price variability therefore becomes an issue relating only to capital assets, bonds and money. Since Keynes treats capital assets as dominated by both bonds and money in terms of liquidity risk, it is reasonable for him to consider only the *net* liquidity premium between bonds and money, even if bonds and capital assets both possess some degree of liquidity. On his own terms of engagement, his treatment of the uncertainty of future prices is complete.

So on this reading, by stability of value Keynes means $\partial V/\partial x$, stability of value in terms of consumable output with respect to changes in an unspecified factor, which I suggest is the state of long-term expectation. We have not in this discussion considered the possibility that stability refers to m/W, the value of money in terms of the wage-unit, corresponding to the 'stickiness' of money-wages W/m. This is because Keynes is explicit that sticky money-wages are a consequence rather than the independent source of the liquidity of money. 'It is because of money's other characteristics—those, especially, which make it *liquid*—that wages, when fixed in terms of it, tend to be sticky' (*G.T.* 233). The stability of the value of money in terms of consumable output is the primary cause of the stickiness of money-wages, although Keynes acknowledges that this stickiness in turn feeds back and reinforces the stability of the value of money in terms of consumable output. When he considers the necessary properties of an alternative commodity wage-good, the need for its liquidity premium to exceed carrying costs in order to absorb excess supply (together with the stability of its normal supply price) is a prior condition for stickiness (*cf G.T.* 238). Liquidity therefore cannot itself be the result of wage stickiness.

A4.4.3 Actuarial vs. liquidity risk

The distinction between actuarial risk, or 'risk proper', and liquidity risk may be understood in the terms of Section A4.3.1. The relationship between actuarial and liquidity risk parallels that between Classical frequency probability and Keynes's logical probability insofar as, in both cases, the former is a subset of the latter. Actuarial risk corresponds to the loss, or gain, that results from the difference between the individual outcome q_i and its expected value,

$$\mathrm{E}_i\left[q_i^{**}\right].$$

By contrast, from the perspective of Keynesian probability, risk may be understood as the loss, or gain, resulting from a difference between the individual outcome q_i^{**} and the expectation $\hat{q}_i$ as the information set approaches completeness, or $\Omega_i \to \overline{\Omega}$. As in Section **A4.3.1**, each q here represents the discounted present value of the asset, rather than its marginal efficiency or running yield as in *G.T.* Chapter 17.

Implicit in the idea of actuarial risk is the assumption that each asset represents a drawing from a large population, whose individual *ex post* fundamental value q_i^{**} follows a relative frequency distribution $\varphi(q_i^{**})$, which can be deduced by repeated sampling. The term 'actuarial' reflects the implicit or explicit use of such frequency tables in the insurance of life and general accident, where there are large populations of events and, within limits, the incidence of a claim by an individual in any given period of time can be treated as random, while the overall incidence of claims by the population as a whole is expected to be stable over time.

A risk-neutral insurer of this type, holding a diversified portfolio of policies, will be indifferent between the individual qualifying risks and in competitive equilibrium will charge a premium reflecting the average loss on the portfolio as a whole (plus any long-period profit margin reflecting the degree of competition), which may be regarded as the premium for 'risk proper'. Implicit in this equilibrium risk premium is the assumption of a steady state, so that the average loss across time periods equals the average loss on the portfolio, and competitive insurers may be expected to base their offers of insurance on the 'rational expectation' of loss. Conversely, a diversified risk-neutral insurer will be satisfied with an expected return from the policy portfolio equal to the expected value; only if the insurer is risk-averse will there be a difference in the total return required from two portfolios, one of bonds with certain yields, and another of policies whose expected yields follow a known frequency distribution. In the latter case, the risk premium will reflect, not only the expected rate of loss implicit in the expected return, but also an additional inducement to overcome the insurer's aversion to the risk resulting from the dispersion of the expected return (this is the point made by Tobin, 1958).

As noted above, Keynesian risk may be understood as the loss, or gain, resulting from a difference between the individual outcome q_i^{**} and the expectation $\hat{q}_i$ as the information set approaches completeness, or $\Omega_i \to \overline{\Omega}$.

In general, of course, complete information is achievable, even in principle, only with hindsight. The expectation (and market value) $\hat{q}_t$ reflects uncertainty, not only about the *ex post* incidence of loss in individual cases, but also about the state of expectation in general.

These two sources of uncertainty can be separated, for illustrative purposes, by assuming for a moment that identical newly produced capital-assets command a fixed money rental for their services over their (known) economic life, but are not transferable, so that the holder of a (necessarily new) asset must value its prospective yield over its expected life, receiving income as rent for its use in production, but unable to take into account its capital value on a transfer. We assume further that some new capital-assets fail irreparably at random after a fixed period shorter than their economic life, that investors have observed a regular frequency of these losses in the past, and that they expect this pattern to continue in the future.

In this artificial case, the *ex ante* fundamental value q_t^* would stand at a discount to the value q_t^{**} which would be placed on an asset if it was known to be safe from failure, a discount equal to the actuarial risk, given risk-neutral investors. Any liquidity risk in this case would arise from a lack of confidence in the historic loss rate as a guide to the future, and the liquidity-premium required to compensate for this risk would be a difference between $\hat{q}_t$ and q_t^*, where the market price corresponding to the expectation $\hat{q}_t$ would stand, in turn, at a discount to the *ex ante* fundamental value q_t^* that reflects actuarial risk. These discounts can alternatively be expressed as margins over the secure interest rate for debts of comparable maturity.

The special assumptions of this example demonstrate the limited application of the concept of actuarial risk outside a subset of the class of insurable events (only a subset, bearing in mind that insurance is often based on a matched book rather than frequency tables). This is because assets are heterogeneous and the incidence of loss depends on historical events, while the prospective yield is not in general fixed by a rental contract for the economic life of the asset and reflects the state of expectation. Furthermore, the market price of a transferable asset represents a conventional valuation dominated, under perfect competition, by expectations of tomorrow's price rather than the prospective yield over the course of its economic life.

The risk of loss on capital-assets cannot in practice be decomposed into actuarial risk and the liquidity risk arising from a change in the state of expectation since, for most types of loss, there exists no basis in frequency tables for calculating actuarial risk. As discussed in Sections **AP.5.1** and **A4.3.1**, the concept of *ex ante* fundamental value is tenable only in an ergodic steady state. While investors may form the best expectation they can of prospective yield, gross and net of expected losses, it is not possible in general to apportion, between actuarial and liquidity risk, the risk premium implicit in the marginal efficiency of capital. This is why Keynes emphasises that:

> There are not two separate factors affecting the rate of investment, namely, the schedule of the marginal efficiency of capital and the state of confidence. The state of confidence is relevant because it is one of the major factors determining the former, which is the same thing as the investment-demand schedule. (*G.T.* 149)

By contrast, it is possible to isolate the liquidity risk on secure bonds, which offer no actuarial risk, and this partly explains why Keynes singles out the rate of interest on money as the principal example of a liquidity-premium. Note, however, that the state of confidence in expectations of future interest rates is only part of the state of confidence in the prospective yield of capital-assets in general. In the case of a long-term bond, let q_t^{**} be the (undiscounted) sum of future payments due. The market value $\hat{q}_t$ reflects the market's discounting of these future payments, thereby determining the structure of interest rates, and the difference between $\hat{q}_t$ and q_t^{**} is a direct measure of the present value of the premium required by investors to accept the liquidity risk. This premium can also be expressed as an interest rate, the (marginal) efficiency of the bond in terms of money. For this premium to be significant requires that Ω_t is a small subset of $\bar{\Omega}$, as in the case of long-dated bonds, notably the undated government perpetuities (Consols and War Loan) which were of particular importance in Keynes's time.

At this point, it is worth considering the relationship between actuarial and liquidity risk, on the one hand, and borrower's and lender's risk (*G.T.* 144–5), on the other. The proportion of the borrower's risk that Keynes refers to as double-counted is the liquidity risk. The borrower's risk includes elements of both actuarial and liquidity risk; the actuarial element can be diminished by 'averaging as well as by an increased accuracy of foresight', while the borrower's liquidity risk is compensated by a 'wider margin between his expectation of yield and the rate of interest at which he will think it worth his while to borrow' – wider than the actuarial risk alone warrants. As an aside, Keynes does not appear to regard as 'risky' an investment subject only to actuarial risk. The lender's risk falls into two main parts, the risks of voluntary and involuntary default, respectively. The risk of voluntary default, or moral hazard, has been emphasised in modern theories of corporate finance, based on agency problems or asymmetric information. The risk of involuntary default derives from the disappointment of expectation, i.e. the borrower's liquidity risk, and is also a problem for the lender, unless 'the borrower ... is in a position to offer an exceptional margin of security. The hope [NB: *not* the expectation] of a very favourable outcome, which may balance the risk in the mind of the borrower [here we are discussing the borrower's 'animal spirits'] is not available to solace the lender [under a risky debt contract].' Section **AE.2.1** to the Epilogue develops further Keynes's concept of lender's liquidity risk, applying it to the issue of equity shares as well as of debts.

NOTES

1. Kregel (1997) identifies the relationship between the marginal efficiency of capital and user cost, the importance of spot and forward prices in production, and recognises that aggregate demand prices should be understood as forward or futures prices.
2. Mankiw's loanable funds approach requires him to follow Fisher in making the *ex ante* real rate of interest the (long-run) causal variable (2003, pp. 89–90).

5. Employment, Money and the Price-Level

G.T. Book V completes the theoretical structure of *The General Theory* by considering the relationship between the principle of effective demand, the levels of money-wages and prices, and the quantity of money. It is appropriate to consider G.T. Chapter 18 here, rather than relating it to investment alone, as Keynes does as part of G.T. Book IV, since it summarises the theory of employment as a whole before considering the price-level. Keynes gives G.T. Book V the title 'Money-wages and prices'; the present title reflects this alternative arrangement of the G.T. chapters.

G.T. Book V touches upon two policy issues which continue to be of great relevance: the relationships on the one hand between money-wages and (un)employment, and on the other, between monetary policy and inflation. The downfall of Old Keynesian economics in the 1970s was associated with the combination of inflation and high unemployment known as stagflation, so that if *The General Theory* is indeed general enough still to be relevant today, it is necessary to identify where stagflation fits within its theoretical structure.

G.T. Chapter 18 (considered here in Section 5.1) summarises the equilibrium model which Keynes has built around the principle of effective demand first set out briefly in G.T. Chapter 3. He then moves outside the equilibrium model, so that G.T. Book V is of a different character to the earlier books. G.T. Chapter 19 (Section 5.2) considers (mainly) the causal link running from money-wages via the quantity of money to employment; G.T. Chapter 20 (Section 5.3) develops the causal link in the opposite direction from employment to prices and money-wages; while G.T. Chapter 21 (Section 5.4) considers the resultant relationship between the quantity of money and the levels of employment, money-wages and prices. However, in contrast to the dependent variables of the model of G.T. Chapter 18, the money-wage and the closely related price-level are not treated as equilibrium values, held continuously in a stable position by competitive forces.

5.1   THE EQUILIBRIUM SUB-SYSTEM OF *THE GENERAL THEORY*

G.T. Chapter 18 is the source of the Old Keynesian representation of *The General Theory* epitomised in Hicks's IS-LM model, as a system equilibrium of the goods and money markets corresponding to certain values of income and the rate of interest. The Old Keynesian IS-LM model and the Classical AD/AS model, derived from it and now found in all macroeconomics textbooks, are discussed further in the Appendix. ▶ **A5.1.1, A5.1.2**

There can be no denying that section I of *G.T.* Chapter 18 describes a set of simultaneous equations and indeed uses the language of mathematics in setting out the parameters, independent and dependent variables of the model. Although Hicks's claim to have Keynes's blessing for IS-LM is controversial, Keynes undoubtedly assented to the interpretation, as far as it went. Note, in particular, that the original model approved by Keynes (Hicks, 1937) illustrates the determination of income, and says nothing directly about effective demand and employment. The dependent (and mutually dependent) variables of income and interest rate are equilibrium values determined by the parameters and independent variables. The equilibrium is, as we have seen in earlier chapters, the outcome of a Marshallian process of individual optimisation in competitive markets with flexible relative prices, and not a matter of the quantity adjustments portrayed in the Old Keynesian interpretation. The equilibrium position is defined by a mechanical model in the Classical tradition, that would have been quite acceptable to Marshall, and indeed Walras.

What is lost in the IS-LM and other simultaneous equation interpretations of *The General Theory* is Keynes's original categorisation of the independent variables as the prime movers of the system, as distinct from the given parameters. For Keynes, these independent variables are ultimately the three psychological factors, the propensity to consume, the state of long-term expectation and the preference for liquidity, together with the quantity of money expressed in wage-units. In the Classical system, the parameters alone (preferences, technology and endowment) determine the relative prices and quantities which in turn correspond to the values of income and employment, and also the quantity of real balances. In Keynes's model, there are independent variables beyond the reach of equilibrium analysis (exogenous, i.e. outside the equilibrium model, yet still variable in the short term), as well as parameters (also exogenous, but not variable in the short term).

Underlying this appears to be an insistence by Keynes that equilibrium analysis can only legitimately be undertaken with reference to a given state of expectation. The future is not determined by the past and present, and has an independent existence reflected in the psychological factors. Thus although the model is deterministic, as all equilibrium models must be, it is not self-sufficient and closed in the sense that the parameters alone determine the outcome; rather it must be understood as a mapping of the independent variables onto the dependent. The model is open-ended, driven ultimately by changing views about the future which cannot be reduced to the parameters of the model or directly expressed numerically. The consumption function and the schedules of the marginal efficiency of capital and liquidity-preference are key analytical devices for translating these complex views about the future into relations between the Classical decision variables of price and quantity, and thus, together with the relatively Classical employment function, determining individual decisions about consumption, investment and employment. Exactly so, indeed, are consumers, investors and employers forced in practice to translate the unquantifiable and the uncertain into firm decisions about the future, and the complexity of these decisions is incorporated by Keynes into his three psychological functions. The long-term future itself cannot be modelled rigorously within the equilibrium system, but nevertheless this does not rule out attempts to explain, without invoking equilibrium, the tendencies of the independent variables over time in terms consistent with historical observations.[1]

G.T. Chapter 18 therefore presents *The General Theory* as a short-term equilibrium model nested within a larger open system, in which comparisons of different positions of static equilibrium of the model can be made, but which cannot itself be modelled in equilibrium terms. Keynes's use of equilibrium and choice of variables is heavily influenced by the observed stability of the system as a whole, on which section III places great emphasis, although these passages have subsequently spawned the 'elasticity pessimism' interpretation. As discussed in the Prologue, if the notion of equilibrium is to be of scientific value in economics, equilibrium positions must be continuous, observable and moderately stable, which also means that equilibrium must be relative to a given state of expectation, and therefore limited either to the static analysis of a point in time, or to short-term dynamics at most. Keynes strikes the right balance between what can, and what cannot, usefully be done with the Classical tools of equilibrium analysis.

5.2 THE INFLUENCE OF MONEY-WAGES ON EMPLOYMENT

Perhaps it is because the money-wage is outside the equilibrium sub-system that the myth has developed that Keynes assumes rigid money-wages, confusing this with their exogeneity in the sub-system, and with his recommendation of rigid or stable money-wages as a practical policy for price stability (*G.T.* 271). Certainly it is true that the money-wage and indeed the rents of all factor services (together making Keynes's 'cost-unit') are not determined by an equilibrium process, and do not clear the factor markets as in the Classical system. *G.T.* Chapters 19–21 consider the nature of the relationship between the money-wage and employment, thus reducing the degree to which the money-wage is exogenous to Keynes's theory as a whole, while it remains strictly so for the equilibrium sub-system. The money-wage is not beyond explanation, but it is not an equilibrium value. This may be why *G.T.* Book V is rarely cited by Classical economists, and why indeed the AD/AS model attempts to force the quantity of real balances and the money-wage back inside a closed equilibrium system.

The primary policy target of *The General Theory* was the Classical prescription that money-wage reductions would reduce unemployment. In *G.T.* Chapter 2 Keynes attacked the Classical theory of employment on two grounds, its implausible prediction of the withdrawal of labour in response to a rise in prices, and its logical inconsistency in asserting that money-wages and real wages are interchangeable concepts. After sixteen chapters of careful argument in presenting his new theory of employment based on the principle of effective demand, Keynes is at last ready to return to the question of money-wages. In large part, his new theory is itself the answer to the question, because his money variables can all be measured in wage-units without affecting their theoretical relationships (*G.T.* 260). So, in an immediate sense, he has already shown that the money-wage has no direct influence on aggregate employment. Nevertheless, given the importance of the wage-cut prescription in Classical thought, Keynes takes pains to identify the indirect repercussions of a change in money-wages, via its influence on the independent variables of the sub-system, notably the quantity of money expressed in wage-units.

Keynes identifies no less than seven possible channels of indirect influence (*G.T.* 262–4) before concluding that the only one that is remotely credible for policy purposes is through real balances (the so-called 'Keynes effect'). By assuming that the nominal quantity of money is exogenous he bends over backwards to accommodate the Classical position, noting that 'if the quantity of money is itself a function of the wage- and price-level, there is indeed, nothing to hope [for] in this direction' (*G.T.* 266), and thus anticipating the Post Keynesian endogenous money critique of monetarism. He notes that a policy of wage-cuts becomes in pure theory equivalent to an expansive monetary policy, and is subject to at least the same limitations and constraints, in particular the risk to confidence. Furthermore, in practice a policy of wage-cuts also brings with it additional problems of enforcement, distributive justice, debt deflation and depression of the state of long-term expectation. The effects of a lower wage and of a falling wage need to be distinguished. ▶ **A5.2.1**

Chapter 3 of this book discussed these adjustment problems in connection with the Pigou effect and identified a debt-free, bank-free economy as the minimum precondition for a positive influence on employment, making it of no practical relevance. In terms of the present theoretical discussion, the Pigou effect represents a postulated relationship between three of the independent variables of Keynes's system, the consumption function and the quantity of money expressed in wage-units. The usual text-book argument, derived ultimately from Hicks's *Value and Capital* (1939), is that the Keynesian system describes the short-term equilibrium, and the Classical system the long-term equilibrium, where the distinction arises from the stickiness of price expectations (including wages) in the Keynesian system compared with the flexibility of prices in the Classical system. While the Old Keynesian system may correctly be described as 'fix-price', *The General Theory* itself is a 'flex-price' system, but not of Hicks's Walrasian type.

Leaving aside Keynes's expectation that increasing wealth leads in the long term to a *reduction* in the average propensity to consume, there is here a 'dimensional problem' in that the principle of effective demand relates to the short period and the Pigou effect to the long term, and if the quantity of real balances is considered part of the capital equipment, to the Classical long period. The Pigou effect simply does not fit into Keynes's equilibrium sub-system, since variables which adjust in the long term cannot bring about equilibrium in the short period. If the Pigou effect were in fact a short-period phenomenon, we would experience the violent instability of the price-level and the shattering of confidence, which are anything but conducive to increased employment, as noted by Keynes (*G.T.* 267, 269).

The Classical argument that the economy is self-adjusting towards full employment cannot be sustained by the incorrect claim that Keynes assumes fixed or sticky prices and wages. It must therefore rest upon the assumptions of a debt-free, bank-free world together with a long-period equilibrium relationship between real balances and the consumption function and its corollary, the absence of a long-term demand for money as a store of value. This long period is of indeterminate length, both empirically and conceptually, since it has no physical foundation in production time, and certainly is not rigorous in the sense and usage of *The General Theory*, which insists that observed values of income and employment be treated as equilibrium values. The short-period employment equilibrium of the principle of effective demand requires only that a state of expectation exists at a point in time, and Keynes's long-period employment differs only from the daily short-period employment because of the relatively short time it takes to produce capital-goods; the long-period equilibrium of the Pigou effect does not have any similar physical basis or limit in the short term for its equilibrium period. It is a purely logical concept against which any and all observed values can be justified as examples of temporary disequilibrium.

In a world with an unknown future, the propensity to consume cannot be derived as an equilibrium value in the style of Fisher (1930) without a fatal loss of realism. The consumption function is caught between the opposing subjective forces listed by Keynes (*G.T.* 108–9), including Precaution, Independence and Avarice, ranged against Miscalculation, Extravagance and Generosity. None of these motives are a simple function of price; here we are dealing with the psychological and sociological fabric of society, quite unsuitable material for cutting with the Marshallian scissors.

5.3   THE INFLUENCE OF EMPLOYMENT ON MONEY-WAGES AND PRICES

Much of *G.T.* Chapter 20 is concerned with fairly complex matters of definition which might equally have appeared in *G.T.* Book II, and are a necessary preliminary to the argument of *G.T.* Chapter 21. The overall theme is the consequences of *changes* in effective demand. Section I returns to the aggregate supply function and its close cousin, the employment function, and defines elasticities of employment, output, money-wages and prices with respect to effective demand. ▶ **A5.3.1** Section II addresses the implications of the distribution of employment and provides another perspective on the short-term dynamics arising from production time, already considered at *G.T.* 50–51 and 122–4. ▶ **A5.3.2** Section III considers the implications of full employment and the definition of inflation, as a rise in prices *pari passu* with money-wages. ▶ **A5.3.3**

Section IV, by contrast, briefly restates the principal theme of *G.T.* Chapter 2, that *The General Theory* is a theory of a competitive monetary production economy based on wage labour, in which firms make the hiring decisions and bargain with workers over money-, not real, wages. Although workers as a whole can demand and may receive higher money-wages in buoyant employment conditions, they cannot demand work at lower real wages when output falls, since accepting lower money-wages will not achieve this objective.

Leaving aside the technical detail, there are three other major points to be made about this chapter. Firstly, this is principally a discussion of the consequences of changes in effective demand, not aggregate demand. Although Keynes does discuss changes in aggregate expenditure or demand, he never loses sight of the fact that effective demand represents the equilibrium between aggregate supply and demand, and cannot be reduced to either one.

Secondly, it has not generally been recognised that the employment function represents the 'macrofoundation of microeconomics'. The fact that Keynes gives *G.T.* Chapter 20 the title 'The Employment Function' suggests an importance beyond its use to analyse the influence of changes in employment on money-wages and prices. The employment function is the inverse of the aggregate supply function, expressed in wage-units, except that it is a relation between effective demand (rather than aggregate supply price) and employment. Effective demand is the resultant of equilibrium across all product markets and is not struck, as often depicted, by the clearing of a market for homogeneous output. When output and the capital equipment are heterogeneous, the repercussions between markets must be taken into account, as Classical general equilibrium theorists have made clear. The Marshallian supply curves of individual industries and firms are no more independent of the volume of output and employment of industry as a whole than are the individual industry demand curves. Something needs to fix the equilibrium level of aggregate employment: in the Classical system this is the combination of factor endowment, technology and preferences, while in *The General Theory* it is effective demand. ▶ A5.3.4

Thirdly, the distinction between income and effective demand emerges once again in section III (*G.T.* 288), when Keynes refers to the windfall gains arising from changes in the state of expectation, in contrast to the profits entrepreneurs expect as a result of their own actions. The first and third points suggest that although Keynes did not consider stagflation, it is in the interstices between income, aggregate demand, aggregate supply and effective demand that it can be located within a Marshallian perfect competition equilibrium model. The big questions are: how can demand-pull inflation exist below full employment, and how can it be generated independently of cost-push pressures from labour and other factors of production? The Epilogue will offer tentative answers to these questions. For the moment, note firstly that if aggregate demand in the expenditure sense (what Chick (1983) calls *D*) at the end of a production period exceeds aggregate demand in the sense of entrepreneurs' expectations (what Chick calls D^e) at the beginning of the production period, realised market prices will exceed the original expectations and the income realised from final output will exceed the effective demand that originally called it forth at the beginning of its production period. Secondly, ordinary supply prices (gross of user cost) may rise independently of aggregate supply prices (net of user cost), through a rise in marginal user cost. User cost provides an unexplored theoretical link from the demand for existing capital-goods to the prices of new output.

5.4 MONEY AND THE PRICE-LEVEL

Section I of *G.T.* Chapter 21 is an important recapitulation of Keynes's claim to offer a theory of the competitive price and quantity equilibrium, a theory of value and distribution based on supply and demand, of a monetary production economy. The passage on *G.T.* 293–4 is similar to Keynes's 1937 summary of *The General Theory* (*C.W.* XIV, pp. 109–23), in making a two-fold division, firstly between what we would now call microeconomics and macroeconomics; and secondly, between a state of expectation which is stationary and objectively correct, and one which is shifting and subject to continual revision as the future unfolds. Modern Classical theory (even in the form of inter-temporal general equilibrium) is a theory of stationary equilibrium in Keynes's sense, which encompasses steady state growth (*G.T.* 48, n1) and stochastic risk ('risk proper') as well as the stationary state; and accordingly reduces macroeconomic analysis to little more than its traditional microeconomic form. Once a shifting state of expectation is admitted, money (and specifically, liquidity-preference) cannot be detached from the theory of value. For Keynes, nevertheless, it remains essentially Marshall's theory of value.

The main purpose of *G.T.* Chapter 21 is to present, in sections III–V, a General Theory of the relation between the quantity of money and the price-level, which includes and replaces the Classical Quantity Theory. Section VI expresses Keynes's theory in an optional 'mathematical concoction', which he takes pains to distance from the theory itself, by defining a Marshallian elasticity of the price-level with respect to changes in the quantity of money, itself composed of a chain of subsidiary elasticities, including those introduced in *G.T.* Chapter 20. This 'money-stock elasticity of the price-level' may be regarded as a replacement for the Classical (Cambridge) quantity equation $MV = Y$. ▶ **A5.4.1** The value of this elasticity can in general lie between zero and unity, while the Classical quantity theory admits only unity. Both Keynes's elasticity and the Classical quantity equation are of course identities, mere definitions with no causal content in themselves.

The relationship of this elasticity to the causal equilibrium sub-system is that it expresses the effect of a change in one of the independent variables of the sub-system (the quantity of money) both directly, and indirectly through the repercussions of changes in employment, on another independent variable, the money-wage. Keynes's emphasis on neglected partial differentials is a reminder that this feedback to the money-wage is only one of the possible indirect channels. Since the direct relationship between the quantity of 'real' balances and the 'real' prices in each industry, both measured in wage-units, is determined by the other independent variables and parameters of the equilibrium sub-system, the only additional causal relation included explicitly by Keynes in defining his elasticity is that between employment and money-wages, and this he takes to be fairly self-evident (*G.T.* 301), although not always open to 'theoretical generalisation' in the form of an elasticity based on a continuous function, let alone as a Phillips curve relation between *un*employment and the rate of growth of money-wages.

In the final section VII Keynes considers the long-term relationship between the quantity of money and the price-level and offers an explanation of its perceived long-term stability. The prohibition of attempts to use equilibrium analysis in this explanation is repeated ('This is a question for historical generalisation rather than for pure theory', *G.T.* 306). The existence of a 'stable proportion ... to which the psychology of the public tends sooner or later to revert' (*G.T.* 307) does not presume or imply a mechanical equilibrium relation between the quantity of money expressed in wage-units and the propensity to consume. The adjustment takes place through a rise in money-wages when employment is buoyant, tending to reduce real balances, offset to a greater or lesser extent by a rise in the efficiency of labour, and by a rise in the nominal quantity of money when the rate of interest is significantly above the psychological minimum acceptable to the holders of wealth. These changes in the wage-unit, technology and the money stock represent changes in the independent variables and parameters of the equilibrium sub-system, but they are not themselves part of the sub-system.

In this final section Keynes permits himself a diagnosis of the nature of the contemporary depression of the 1930s and the relative prosperity of the nineteenth century, returning to the themes sounded at the ends of *G.T.* Chapters 16 and 17. However, these are taken up in earnest in *G.T.* Chapter 24, which is part of the subject of our next chapter.

NOTE

1. There is a considerable literature on the appropriateness of the use of formal closed models to describe open systems, characterised by time, human agency and/or complexity. See O'Donnell (1997), Chick and Dow (2001) and Lawson (1997, 2003) for an introduction.

Appendix to Chapter 5

A5.1   THE EQUILIBRIUM SUB-SYSTEM

A5.1.1   Hicks's IS-LM diagram

Hicks's IS-LM model has been so important in the teaching of Keynesian economics that an assessment of it from the perspective of this book cannot be avoided. How many different theories have been read into this familiar diagram in (Y, r) space! Let us begin by considering why Keynes himself 'found it very interesting and really [had] nothing to say by way of criticism' (*C.W.* XIV, p. 80). For Keynes the rate of interest (as proxy for the state of liquidity-preference and the quantity of real balances, i.e. the quantity of money measured in wage-units) is the dominant influence on investment and therefore income, so it is fair enough to isolate the relation between the two. The IS-LM diagram is of particular interest as a contrast with Keynes's own diagram (or was it Harrod's? – see O'Donnell, 1999) of the Classical equilibrium between investment and saving, cleared by the interest rate (*G.T.* 180), and indeed with a loanable funds diagram, which would look identical to the IS-LM but with the abscissa labelled I,S rather than Y.[1]

As with all Marshallian diagrams, the only observable point is the equilibrium intersection: the lines themselves represent only the stability conditions of the equilibrium. A change in any of the independent variables (which may interact with one or more of the others outside the equilibrium model) defines a new position of equilibrium. There is no question of ever being out of equilibrium if buyers and sellers act in accordance with their expectations and interests.

The drawback of IS-LM is that so much of *The General Theory* disappears behind the scenes. The IS curve represents both the propensity to consume and the marginal efficiency of capital, while the LM curve covers both liquidity-preference and the quantity of real balances. Putting the spotlight on the relation between the rate of interest and income leads easily to neglect of the many other influences on both variables which are captured in Keynes's own more subtle variables, but can only be expressed in the diagram by shifts in the schedules. It also compounds the downgrading of

Keynes's independent variables to the same status as the Classical parameters.

Worse still are the consequences of redefining the variables and the meaning of the schedules. As we have seen in Hansen's interpretation (Section **A2.3.1**), Y can quickly go from representing income to effective demand, and thence to real output. In this process flexible relative prices, the determination of employment by expectation and the supply side all disappear; 'goods market equilibrium' becomes interpreted in terms of *ex ante* and *ex post*, and mixed up with loanable funds thinking; and equilibrium, rather than being observable in the value of income and the level of employment on any given day, becomes a state of tranquillity achieved only over an indefinite period of time, in which there are no surprises (Hicks, 1980, p. 152). In fairness, by the time he made this last point, Hicks was less than enamoured of his creation, although it is not so much the model as its abuse that is the problem.

A5.1.2   The AD/AS diagram

One might be forgiven for thinking, on first hearing the term 'AD/AS model', that Keynes's principle of effective demand and the Weintraub and Davidson Z diagram had been accepted by the profession. Very much like the New and the Post Keynesians, it is extraordinary how little the two models have in common.

The AD/AS diagram is drawn in (Y, P) space rather than (N, Z) space. The substitution of P for Z neglects user cost (although so do Weintraub and Davidson), and also the distinction between the spot market price P of aggregate (homogeneous) output (the general price-level of realised income) and the expected value of (heterogeneous) output at the various future dates of Z (effective demand). The substitution of Y (meaning real output, not money-income measured in wage-units) for N eliminates the distinction between aggregate and effective demand, the decision-making process of entrepreneurs and the supply side, as noted earlier. The AS curve in turn is something altogether different from the Z curve.

The derivation of the AD curve begins from the IS-LM relationship, plotting the different points of IS-LM intersection for different quantities of real balances. Note that while a correct IS-LM model (correct as a representation of *The General Theory*) deflates the nominal money supply by the wage-unit (along with the implicit aggregate demand and supply prices), real balances in the AD/AS model are calculated by deflating nominal money by the theoretically inadmissible price-level. This reflects the importance in the AD/AS model of the real balance (Pigou) effect on the consumption function, and of the real wage, both of which are absent from a correct IS-LM model. The Pigou effect must be taken to affect, in the first instance, the prices of consumption goods, i.e. the price-level, rather than the money-wage.

The AS curve in fact really represents, not the supply decisions of firms as usually maintained, but our old friend the Classical supply curve of labour available to firms S_U (see Figure 1.1 on page 52). It is assumed that flexible prices and money-wages *can* clear the labour market, in stark contradiction to *The General Theory*, so that in the absence of nominal and real rigidities, there would always be full employment, with the natural rate of observed unemployment being wholly voluntary (in the sense of Professor Lucas) and determined on the supply side. This corresponds to the vertical AS curve (or line). Under the perfect competition assumption shared by both Keynes and Lucas, there is no elastic short-run AS curve; for Keynes the supply function of labour is given (allowing for voluntary and frictional unemployment), but does not determine employment, while for Lucas, the supply function of labour alone determines the level of employment.

Variations in employment depend for Keynes on changes in effective demand, which is not adequately accounted for in the AD/AS model. For Lucas and the New Classical school, variations in employment depend, unanticipated monetary shocks aside, mainly on shocks to labour supply or productivity ('real business cycles'), corresponding to shifts in the vertical AS curve, with the economy always in equilibrium at the AD/AS intersection. The New Keynesians, in the interests of realism, postulate a short-run AS curve based on sticky prices (including wages), which allows the economy to be in equilibrium in the goods and money markets with reduced output but involuntary unemployment in the labour market. Implicit in this pragmatic approach remains the assumption that flexible labour markets and money-wages would lead to full employment rather than gross price instability, however much this possibility is discounted in practice. The many sophisticated New Keynesian explanations of temporary involuntary unemployment remain essentially studies of imperfections in competition, yet this is not the source of involuntary unemployment in *The General Theory*.

A5.2   THE INFLUENCE OF MONEY-WAGES ON EMPLOYMENT

A5.2.1   The money-wage in an open economy

Keynes's argument that the openness of the Australian economy helped to stabilise prices in the context of a legal real wage (i.e. strict indexation, a money-wage pegged to the value of a basket of commodities) can be clarified by expanding it beyond his single sentence. The enforcement of a legal real wage would mean that only one level of employment was consistent with equilibrium. In a closed economy, this would lead to price instability, since competition would drive prices to zero or infinity as money investment demand fell below or above the critical level corresponding to the equilibrium level of employment. In Australia, Keynes argues 'the level of money-wages was itself a determinant of the level of foreign investment and hence of total investment, whilst the terms of trade were an important influence on real wages' (*G.T.* 270).

Keynes is not explicit about the link between money-wages and foreign investment. The logical steps here, partly anticipating the arguments of *G.T.* Chapter 23, appear to be that an increase in money-wages reduces the balance of payments by reducing lending from abroad, which was significant in the case of Australia. Lending from abroad is partly a function of the marginal efficiency of capital in export industries (e.g. wool and mining), reducing if domestic money-wages increase against a given world price and exchange rate. A balance of payments deficit reduces the domestic money supply (by outflow of reserves) and so tends to increase the interest rate, reducing domestically financed investment as well. Higher money-wages also increase the demand for imported wage goods (tending to reduce the balance of payments) and the transactions demand for money (tending to increase the interest rate), although Keynes does not mention these two additional factors here. These forces stimulate two countervailing and stabilising processes. First, a reduction in total investment demand and so aggregate output tends to reduce domestic prices and under strict indexation this means money-wages are reduced. Second, an increase in domestic interest rates attracts lending from abroad, thus tending to increase the exchange rate, reduce the price of imported wage goods, and therefore reduce money-wages.

Interestingly, provided that lending from abroad is sufficiently elastic with respect to the domestic marginal efficiency of capital, this argument implies that in an open economy a legal minimum real wage fixed, with the primary aim of overcoming employer monopsony, no higher than the marginal disutility of labour, will also deliver full employment, given perfect competition in product markets.

A5.3   THE INFLUENCE OF EMPLOYMENT ON MONEY-WAGES AND PRICES

A5.3.1   Measuring changes in the price-level

Section I of *G.T.* Chapter 20 returns to the aggregate supply function and its inverse, the employment function, and defines elasticities of employment, output, money-wages and prices with respect to effective demand. An important aspect of this section from today's perspective is that the employment function and the various elasticities are all stated in terms of effective, and not aggregate, demand. Furthermore, in the first part of the discussion (*G.T.* 282–3) effective demand is expressed in wage-units rather than money, and Keynes is careful in his discussion of the elasticity of output or production to distinguish between the individual industry and industry as a whole. It is possible for effective demand in terms of wage-units to increase when the output of an individual industry is perfectly inelastic, if other industries retain some elasticity, so that the increase in effective demand for the output of that industry translates wholly into increased profits; but effective demand in terms of wage-units cannot increase when the output of all industries has become perfectly inelastic, a state corresponding to full employment. This discussion therefore deals solely with increases in 'real' prices in terms of wage-units (and so, falls in real wages), corresponding to the general assumption of diminishing returns, and is separate from any increase in money prices consequent upon changes in money-wages, let alone true inflation. It helps to clarify Keynes's rejection of the idea that inflation means 'merely that prices are rising' (*G.T.* 304).

A change in the price-level is not a scalar quantity like the units of money-value and standard labour in which Keynes has carefully developed his theory of employment. Although the price-level itself may be defined as the scalar product of industry price and quantity vectors, the measurement of changes in the price-level involves inherent approximation by means of an index involving some regime of weighting of the individual prices. Nevertheless the price-level is of great practical importance, so that Keynes introduces the 'elasticity of money-prices' and the elasticity of money-wages, in both cases with respect to changes in effective demand in terms of money (*G.T.* 285). The elasticity of money-prices is a methodologically difficult concept, since a change in the price-level (as opposed to a price index) cannot necessarily be represented by a single number. It is acceptable provided that it is understood as an exercise in comparative statics, comparing the proportionate change in a defined price index with the proportionate change in effective demand corresponding to two different equilibrium employment vectors. Strictly the equations

$$e'_p + e_o = 1, \; e_p = 1 - e_o \left(1 - e_w \right)$$

are only correct either if the composition of output (the pattern of index weights) is constant, which is the tacit assumption behind any assumption 'that we have a unit in which output as a whole can be measured' (*G.T.* 285), or when the elasticity of output is either zero or unity.

A related problem was raised by Townshend (*C.W.* XXIX, pp. 240–45) when he pointed out that the prices of which the price-level is composed are not the aggregate supply prices embodied in effective demand, differing by the marginal user cost. The assumption slips in that the price-level would be the price of current output as a whole O (if output as a whole could be measured, especially net of user cost in accordance with *G.T.* Chapter 6), at an early stage of the argument (*G.T.* 209) when Keynes defines $Y = OP$ so that P here can only mean unit aggregate supply price or Z/O (at this point only, Keynes uses P instead of p for the price-level; elsewhere (*G.T.* 283) P stands for profits). For the purposes of the formal algebra, the 'prices' to which Keynes refers at *G.T.* 283–6 and 304–6 should all strictly be read as 'marginal proceeds', and the references to 'prime cost' at *G.T.* 283 should read 'factor cost'; Keynes's conclusions about the relation between the quantity of money and the price-level do not take account of any relationship between marginal user cost and the quantity of money, a point to which we will return in the Epilogue. As Keynes admits in his reply to Townshend, he has 'got bogged in an attempt to bring [his] own terms into rather closer conformity with the algebra of others than the case really permits' (*C.W.* XXIX, pp. 245–7).

Unlike the wage-unit of standard labour, changes in the price index of heterogeneous output play no part in Keynes's causal equilibrium model. It is not possible to eliminate the heterogeneity of output by the device Keynes uses in the case of labour, by which any residual heterogeneity of standard labour units can reasonably be subsumed into the heterogeneity of capital-goods.

A5.3.2   The long period, the short term and the period of production

Section II addresses the implications of the distribution of employment and provides another perspective on the dynamics arising from production time, already considered at *G.T.* 50–51 and 122–4. We have already covered the distribution of employment (*G.T.* 286) in the exposition of the principle of effective demand using vector quantities. ▶ **A1.3.1** *G.T.* 287–8 covers much the same ground as the earlier passages in *The General Theory* on the dynamics of production, with the emphasis here on the period of production rather than the state of expectation or the multiplier relationship. This book has already provided a framework for understanding these dynamics. ▶ **A2.2.2** There are a few subtle additions in this final development of the theme worth noting.

First, Keynes notes that a growth in effective demand directed towards industries with a low elasticity of employment may reduce the propensity to consume as a result of a redistribution of income from workers to entrepreneurs. Secondly, if an increase in effective demand arises in a state of surplus stocks and spare capacity at every stage of production, the long-period elasticity of employment may not recover to its initial high level because of the absorption of expenditure by rent factors as employment increases, and in particular the rate of interest may increase. The introduction of these further elements of simultaneity does not make the system unstable, since the effect on the propensity to consume and the inducement to invest in each case is opposite to the effect of the increase in effective demand.

Thirdly, Keynes's definition of the 'period of production' here (*G.T.* 287) is not identical to the 'production period' to which he refers (although not by that name, at least in *The General Theory* itself) at *G.T.* 46, and he acknowledges this difference of usage (*G.T.* 287, n1; see also Pigou, 1933, pp. 56–60). The period of production allows for the time required for the production of not only an individual good (what this book has called the production period), but for the further delay resulting from the need to increase production of the necessary production inputs, which involves economic as well as purely physical considerations, since the increase in production will depend on the expected price. Thus Keynes's period of production defines the horizon of the short-term expectation for an individual industry, and for industry as a whole it defines the length of the long period. This correspondence between the long period, the short term and the aggregate period of production has a certain elegance.

A5.3.3 'True' inflation at full employment

Section III considers the implications of full employment and the definition of inflation, as a rise in prices *pari passu* with money-wages. The second part of this section (*G.T.* 290) is somewhat dense and merits expansion. In this passage Keynes considers the implications of an attempt to raise effective demand above the level consistent with full employment, through increases in aggregate demand. Having noted that the conditions of strict equilibrium imply a state of true inflation (*cf G.T.* 303) in these circumstances, he notes two practical qualifications.

First, employers may suffer money illusion, underestimate their marginal user cost and increase employment beyond the point of maximum expected profit. This temporary disequilibrium is reminiscent of Milton Friedman's later discussion of 'the expectations augmented Phillips curve', although quite different in substance.

Second, rising prices may redistribute income from rentiers on fixed incomes to entrepreneurs, an effect which occurs both at full employment, with true inflation, and as employment rises towards this level, on account of diminishing returns. Assuming that full employment can be reached by means of monetary policy, the implications depend on the effect on the propensity to consume. If entrepreneurs consume more out of an increase in income than do rentiers, full employment will be more easily reached as prices rise, i.e. a smaller increase in the quantity of money and reduction in the rate of interest, and a smaller consequent rise in investment, is required than otherwise. At full employment, the rate of interest will have to rise more than would otherwise be necessary to avoid inflation, so that current investment is reduced to offset the higher propensity to consume. In both cases, the adjustment to full employment with price stability can be achieved with smaller changes in monetary policy than in the absence of the redistribution effect of higher prices. If the relative propensities to consume of entrepreneurs and rentiers are reversed, so that rentiers consume more than entrepreneurs at the margin, monetary policy is correspondingly weaker. The redistribution effect may change direction below or at full employment, giving four possible permutations.

This discussion makes it clear that it is not possible to raise effective demand, as an equilibrium value measured in wage-units, above the level corresponding to full employment. Increases in money aggregate demand above this level will be matched by increases in the money aggregate supply price as a result of increases in money-wages. At full employment we reach the position, described by Keynes in terms which anticipate New Classical economics, that it is impossible to increase expenditure in terms of wage-units (*G.T.* 284), and which is implicit in the Classical theory that output is constrained by the supply of available labour.

A5.3.4   The employment function

The employment function $F(D_w)$ is the inverse of the aggregate supply function $Z_w(N)$, except that it is a relation between effective demand (rather than aggregate supply price) and employment. At first glance, the employment function seems superfluous, if its inverse already exists. Once again, the distinctions between aggregate demand and supply and effective demand are essential, and also that between aggregate effective demand for the output of industry as a whole and the effective demand for an individual firm or industry. We have noted earlier that the aggregate supply function for an individual firm or industry can, like the ordinary supply curve, only be defined *ceteris paribus:* a change in aggregate employment must shift the industry supply (and demand) curves. By contrast, the aggregate supply function for industry as a whole can be defined uniquely in terms of aggregate employment under certain conditions.

First, either the distribution of capital equipment and the number of firms must be fixed (which Keynes does not assume), or there must be free movement of capital-goods between firms, subject only to any closed shops of employers and similar obstacles, captured by the degree of competition. In the latter case, the number of firms is endogenous, and the capital-goods move to where they are expected to be most profitable, subject to the closed shops, which may partly be based on restricted access to proprietary technical knowledge. Thus, given the degree of competition, the aggregate supply function for industry as a whole is a matter of the physical characteristics of the capital-goods and the marginal prime cost of each firm in a given state of its technical knowledge for using each combination of capital-goods in production, together with (homogeneous) labour.

Secondly, as discussed in Section **A1.3.1**, any given level of aggregate employment may be associated with an indefinitely large number of distributions of employment across industries. This is the idea represented by the modern Walrasian concept of a production possibility surface, defined for any given set of factors of production including labour. For Keynes, there are many production frontiers nested inside one another, each representing all the possible distributions of employment that correspond to any given level of aggregate employment offered by entrepreneurs, while the Walrasian model considers only the full employment frontier, where the level of employment is determined by the endowment and preferences of households, and not by the expectations of entrepreneurs. Keynes's employment function necessarily assumes Keynesian involuntary unemployment throughout its range except at the limit of full employment; the Walrasian model considers only the limiting point of general equilibrium (leaving aside the question of its uniqueness). In both cases, each possible distribution of employment **n** is related to a different price vector $\mathbf{p}^s$, given the usual assumption of strict convexity or continuously diminishing marginal rates of substitution and transformation, and also in general, to different aggregate supply prices Z (see Figure 1.3 in Section **A1.3.1**). Thus, although the aggregate supply function for industry as a whole is determinate for any given employment vector, the functional relation $Z_w(N)$ is an approximation (*G.T.* 286), since each value of N may represent many different vectors **n**. However, the employment function $F(D_w)$ can be defined, on the assumption 'that corresponding to a given level of *aggregate effective demand* there is a unique distribution of it between different industries' (*G.T.* 282, emphasis added), a simplification which permits the derivation of the elasticity of employment as part of Keynes's restatement of the quantity theory of money. If the level of aggregate effective demand were specified as a vector rather than a scalar, the additional assumption of its unique distribution would not be necessary.

Thus the principal difference between $Z_w(N)$ and $F(D_w)$ is that the latter can be uniquely defined as a functional relation because it takes into account the pattern of aggregate demand as well as the conditions of supply, while (strictly) the aggregate supply function cannot be so defined. In Walrasian terms, the employment function introduces the preferences of households contingent upon any given level of income (via the expectations of entrepreneurs), thus picking out the point on the production possibility surface, for any given level of employment, that dealers collectively expect to be preferred by consumers and investors: the point of effective demand.

Thirdly, the changing value of the elasticity of employment over time reflects the difference between the short and the long periods resulting from production time. In the terms of the notation of Section **A2.2.3**, the short-period employment on any day converges to the long-period employment in a given state of expectation by the process $\mathbf{n}^{\cdot}(t|\Pi) \to \mathbf{n}^{\cdot\cdot}$. Thus the employment function for each day of the long period is uniquely defined in a given state of expectation, although the long-period elasticity of employment may be significantly greater than its short-period value (*G.T.* 287).

Fourthly, and implicit in the foregoing, the employment function is objectively defined, given the parameters of Keynes's system (*G.T.* 245), only under conditions of perfect competition in the markets for current output as well as for existing capital-assets (consistent with a degree of competition understood as in Section **AP.2.5**). Perfect competition in this sense is a necessary and sufficient condition for the state of short-term expectation to be defined objectively as a shared expectations matrix (see Section 1.3 and Section **A2.2.2**), and for these expectations to determine employment in each firm as a function of physical supply conditions and the prices of factor services. The distribution of employment and capital-goods across firms within an industry is not addressed by Keynes at this plane of abstraction, and may well not be unique, but it is endogenous, given the industry price and physical supply curves.

Various authorities have argued that *The General Theory* is compatible with both perfect and imperfect or monopolistic competition (Kregel, 1987; Davidson, 1962, 2002). Chick (1992b) has developed a theory of pricing, based on separate concepts of hypothetical and expected demand, in which the supply curve of a firm is constructed from an amalgam of its physical supply curve and the 'hypothetical' demand curves, which determine the mark-up at each point. The corollary is that employers' short-term expectations are taken to be individual and entirely subjective, not shared or 'rational' in the technical sense, as I have argued here to be the case in *The General Theory*.

Since the effective demand for each industry is derived from aggregate effective demand, which depends on a physical aggregate supply curve for industry as a whole, there is no room to slip in a degree of monopoly at firm level, since this would change the supply curve, and so the effective demand, for each industry and for industry as a whole. Moreover, an aggregate degree of monopoly cannot be derived from the elasticities of individual objective industry demand curves, since the latter are not independent of aggregate employment, which therefore cannot itself be determined as a position of monopolistic equilibrium. Keynes appears to have recognised that the theory of monopolistic competition is an exercise in partial, not aggregate, analysis (essentially an extension of *Classical* theory), and that an aggregate theory can be based on monopolistic competition only if you are prepared to follow Kalecki and take the mark-up(s) as exogenous (i.e. outside the equilibrium model), thereby departing from the Marshallian tradition of treating industrial structure as endogenous. Thus in his reference to imperfections in competition at *G.T.* 5 (the reference at *G.T.* 6 is covered by the degree of competition between workers) I suggest Keynes is saying, 'first work out aggregate employment under competitive conditions based on a physical supply curve with a given degree of competition between entrepreneurs; then, in particular industries, monopolistic competition will lead to a restriction of supply (assuming diminishing returns) and some departure of aggregate employment from the competitive short-period position, although I cannot give you an equation for that'. So the principle of effective demand, if it is to be based on objective supply and demand conditions in the sense just defined, *requires* either the assumption of perfect competition between firms in the markets for current output (zero degree of monopoly), or else additional auxiliary assumptions not made by Keynes, even if widely adopted by Post Keynesians; although one can envisage super-imposing monopolistic competition at and below industry level for the purposes of partial analysis, taking the level of aggregate effective demand as part of *ceteris paribus*.

The principle of effective demand brings determinacy to the Marshallian system below full employment and is the essential foundation for the competitive theory of value in a monetary economy. As in the limiting Walrasian case, Keynes's system equilibrium requires simultaneous solution of production possibilities and household preferences, but these are circumscribed by the shifting state of expectation, rather than by the gradually changing endowment of factors of production alone. Once the functional relation between the levels of aggregate expected income and employment is established as a matter of system equilibrium, the individual employment functions for each industry follow directly, since the values of effective demand and employment for each industry can properly be summed, and conversely, the assumption of a unique distribution of effective demand makes employment in each industry a function of aggregate effective demand (*G.T.* 282). The principle of effective demand and the employment function truly provide the macroeconomic foundations of microeconomics outside the Classical special case.

A5.4   MONEY AND THE PRICE-LEVEL

A5.4.1   A mathematical slip

It is regrettable that Keynes's major mathematical error in drafting *The General Theory* appears in the section offering a formal definition of the 'money-stock elasticity of the price-level' e, which replaces the Classical Quantity Equation, and from that perspective is the theoretical climax of the work. In terms of 'public relations' the error is compounded by his statement that he does not himself 'attach much value to manipulations of this kind', contributing to his image in some quarters as a cavalier theorist incapable of rigorous analysis, and obscuring his well-founded methodological objections to the inappropriate use of equilibrium analysis.

As observed by Naylor (1968), the inclusion of the 'demand elasticity of employment' e_e in the final equation for e is incorrect and in fact inconsistent with the equation at *G.T.* 285. The slip and the discussion at *G.T.* 305–6 suggests that Keynes originally defined the 'demand elasticity of output' e_o as an 'employment elasticity of output'

$$\frac{dO}{dN} \cdot \frac{N}{O}$$

so that the demand elasticity of output would then be given as the product of the 'employment elasticity of output' and the 'demand elasticity of employment' e_e, as it appears at *G.T.* 305. The final equation should read

$$e = e_d(1 - e_o + e_o.e_w)$$

When an elasticity is written in the form of a derivative in this way, it is strictly a point-elasticity whose value is defined only at the point of equilibrium, which here means the point of effective demand. Without some specification of the functional forms, including an assumption of continuity, the elasticity represents the increase in the price-level corresponding to an infinitesimal increase in effective demand. This indeed is the formally correct response to the problem of defining an elasticity of the price-level, on account of its nature as an index, in the absence of an express assumption of constancy in the composition of output. My point is that Keynes appears to have been fully aware of the subtleties and pitfalls surrounding the mathematical expression of his ideas, despite his 'arithmetical' error in the manipulation of these equations between drafts of *The General Theory*.

NOTE

1.   Precisely this conflation of the IS-LM diagram (or at least the IS curve) with the loanable funds diagram is perpetrated by Mankiw (2003, p. 270).

6.   Policy Implications

This chapter considers *G.T.* Book VI, in which Keynes addresses the policy implications of the theory developed in the previous Books. *G.T.* Chapter 22 on the trade cycle (considered in Section 6.1) examines the nature of fluctuations in the level of employment, while *G.T.* Chapter 23 (Section 6.2) reviews pre-Classical orthodoxies and contemporary heterodox thought as to the causes and remedies for the chronic level of under-employment that Keynes perceives to be the normal state of the *laissez-faire* market economy. *G.T.* Chapter 24 (Section 6.3) concludes by outlining the political implications of a policy of full employment and maximum investment.

Keynes's tool for addressing these questions is the equilibrium sub-system or model described in our previous chapter, which maps his three psychological independent variables onto the level of employment at any time. These independent variables are schedules rather than numbers, as Keynes reminds us in the case of the marginal efficiency of capital (*G.T.* 315, n1). As in *G.T.* Book V, we are no longer considering relationships amenable to formal modelling, and have moved outside the domain of equilibrium theory into that of psychology and history. Part of the modern Classical aversion to the last two books of *The General Theory* undoubtedly stems from a refusal to admit the limits of the competitive equilibrium method and the need, beyond a certain point, for a different kind of discussion. A benefit for the new reader of this change in tone is that *G.T.* Book VI is written for the most part in ordinary language and is comparatively accessible.

Three aspects of *G.T.* Chapter 22 deserve particular attention: the nature of the discussion of the dynamics of the trade cycle; the two senses of the term 'over-investment'; and the discussion of policies for managing fluctuations, which sheds light on modern monetary policy. In *G.T.* Chapter 23, the discussion of mercantilist policy is not principally about export-led growth, but about the quantity of money, while the discussion of usury laws and Gesell's proposal is about the state of liquidity-preference. The discussion of Hobson and theories of under-consumption takes up the question of the policy trade-off between present consumption and the date of capital-saturation at full employment, a trade-off that seems remote from present conditions and reminds us how resigned we have become to the failure of full employment policy. This leads in *G.T.* Chapter 24 to the conclusion that free enterprise can be reformed and Classical economic theory can become more useful as a guide to policy, if the three independent variables of Keynes's model can be so influenced as to achieve full employment and the reduction of inequality through the 'euthanasia of the rentier'.

6.1 NOTES ON THE TRADE CYCLE

Of the three chapters of *G.T.* Book VI, the discussion in the first (*G.T.* Chapter 22) of fluctuations in employment appears closest to the formal method and has accordingly been misunderstood from the outset simply as an elementary exercise in dynamic modelling, which can be much improved by the application of more sophisticated techniques. Keynes's definition of a cycle certainly begins with a mechanical analogy, typical of the swinging of a pendulum, and places an emphasis on physical characteristics (such as the length of life of durable assets, the carrying-costs of surplus stocks, the acceleration in the movements of stocks of finished goods and working-capital, and the rate of population growth) as determining the length of the down-swing at between three and five years. These characteristics played a central role in the dynamic theories subsequently developed by Harrod and others, all the way down to real business cycle theory.

Yet to treat Keynes's discussion of the trade cycle as a first stumbling attempt to specify a differential equation is to miss the point entirely. His introductory paragraph emphasises the complexity of the trade cycle and the manner in which all three of his independent variables interact, even if fluctuations in the marginal efficiency of capital are the essential feature. A formal model of the cycle requires an equilibrium position about which oscillations take place, which would mean an equilibrium relationship between the independent variables of Keynes's system which is completely absent (and not to be confused with the equilibrium relation between the independent variables and the level of employment). A formal model requires cardinal numerical variables, but the independent variables all depend upon the state of long-term expectation and especially the state of confidence, which cannot be measured or modelled numerically in any meaningful manner. Finally, a formal model usually requires continuous functions, while discontinuity and crisis is for Keynes an intrinsic part of the cycle, as subsequently emphasised by Minsky (1975, 1983).

Having identified fluctuations in the marginal efficiency of capital as the essential feature of the trade cycle, Keynes proceeds to distinguish two senses of the term 'over-investment'. In a so-called 'real business cycle', the fluctuations in the marginal efficiency of capital would represent disequilibrium oscillations about a long-term long-period equilibrium position in which the return on investment equals the (normal) rate of interest. In a steady state dynamic equilibrium with continuous investment, over-investment can be understood as running ahead of the warranted rate, leading to a depression of the rate of return on investment, then recovery and cyclical oscillation. Keynes has already emphasised that the marginal efficiency of capital is an expectation, which is not a simple function of the current rate of return or existing stock of capital-goods (*G.T.* 141). Expectations are destined to disappointment, partly because they become over-optimistic and speculative at the height of the boom. The benchmark, against which expectations must be judged, itself moves with the fluctuations in the marginal efficiency of capital and the consequent level of employment, so that both optimism and pessimism are self-fulfilling to a degree. While doubting that full employment had ever been experienced outside time of war, let alone a state of full investment, even at the height of the 'roaring twenties' in the US, Keynes is remarkably sanguine about the prospects of capital-saturation within a generation, given full employment, returning to his theme at the end of *G.T.* Chapter 16.

Given his diagnosis, Keynes is pessimistic about the prospects for managing the trade cycle in a market economy by monetary policy alone. The range of fluctuation in the marginal efficiency of capital is too great to be offset by changes in the rate of interest; like the rudder on *Titanic*, monetary policy can cope only with small deviations from a straight course and only with sufficient notice. His discussion of Robertson's view (*G.T.* 327) sheds an interesting light on modern monetary policy based on an inflation target. Keynes holds that the ideal remedy for the boom is not a higher, but a lower, rate of interest, but grudgingly accepts the force of Robertson's argument (Robertson, 1926) that the only practical policy for stability (if 'dangerously and unnecessarily defeatist') *may* be to check the outbreak of speculative and inflationary conditions by restraining the pace of expansion by a rise in the rate of interest; although he doubts this would have worked in the conditions of 1929 in the US.

Modern conditions appear to vindicate both Keynes and Robertson to some extent. On the one hand, the growth of government employment, both directly and through contractors, has 'socialised' and stabilised a substantial part of the propensity to consume and the inducement to invest, reducing the range of fluctuation arising from the private sector alone. On the other hand, monetary policy has once again become concerned primarily with the trend in the price-level, and regards the level of employment as determined essentially by Classical forces. With long-term stability (rather than full employment) now considered the only politically feasible objective, the helmsmen on the Bank of England's Monetary Policy Committee attempt to scan the horizon two to three years ahead, through the fog that enshrouds the future, giving a touch on the tiller to keep the economy on course, as it is buffeted by unexpected squalls.

Keynes's vulnerable spot is his admission, in the course of this argument with Robertson, that the cost-unit tends to rise in terms of money when output increases (*G.T.* 328). Robertson's argument anticipates the doctrine of the 'non-accelerating inflation rate of unemployment' (NAIRU) which underpins modern policy and has displaced the concept of involuntary unemployment. When Keynes writes that 'no-one has a legitimate vested interest in being able to buy at prices which are only low because output is low', he underestimates the persuasiveness of the view that low unemployment leads to wage-push inflation, to which the later experience of stagflation lent credibility. So was the Classical linkage between money-wages and employment restored, and NAIRU became the new definition of full employment.

Nevertheless, the existence of a barrier to full employment in the form of the NAIRU does not mean that the theoretical analysis of *The General Theory*'s equilibrium model is flawed, still less that we should revert to the Classical theory of employment and describe any observed level of employment as full employment. A linkage between the cost-unit and the level of employment simply represents a relation between the independent variables (including the cost-unit) of Keynes's system that he did not fully develop. It may be that a 'rigid money-wage' is a practical condition of achieving full employment through demand management alone, but this does not mean that the money-wage can ever clear the labour market. The relation between employment and the cost-unit is not amenable to equilibrium analysis, as those have found who have tried to place a figure on the erratic NAIRU as a 'natural rate' of frictional unemployment.

6.2 OTHER REMEDIES FOR CHRONIC UNDER-EMPLOYMENT

Having considered in *G.T.* Chapter 22 the nature of *fluctuations* in employment, *G.T.* Chapter 23 moves on to consider the *level* of employment, and reviews pre-Classical orthodoxies and contemporary heterodox thought as to the causes and remedies for the chronic under-employment that Keynes perceives to be the normal state of the market economy. He sets out an intellectual heritage for his insights while retaining a critical eye for the weaknesses as well as the strengths of the views of his non-Classical predecessors. His literature review falls into three parts, two dealing with investment from the perspectives of mercantilism and of measures against usury and hoarding, and the third with theories of under-consumption.

The received wisdom, as we noted in Chapter 3 of this book, is that *The General Theory* is a special case in the sense that its model describes only a closed economy: no explanation is offered as to why Keynes would devote a major part of his discussion of policy to mercantilism, using a theoretical model that cannot accommodate international trade. As we noted, Keynes's concern is with the employment consequences of decisions to consume and invest, so that the identity of the consumers and investors is not of fundamental importance. The demand of the foreign sector for consumption goods, and the domestic demand for imports, are both accommodated within the aggregate propensity to consume. The discussion of mercantilism is not an informal extension, but an application, of the model developed in the main body of *The General Theory*.

Keynes defines mercantilism as, broadly, the view that the balance of trade is not in self-adjusting equilibrium and is a legitimate object of policy. His main concern is not with practical policies, over which there is in fact much common ground between the mercantilists and the Classical school, but with the intellectual basis of mercantilism that Classical thought firmly rejects. Keynes's interpretation of mercantilist thought does not, as might be expected by a modern reader, focus primarily on the contribution of net exports and export-led growth to aggregate demand, but on the effect of the balance of trade on the quantity of money, the rate of interest and the inducement for domestic investment. 'Foreign investment' does not refer to investment by foreigners, but mainly to the acquisition of foreign bullion, so that 'aggregate investment' does not here correspond to the value of the output of the domestic capital-goods industries. In the absence of developed international capital markets and central banking, a favourable balance of trade thus promotes investment under both kinds, since it is identical with the net acquisition of bullion and simultaneously increases the domestic monetary base, tending to reduce the rate of interest. The policy can be taken too far, so that the domestic rate of interest is reduced below rates elsewhere and the domestic cost-unit rises at high levels of output; the former may encourage foreign investment in the form of loans rather than bullion, reducing the increase in the domestic monetary base for a given balance of trade, while the latter will reduce the balance of trade itself. Keynes cites the history of imperial Spain and Edwardian Britain as examples of these counter-effects, and India as an example where a chronic trade surplus failed to translate into a reduction in interest rates because of excess liquidity-preference. Yet a moderate application of mercantilist policy will increase the wealth of the nation, and not merely its hoards. By contrast, the gold standard was based on the assumption, partly on the strength of the quantity theory of money and the price-level, that the balance of trade was self-adjusting, and that the balance of payments could be held in (full-employment) equilibrium by the domestic rate of interest.

Neither the gold standard nor mercantilism have much relevance to the modern world of fiat money and flexible exchange rates. Yet Keynes's review of these past controversies remains relevant for its argument that throughout most of recorded history 'practical men' have been rightly aware of the dangers of liquidity-preference and of the chronic tendency for the propensity to save (i.e. not to consume domestic output) to exceed the inducement to invest (in newly-produced domestic capital-goods). According to Keynes, this was also true of those, most of whom the Classical school would scarcely admit to be economists, the ancient and modern writers on usury.

Keynes pays tribute to the medieval scholastics for their recognition of the distinction between the marginal efficiency of capital and the rate of interest, and the need for measures to counter the high degree of liquidity-preference resulting from the risks of life in the medieval world. While Bentham argued that usury laws were counter-productive because they led to the rationing of potential borrowers with legitimate investment projects, such restrictions may equally encourage a holder of money to invest directly rather than to lend, as Adam Smith noted. Keynes praises Gesell for recognising the importance of low carrying-costs as one of the essential properties of money, while noting his failure to provide an explanation of a positive rate of interest and to recognise that liquidity is a matter of degree, hinting once again at the historical importance of land as the dominant liquid asset.

Having considered the arguments of other opponents of the Classical view of investment, Keynes turns to consider the theories of under-consumption put forward in particular by Mandeville, Malthus and Hobson, returning (in the latter cases at least) to the language and terminology of modern economic thought. Keynes defines under-consumption strictly, as a propensity to consume insufficient to sustain full employment in a state of capital-saturation, and thus not simply a low level of consumption resulting from under-employment. Keynes notes with approval the awareness, underlying

Mandeville's poetry, of the fallacy of composition in the relation between saving and current investment, together with his advocacy of full employment as the means to prosperity. Keynes's discussion of Malthus ('the first Cambridge economist') and Hobson makes explicit their joint opposition to Say's Law, including the archetypal quotation from Ricardo that

> Productions are always bought by productions or services; money is only the medium by which the exchange is effected. Hence the increased production being always accompanied by a correspondingly increased ability to get and consume, there is no possibility of Over-production. (*G.T.* 369)

Keynes notes with approval Hobson and Mummery's recognition that the demand for capital-goods cannot be separated from the demand for future consumption; of the nature of capital-goods as the reflection of production through time; of the nature of interest on money; of the tendency of a highly organised industrial society to excessive thrift relative to the need for investment; of the relation between consumption and income; and that production and employment are limited by effective demand and not by the Classical endowment. He finds flaws in their understanding of the relation between saving and current investment (so that they believe excess saving is realised in the form of excess accumulation) and their lack of an independent theory of interest and the state of expectation.

In conclusion, what these theories have in common with *The General Theory* is their diagnosis that the under-employment observed in a monetary economy reflects structural characteristics of society that are impervious to market forces, in contrast with the Classical view that free competition will deliver full employment. The political corollary is that labour, individually or collectively, is not usually to blame for its under-employment, in contrast with the Classical view that unemployment is, apart from frictional unemployment, essentially voluntary (where this usage follows Keynes in covering defects in labour market institutions of any kind that impedes competition).

6.3 POLITICAL IMPLICATIONS

Only just below the surface of *G.T.* Chapter 24 lies Keynes's passionate commitment to the Liberal view that the purpose of economic activity is to allow every person to exercise their liberty and to pursue happiness, free from the scourge of under-employment, even if the fulfilment of this objective entails a reduction in the return to accumulated wealth. This view remains as relevant and as controversial as ever today, in a world of poverty and inequality on a global scale.

Keynes's prescription was no more than to take the necessary steps to make the Classical parable a reality. Few, at least in a modern liberal democracy, would openly question as undesirable or inappropriate the implications of Marshall's long-period equilibrium, that no-one would need to work more (or less) than they chose, and that the return on capital and to individual talent would reflect only genuine sacrifice, enterprise or skill. What raises hackles is the brazen claim that the parable describes the world in which we live, or would live if labour was more docile.

The enduring technical contribution of *The General Theory* is to refute the Classical view of the 'nature and necessity of interest' (*G.T.* 176), and show that the avowedly shared aim of full employment and maximum investment is thwarted, not aided, by policies such as the Gold Standard and its modern equivalents; and that the misery to which working people were subjected during the 1920s and 1930s (and not only then) in the form of welfare and wage cuts was not only regrettable, but futile. The political contribution of Keynes's book was to legitimise the use of monetary and fiscal policy and the provision of goods and services by the State in order to secure full employment. Keynes won the political argument and helped to secure the unparalleled prosperity of the post-war period until the cost-unit finally broke free in 1973. The breakdown, first of the 'cheap money' policy which died with Keynes and much later, of demand management as the basis of full employment, has led to the resurgence and current dominance of Classical ideas in the academy, although the attitudes of policy-makers as revealed by their monetary and fiscal policies continue to be far more eclectic.

In reviewing Keynes's political vision with the benefit of 70 years of hindsight, it is important to recall that the policy measures associated with Old Keynesian economics were but one way of 'adjusting to one another the propensity to consume and the inducement to invest' (*G.T.* 380). The partial failure of one particular set of policy tools is not an excuse for reverting to an obsolete theory of the competitive monetary economy; nor for accepting inhumane and wrong-headed policies on labour rights and international trade, based on a confusion of the Classical parable with reality; nor for admitting defeat in the search for a better understanding of the workings of the economy, and for structural reforms capable of improving its performance in the service of genuine human freedom.

6.4 CONCLUSION

G.T. Book VI is a classic demonstration of the powerful use of economic theory in the hands of a master. The limitations of equilibrium analysis do not mean that nothing can be said about change over time (dynamics in the wider sense), but we need to take our heads out of the engine compartment, stop tuning up the equilibrium model, and take the model for a spin through a social landscape embedded in history. There can be wisdom in the insights of practical men and thinkers, who see the world without the aid of equilibrium analysis, and have often perceived enduring social realities more clearly than the economists. Full employment is a necessary condition of human liberation, but remains elusive; yet it will not help to pretend that we already have it. Keynes offered some specific proposals which have largely been put into practice with unparalleled success, but these have not proved adequate for the securing of permanent full employment on a global scale. The next chapter will consider, by way of epilogue, what the interpretation of *The General Theory* developed in this book now suggests, in the light of the events and debates of the last 70 years.

Epilogue

With the help of the Five Propositions, this book has sought to demonstrate that *The General Theory* is a difficult, but not an incoherent or tendentious, text, which is rightly regarded as a landmark in the development of economic theory, and not merely an essay in persuasion. My aim has been to show more clearly how Keynes extended Marshall's theory of supply and demand, or competitive equilibrium, to take account of the true nature of the monetary production economy, as 'one in which changing views about the future are capable of influencing the quantity of employment and not merely its direction' (*G.T.* xxii). The major corollary is that equilibrium analysis in economics can be rigorous (in the old sense of compliance with the facts, as well as in the modern sense of internal consistency) only in a given state of expectation, which for most purposes means only at a point in time. The use of the concept of long-term long-period equilibrium is 'misleading and disastrous if we attempt to apply it to the facts of experience' (*G.T.* 3).

The implications for modern economic theory are indeed fairly devastating. One can understand the reaction of the immediate followers of Keynes, particularly at Cambridge, in regarding the entire Classical structure as having been 'smashed up' and in seeking to rebuild economic theory on entirely different foundations. One can also understand, as more than an act of mere obstinacy or partiality, the refusal of Classical scholars to accept that the previous hundred years of formalisation of economic thinking since Ricardo had been fundamentally misguided. In the resulting hubbub, Keynes's own voice appears to have been drowned out. The above quotation is followed by the words:

> But our method of analysing the economic behaviour of the present under the influence of changing ideas about the future is one which depends on the interaction of demand and supply, and is in this way linked up with our fundamental theory of value. We are thus led to a more general theory, which includes the Classical theory with which we are familiar, as a special case. (*G.T.* xxii)

There is a great deal more common ground between the formal methods of Keynes and the modern Classics than is commonly allowed. In the Appendix to Chapter 1, vector mathematics has been used to represent the principle of effective demand and clarify the points of departure from the Classical conception of system equilibrium. In the Appendix to Chapter 2, the transition from short- to long-period equilibrium has been described with differential equations. In the Appendix to Chapter 3, the nature of the multiplier as an equilibrium condition has been clarified with vector calculus. In the Appendix to Chapter 4, the difference between fundamental and conventional value, and the nature of the latter as an equilibrium between 'bulls and bears', has been defined using the logical symbols and relations of Keynes's *A Treatise on Probability*. The microeconomic foundations of *The General Theory*, such as the aggregate supply function and user cost, have been largely ignored by the profession, which has grossly underestimated the degree of continuity between Marshall, Pigou and Keynes.

On the negative side, the implication of *The General Theory* is that any theory, especially a macroeconomic theory, which depends upon a constant state of long-term expectation (which includes both stationary and steady states of the economy), is fundamentally flawed from a scientific perspective, that is, as an attempt to explain the world. The most serious objections are to the concept of competitive equilibrium over time and its ultimate expression in dynamic inter-temporal general equilibrium; to models with homogeneous output and capital and clearing factor markets, which implicitly avoid the problems of a shifting state of expectation, including the monetary nature of production and the durability of capital-goods; to the concept of fundamental value in finance and investment theory; and to the intrinsic assumption of statistical regularity in time-series econometrics. At the very least, the special assumption of a constant state of expectation must be justified as the first step in any such argument, and the onus of proof must fall upon those who argue that such an assumption can help to explain the world of unceasing and unforeseen change in which we find ourselves.

Does *The General Theory* therefore mark the end of Classical economics? Should economists follow the dictum of Wittgenstein, that 'whereof one cannot speak, thereof one must be silent', and limit themselves to considerations of static equilibrium at a point in time? Certainly, we should hear a lot less about Pareto-efficiency, but *The General Theory* is the beginning and not the end of a research programme. The following sections offer some tentative observations as to what can properly be said.

The first section returns to the equilibrium sub-system of *The General Theory* and explores whether the understanding of liquidity and user cost developed in this book provides a neglected link between monetary policy and the price-level that may help to explain the phenomenon of stagflation. The second section applies that understanding of liquidity to corporate finance, and considers whether it is in this area, rather than in the propensity to hoard money, that liquidity-preference may produce an obstacle to full employment, in a modern economy of transnational corporations and central banks. The third section suggests the need for a rapprochement between elements from both sides of the orthodox/heterodox divide, based on the need to move beyond equilibrium analysis after a certain point has been reached, notably in the theory of accumulation and innovation.

E.1 STAGFLATION

The downfall of Old Keynesian economics in the 1970s was associated with the resurgence of inflation in the real world and of the quantity theory of money and the price-level in economic theory. It is true that neither in *The General Theory* nor in his later writings on inflation (*How to Pay for the War*, *C.W.* IX, pp. 367–439) does Keynes explicitly address the possibility of a sustained rate of increase in the price-level under conditions of Keynesian involuntary unemployment that has come to be known as 'stagflation'. Keynes's own analysis of inflation relates to conditions of excess effective demand at full employment (his 'true inflation', *G.T.* 303).

In order to incorporate stagflation within the framework of *The General Theory*, we begin by distinguishing three cases: anticipated inflation, and unanticipated inflation arising from cost-push and demand-pull respectively (although we shall find that the latter two are not so easily disentangled from each other). The case of anticipated inflation is readily incorporated by extending Keynes's working assumption, of basing expectations of prices on realised prices, to basing expectations of the rate of change of prices on the realised rate of change of prices. Thus, in a given state of expectation and employment, if today's rate of change of the cost-unit is expected to continue unchanged, the rate of change of the forward prices of effective demand and their relation to the cost-unit at each future date will remain unchanged, and the level of today's employment will remain unchanged.

Anticipated inflation is thus wholly compatible with Keynesian involuntary unemployment. The fulfilment of expectations will depend on aggregate demand increasing as expected, and increases in the cost-unit are not in general sufficient to guarantee this. Although the factor incomes represented in the cost-unit will increase in proportion, there is not of course a one-to-one relationship between factor incomes and expenditure, so that the fulfilment of the inflationary expectations requires 'accommodation' by increases in the money-value of current investment and the autonomous elements of consumption expenditure (including public sector employment), both of which may involve increases in credit. The increase in transactions demand as money-income increases, together with the maintenance of the reserve ratios of the monetary system as credit expands, may require (and indeed, endogenously create) an increase· in the supply of bank and base money.

It follows directly that a non-accommodating fiscal and monetary policy (or an adverse change in the balance of trade through a loss of competitiveness as the cost-unit rises relative to that of other currency areas) may lead to the disappointment of expectations. Whether this disappointment leads simply to a readjustment of expectations or also involves a decline in effective demand depends on the exact incidence of disappointment and adjustment, and is inevitably a messy business, particularly if the shift in policy is sudden or large. If the disappointment of expectations leads entrepreneurs to revise downwards their expectations of increases in forward prices but not their expectations of increases in the wage-unit, this will clearly mean a reduction in effective demand and employment. It is thus in the interests of labour to take careful account of changes in the inflationary expectations of employers, and here is a case for proposals for the indexation of prices and incomes (that can unfortunately cut the other way, leading to the acceleration of inflation rather than the maintenance of employment). Such policies seek to avoid unemployment caused by divergent expectations in a changing situation; note the conceptual difference from attempts to use money-wage-cuts to achieve full employment in a given state of expectation.

So far, this discussion of inflationary expectations and their accommodation or disappointment should not have been controversial, in terms either of received wisdom or of the interpretation of *The General Theory*. The difficulty arises over the genesis of unanticipated inflation in the first place, and in particular the relative roles of cost-push and demand-pull, specifically monetary, factors. The Old Keynesian position, shared by Post Keynesians, is that the source of unanticipated inflation lies in the movement of the cost-unit; while the Classical position, maintained by Keynes himself before *The General Theory*, locates it in demand, meaning monetary policy. Policy prescriptions follow accordingly: Keynesians recommend different forms of incomes policy for the management of inflationary expectations so that demand management can be used to promote employment without inflation; the Classicals regard inflation as essentially a monetary phenomenon, and the level of employment as, ultimately, a separate matter.

Policy-makers now tend to take a pragmatic line between the two extremes, seeking stability in the growth of aggregate demand and the price-level, without any longer using demand management as an instrument of full employment policy, while seeking to influence inflationary expectations through policy transparency and moral suasion, and advocating labour market flexibility to promote employment.

Movements in the cost-unit can indeed be autonomous. Many Keynesians ascribe inflation primarily to conflict over income shares between labour and capital, leading to upward pressure on the wage-unit. Another example of a purely cost-push source of inflation based on distributional (and military) conflict might be the OPEC oil cartel in the 1970s. Into this category also fall 'real shocks' such as natural disasters, for example the effect of a hurricane on the US oil industry. However, the cost-unit may also be influenced by changes in the level of employment and output, thus blurring the neat distinction between cost-push and demand-pull. Keynes is very clear that he expects the money rewards of different factors of production to respond to changes in demand: he notes the likelihood of 'bottle-necks' arising from the heterogeneity of capital-goods, and the existence of semi-critical points at which increasing effective demand tends to raise money-wages discontinuously. He also notes that the elasticity of supply, or conversely the sensitivity of the cost-unit to demand, is a function of the rate of change of demand, so that a rapid increase in effective demand is more likely to raise the cost-unit than the same increase in money terms spread over a longer period (*G.T.* 300–301).

It is thus conceivable from a traditional Keynesian perspective that an inflation can begin with a shock to the cost-unit from any one of these sources, which is then accommodated by a permissive, and at least partly endogenous, fiscal and monetary policy. The inflation in turn exacerbates the distributional conflicts and provokes further unanticipated inflation and a wage-price spiral. The process can be ended only by the abatement of wage-claims and profit mark-ups, either directly by collective bargaining and political means, or indirectly by a deflationary war of attrition, reducing the bargaining power of labour through the threat or prospect of unemployment. The Keynesian may accept that a permissive fiscal and monetary policy is a necessary condition for the original shock to be translated into a sustained inflation; although this would be expressed in different terms, that unemployment must be kept at a high enough level to moderate wage bargaining, and that the quantity of money at least, if not the fiscal balance, is endogenous, given interest rate policy.

What cannot be admitted as part of the traditional Keynesian story (including here Friedman's) is the idea that *excess* demand can initiate the process of inflation in a state of involuntary unemployment, where labour and other resources are in excess supply, i.e. nearly always except during time of war. High, and rapidly increasing, levels of demand may affect the cost-unit and unleash latent distributional conflicts, yet this must not be construed as the state of excess demand for inelastic output that applies at full employment. Thus the excess demand story that lies behind the quantity theory of money and prices (and the other softer varieties of monetarism) must be ruled out of the Keynesian court: excess demand and Keynesian involuntary unemployment are logically incompatible. This denial that inflation is essentially a monetary phenomenon has been matched by the countervailing New Classical denial of involuntary unemployment of any kind. ▶ **AE.1.1**

Our purpose here is not to assess the past debate, but only to reconsider the theory of stagflation in the light of the present reading of *The General Theory*. An idea that has so far been neglected in that debate is that of user cost, as a link between the demand for capital-assets and the price of newly produced goods. In accordance with our interpretation of liquidity as stability of value with respect to changes in the state of expectation, stocks of liquid capital-goods (where liquid is Keynes's term) may come to command a liquidity premium under conditions of uncertainty and low money interest rates. For example, a heightened precautionary demand for stocks of raw materials with long production periods may arise from the fear of losses through price volatility and disruption in production, as a result of shortages of capital-goods at particular points in the supply chain (see McCracken et al, 1977, pp. 58–61). The liquidity premium on such stocks, as a hedge against such losses, may come to offset their carrying costs, including the cost of finance. This is particularly likely if 'real' interest rates are negative, owing to a positive rate of anticipated inflation. ▶ **A4.4.2** Marshall certainly believed that the primary link between the money supply and the price-level was through speculation in commodities when the interest rate fell below the natural rate determined by productivity and thrift (Marshall, 1926, pp. 129–31; see also Brown, 1992, p. 168). Even if money (including interest-bearing deposits) remains the best hedge against the general price-level, stocks of particular commodities may well be superior to money for the purposes of the entrepreneur producing particular types of output.

Given a low elasticity of production, an increase in liquidity-preference for liquid capital-goods relative to money will increase the price of the capital-goods and thus increase their user cost in production. Since the level of employment depends on expected income net of user cost, an increase in user cost does not affect the aggregate supply price of any given level of employment, although it does affect the price-level of output (*G.T.* 302). Provided that the increase in user cost does not affect expected income, the increase will not affect employment. Thus we have a theoretical link between the quantity of money and the price-level of output, via liquidity-preference and the liquid capital-goods employed in production, which does not assume full employment. Given that the wage-unit rises much more easily than it falls, an initial shock to user cost may lead to a permanent increase in the price-level and even trigger a continuing wage-price spiral.

One implication is that there may exist an inflation barrier to the reduction of the money rate of interest. While liquidity-preference for money can be satisfied by a modern banking system, low interest rates (particularly in real terms) may allow liquid capital-goods to acquire a higher liquidity-premium than money, at least for the purposes of production. This liquidity-premium will exist so long as there is uncertainty in the state of expectation about the balance of supply and demand over the period of production, the shifting state of expectation reflected in the price volatility typical of such commodities. The prices of capital-goods not directly used up in production cannot affect the price-level of output; nor can an increase in the demand for the goods themselves, as a store of value, directly increase the price of the factor services they offer. Yet it is to be expected that in circumstances of very low or negative real interest rates, not only will liquid capital-goods have acquired greater liquidity than money itself for the purposes of production, so also will other scarce and tradable capital-goods such as 'foreign currency, jewellery and the precious metals generally' and of course land (*G.T.* 358), as hedges against unanticipated inflation of the general price-level. Increases in the prices of other such capital-goods may therefore fairly be taken as a rough indicator of inflationary pressure that is likely to spill over into the demand for liquid capital-goods and thus into production cost via user cost. The quantity of money has no direct significance here; the shift in the hierarchy of liquidity-preference arises from the low rate of interest on money.[1]

The other main implication of this argument is that even if inflation were to be accepted as essentially a monetary phenomenon, the source of under-employment is not to be found in the labour market, and the mantra of 'labour market flexibility' is insufficient. If under-employment is nearly always involuntary and a matter mainly of inadequate effective demand (rather than of the frictional resistances that may, in part, reflect 'inflexibility'), but the use of monetary policy to promote employment faces a limit in the form of an inflation barrier, an alternative remedy is required.

E.2 FULL EMPLOYMENT

Keynes's definition of involuntary unemployment is not limited to registered jobseekers, but encompasses all forms of under-employment and mis-employment where the marginal product of any given type of labour in industry as a whole exceeds its marginal disutility. Thus a competent (and usually highly-paid) accountant working as a cab-driver is under-employed, as is much of the population in the so-called Third World, where registered unemployment is unusual. The Classical concept of full employment is in fact rather radical from the perspective of most employers, since it implies, in practice, a significant number of unfilled vacancies and the ability of a competent employee to take another job at any time. A world in which all employers have to compete for labour, as much as do employees for jobs, would be rather different from the one to which we are accustomed.

The previous section has suggested that the use of monetary policy to promote employment may face an inflation barrier, even if the liquidity-preference, identified as an obstacle by Keynes, has been overcome by a modern banking system. Does a similar obstacle apply to fiscal policy? Can full employment be reached by government deficit finance, provided that interest rates are kept high enough to avoid inflationary pressure? If there is no significance in the quantity of money *per se*, but only in its effect on interest rates, it ought to be possible in principle to decouple fiscal from monetary policy, allowing the former to be used to promote employment while maintaining more or less the present line on the use of monetary policy for inflation targeting via interest rates.

I do not here consider the political arguments about the tax and debt-service burdens, which may present an important limit to government expenditure and deficit finance in themselves, particularly if the minimum feasible interest rate is quite high (see Arestis and Sawyer, 2004; Sawyer, 1998). The member states of the European Union have deliberately limited their use of deficit finance to promote employment by their 'stability and growth' pact (this may perhaps be reversible to the extent that the treaty is based on Classical economic theory). The purely economic obstacle to the use of fiscal policy by an individual state to promote employment lies in the balance of payments, given the propensity to import out of a rising income (our analysis has ruled out the hypothesis, based on the loanable funds fallacy, that public deficits can 'crowd out' private investment, provided that interest rates are managed). Historically, attempts by individual currency areas to fix aggregate demand at a level in excess of that consistent with balance of payments equilibrium have faced either an external finance constraint, or currency depreciation leading to the inflation barrier in another form (McCombie and Thirlwall, 2004). Countries with relatively high levels of employment such as the UK and US in recent years have run significant and widening trade deficits, but have not faced a finance constraint because of inflows on capital and financial accounts, including in the case of the US the acceptance of dollars as monetary reserves by other central banks. Other countries, notably heavily indebted poorer countries, have not been so fortunate. There is an established Post Keynesian literature on the implications of payments imbalances for effective demand and possible remedies by way of reform of the international financial system along the lines Keynes originally proposed for the Bretton Woods institutions (Davidson, 2002, 2006).

If the use of fiscal policy to promote employment is ruled out or limited by political or balance of payments constraints other than in exceptional cases, and interest rates have been reduced by monetary policy to the minimum level consistent with price stability, what else does the logic of *The General Theory* suggest can be done to eliminate involuntary unemployment?

Keynes recognised the importance of frictional unemployment, i.e. 'Classical involuntary' unemployment, and there is no denying the value of labour market flexibility, provided this is understood to mean measures to overcome obstacles to the voluntary free movement of labour, in terms of information and mobility costs (*G.T.* 7). On the other hand, the interpretation of 'flexibility' as a reduction in employment protection, individual and collective labour rights, and welfare benefits, reflects the Classical understanding of unemployment as 'voluntary', and must be rejected not only as mean-spirited and illiberal, but as ineffectual, in all but a very small minority of cases. Voluntary unemployment is likely to be the exception and involuntary unemployment, in one form or another, the general rule. If a lack of employment as a result of an individual refusal of employment at the market rate, in the market for which the individual is best suited, is deemed not to be unemployment (i.e. the accountant who turns down a job, not as a cab-driver, but as an accountant), and any effects of restrictive practices or minimum wages are redefined as involuntary (as they are from the individual perspective), the prefix becomes redundant, not because all unemployment is voluntary, as Lucas would have it, but because it is all involuntary. The measures required to reduce Classical involuntary unemployment, arising from frictional resistances and from the phenomena explored by New

Keynesian economics, such as asymmetric information, are of a different nature from those required to reduce Keynesian involuntary unemployment, arising from a deficiency of effective demand.

The realisation of the Classical full-employment parable (involving an absence of Keynesian involuntary unemployment) would mean a quasi-stationary or steady state, in which change in employment arose only from changes in tastes, technology or the endowment of factors of production, notably population (*G.T.* 220–21). Such a state would, sooner or later, in the absence of unbounded technical change and natural resources, produce a state of full investment or capital-saturation, where the marginal efficiency of capital was equal to zero, since there are no intrinsic reasons for the scarcity of producible capital-goods.[2] Yet as Keynes asks, 'what would this involve for a society … possessing a monetary system such that … interest cannot be negative; and in conditions of full employment, disposed to save?' (*G.T.* 217).

It can be fairly argued, I think, that Keynes's remedies of a low interest rate policy, redistributive taxation, deficit finance and the partial socialisation of investment (notably in health and education) have been implemented and extended, after some over-shoot and correction, as far as they can be in a free society, without eliminating Keynesian involuntary unemployment. Unresolved problems remain with the imbalances of the international financial system, and there are other differences between the circumstances of the industrialised and developing regions that are considered in Section **AE.3.1**. Yet at this point we need to begin to move, at least at the theoretical level, beyond Keynes's abstraction from financial and industrial structure, and consider whether there are intrinsic features of our system of business ownership that present a barrier to full employment, even with interest rates at the minimum level consistent with price stability. There are some compelling reasons for believing that our system of ownership is, in fact, incompatible with the realisation of the Classical full-employment steady state in practice.

The bulk of industrial investment is undertaken by large 'capital-driven' corporations, whose managers control the business and investment decisions, while financial investors own most of the shares. This separation of control from ownership corresponds also to a division between the forces of enterprise, on the one hand, and thrift (and speculation) on the other. In Kalecki's theory of employment (which most Post Keynesians have followed in preference to *The General Theory*), the relationship between profits, saving and investment is central, and it is the rate of profit, rather than the propensity to consume as such, that determines the level of employment in conjunction with the rate of current investment. Furthermore, there is a two-way relation between current investment and profits, the former creating the latter, and the latter financing the former. It is not difficult to use an aggregate model, such as Kalecki's or Robinson's, to demonstrate the difficulty of sustaining full employment as well as the likelihood of the system becoming stranded in under-employment equilibrium, although these models are open to the criticism that they abstract from the forces of competition.

Keynes recognises the importance of corporate profits in the form of depreciation allowances or 'sinking funds' as a form of saving (*G.T.* 98–104), but is silent on the accumulation of net profit, as reflected in the modern target of 'compound growth of earnings per share' which appears in nearly every corporate mission statement. As Joan Robinson writes, 'It would be the height of imprudence for a business to distribute the whole of its net profit to the family or to shareholders' (1977, p. 1324). This is true, not only of dividends, but also of capital distributions through acquisition and otherwise, with their consequent substitution of debt for equity. Corporate objectives may require a rate of profit corresponding to an average propensity to save inconsistent with full employment, except under conditions of continuous growth and accumulation. It is hard to reconcile such objectives with a steady state, in which no net investment per head is taking place and the marginal efficiency of capital is at the minimum level consistent with price stability.

Our reading of *The General Theory* suggests that some of the key insights of Kalecki can be incorporated within Keynes's competitive framework, and thus used to extend rather than supplant the Marshallian framework, at least in certain respects.[3] This 'reconciliation' hinges on our interpretations of the degree of competition and of Keynes's liquidity. Keynes's degree of competition refers to the obstacles, associated with closed shops in one sense or another, to the entry of entrepreneurs and workers into particular industries and occupations. Of particular relevance to the modern knowledge-based economy, the possession and control of technology, brands and distribution channels, whether through formal intellectual property or otherwise, represent formidable barriers to the entry of new firms. It is quite clear that these can lead to a rate of profit above the normal long-period cost of production, including depreciation and finance costs, if this can meaningfully be defined in such circumstances, and equally clear that there is no formal equilibrium method for deducing such a rate of profit from the parameters of the Marshallian model. It is quite proper for both Keynes and Kalecki to treat it as an exogenous factor, given from outside the equilibrium model. Keynes's under-employment equilibrium does not depend on the assumption of a degree of competition less than 100%, but if the implications for the propensity to consume cannot be offset by fiscal means, the degree of competition may be inconsistent with full employment.

Furthermore, there may be a tendency for any rise in the degree of competition to be offset by the deliberate destruction of capital-goods so as to maintain their scarcity. A rise in the degree of competition will reduce current returns on existing capital-goods and is likely to influence adversely the marginal efficiency of capital, with a consequent fall in investment in turn reinforcing the decline in current profitability. Current profitability can be improved by scrapping existing equipment, either by way of the formal schemes for industrial re-organisation mentioned by Keynes (*G.T.* 71), or through the mergers and acquisitions process of the modern market for corporate control. Many acquisitions are motivated by the need to capture market share and 'consolidate' production, eliminating 'excess capacity' – capacity that is excessive only in relation to the profit targets of corporations and to a depressed level of effective demand, and not necessarily to the needs of a full employment steady state, where the marginal efficiency of capital must be zero. Conversely, high current rates of profit are likely to draw in fresh competition and investment in new capital-goods. These countervailing forces must not be interpreted as leading to an 'equilibrium' rate of profit, since they operate over long stretches of time during which the state of long-term expectation will inevitably shift.

Another aspect of Kalecki's model is that investment is financed by cashflow, to some extent geared up with debt, rather than by new issues of equity. This is in fact a good representation of the empirical evidence from the private non-financial corporate sector in the UK and US over the last 50 years. Apart from Kalecki's own explanation in terms of imperfect competition in equity new issue markets, various explanations based on competitive markets have been put forward for this well-established 'pecking order', including tax bias, bankruptcy and agency costs and asymmetric information. None of these are wholly satisfactory, and a stronger hypothesis can be built upon the concepts of borrower's and lender's risk upon which Keynes touches briefly (*G.T.* 144–5). His insights have been partly developed by Minsky (who treats equity as a form of risky debt) and by Myers and Majluf (who build on the moral hazard element of lender's risk in new issues of equity), but neither of these can explain the observed 'differential equity new issue discount' that appears to lie behind the extensive use of new equity issues by large corporations for acquisitions of existing and financial assets, but not for investment in capital formation.[4] This phenomenon can be explained through the recognition that borrower's and lender's risk are composed at least partly of liquidity risk, the risk that the best estimates prove to be quite wrong. ▶ **A4.4.3** A differential new equity issue discount reflects systematic divergences in the liquidity risk attached to new and old or financial assets, on the one hand, and in the confidence of managers of corporations and financial investors, on the other. Differences in confidence (or 'animal spirits') make financial investors more averse than managers to the liquidity risk of new assets, so that if managers act in the interests of financial investors, they will avoid the dilution of shareholder value by new equity issues for capital formation, except in the cases of exceptionally profitable opportunities or of the acquisition of assets with low liquidity risk. ▶ **AE.2.1**

The concepts of the degree of competition and of liquidity risk can thus encompass, as an endogenous phenomenon, the accumulation of capital by the modern corporation, and thereby lend greater importance to the distinction between employers and workers, already implicit in the principle of effective demand. Keynes himself chose not to develop this theme, perhaps in the belief that his policy proposals would be sufficient to achieve full employment without modifying the basic fabric of the private ownership of the means of production. Nevertheless, this interpretation of *The General Theory* provides a justification for using Kalecki's short-hand macro-modelling based on the historical nature of time while retaining, unlike Kalecki, the assumption of perfect competition in the markets for current output and securities (thus avoiding the need for particular assumptions about industrial and financial structure).

Kalecki's approach reinforces Keynes's diagnosis that full employment depends on continuous accumulation, and that the economy cannot easily break out of under-employment equilibrium, because 'the odds are loaded' against the entrepreneur (*G.T.* 381). Investment opportunities, which might be profitable at full employment and the current cost of capital, will not be profitable because of the low level of effective demand. In slump conditions, it will be in the best interests of corporations to limit the investment of their cashflow to financial and existing assets, especially to paying off debt and buying up each other to destroy 'excess capacity' so as to improve the rate of profit. Even if sophisticated managers were capable of making estimates of the marginal efficiency of capital-goods in their own businesses, on the assumption of full employment, and could somehow co-ordinate their investment with those of other businesses (perhaps along the lines of the old-style French indicative planning), it would not be in the interests of their financial shareholders to make new equity issues to kick-start the process of investment. Recovery of private investment is therefore likely to depend on technological innovation that creates new investment opportunities which can be financed from debt or cashflow, together with a return of confidence in the profitability of capital-goods with low liquidity risk, such as residential and commercial buildings, aided by falls in the relative cost of development land. Some writers would in addition regard military expenditure, and other government contracts funded by taxation or fiscal deficits, as an essential alternative or complement to accumulation, in the maintenance of corporate profits.

These considerations lead to the conclusion that the capital-driven corporation is not a form of ownership that is likely to be compatible with the steady state that may well be, sooner or later, in the best interests of society, not only on the economic grounds of maintaining full employment under conditions of capital-saturation, but also on the grounds of the social and environmental objections to unlimited growth. That is by no means to be taken as an attack on enterprise, nor as a suggestion that we are anywhere near capital-saturation in most parts of the world. The modern corporation is a triumph of human co-operation and large-scale enterprise: the trick will be to bring about the euthanasia of the rentier without the enervation of the entrepreneur. Even in the steady state, let alone while the necessary accumulation of physical capital continues, competition between entrepreneurs will play a vital role in society, in anticipating changes in tastes, technology and natural resources and in ensuring that capital-goods are used to the best effect. The profound questions are whether the capital-driven corporation delivers accumulation where it is most needed; whether it encourages instability of investment with subsequent slumps and destruction of capital-goods; at what point physical accumulation becomes no longer necessary, in the social interest, as opposed to the interests of corporate profitability and merely financial accumulation; and how would the corporation need to change in order to accommodate the steady state of the Classical parable? ▶ **AE.2.2, AE.3.1**

E.3 GROWTH AND INNOVATION

Our analysis indicates that modern growth models, based on long-period dynamic inter-temporal equilibrium in various forms including endogenous technical change, simply assume the long-term full-employment steady state of the Classical parable, which for Keynes is indeed a desirable object of policy, but like Candide's garden, not the world in which we find ourselves. In our terms, this happy state requires both a level and variety of capital-equipment in every region sufficient for the population to meet its own heterogeneous consumption needs competitively at global prices, together with its balance of trade in consumption-goods with other regions; a continuing level of investment in new capital-goods to replace capital consumption, meet changes in the composition of demand, in technology, and in population; and an aggregate propensity to save out of global income no more than is required by the needs of investment.

As we have seen, Keynes regards the concept of long-term long-period equilibrium based on a fixed and reliable state of expectation as wholly misleading. Indeed the most cursory reading of economic history, and of the continuing industrial revolution of the last 250 years, shows that growth is inextricably linked with unpredictable technical change in products and processes. *The General Theory* says very little about the process of growth and almost nothing about technical and social change, not because they are unimportant matters, but because meaningful formal equilibrium analysis is necessarily based on a given stock of capital equipment and a given state of expectation, technology and preferences. Steady state growth, of which so much has been made since 1936, by both the followers and the critics of Keynes, is considered only in a brief footnote (*G.T.* 48). Keynes doubts very much that investment outcomes bear any reliable relation to the expectations that prompted them, and his analysis encourages the view expressed in the previous section that the risks of industrial capital formation are such as to require funding from retained profit over short horizons, and that society's accumulation of industrial capital equipment must take place mainly at the level of the individual firm, assisted to a modest extent by the issue of debt, but not by the issue of equity to individual savers. Individual time-preference does not remotely enter into the matter, and as policy-makers have recognised, continued investment by capital-driven corporations (and thus high employment) depends on a constant stream of successful innovation, fed to some extent by publicly-funded research and development, and the continuous expansion of markets through globalisation.

Since *The General Theory* is necessarily silent on the subject of historical growth and technological change (and Classical theory ought to be), a recognition of the limits of equilibrium theory should encourage, in a spirit of scientific enquiry, the study of the non-market institutions through which accumulation and innovation in fact take place; the Classical insistence on the inappropriate application of equilibrium analysis beyond its legitimate static role has displaced such research from the orthodox programme. Indeed it is only if, and when, Keynes's critique is finally accepted, that orthodoxy is likely to accept the legitimacy, as part of economics proper, of research programmes based on methodologies wider than individual optimisation, including historical, psychological and sociological studies. This interpretation of *The General Theory* also cuts the other way too, since it represents a critique of any form of long-term long-period equilibrium theory, including neo-Ricardian theory (e.g. Eatwell, 1983). It is conceivable that the insights of Sraffa provide the prelude for an alternative theory of value and distribution, as he intended, and a stronger platform for the principle of effective demand, on the foundation of specific assumptions about financial and industrial structure and the degree of competition, rather than those of Marshallian marginalism; yet the lesson of *The General Theory* is that any equilibrium theory of value must remain of the short term, if it is to be compatible with the historical nature of time.[5]

E.4 CONCLUSION

The purpose of this book has been to set forth a perspective on *The General Theory* which resolves many puzzles and paradoxes that have been found in it by other writers over 70 years, and enables the reader to appreciate its intellectual coherence and true significance. The result, I believe, is to establish that *The General Theory* is what Keynes claimed it to be: a major step forward in the development of economic theory, 'essentially in the Classical tradition' of competitive equilibrium theory, that ought to have transformed that tradition and increased its scientific value. For many historical reasons, *The General Theory* was not received as a platform for development, but as a revolution that has fractured the study of economics for two generations. The wholesale rejection of 'supply and demand theory' by many of Keynes's followers was premature, and the subsequent counter-reformation has merely reinstated an intellectually more powerful version of the *status quo ante* Keynes. ▶ **AE.4.1**

Yet, if this book has made one thing clear, I hope it is that we cannot return to the past. *The General Theory* demonstrates that Classical theory depends on the special assumption of a constant state of expectation, while in general, 'our previous expectations are liable to disappointment and expectations concerning the future affect what we do today. It is when we have made this transition that the peculiar properties of money as a link between the present and the future must enter into our calculations' (*G.T.* 293–4). As Pigou initially observed rather caustically in his original review (1936), Keynes seems to have chosen his title as an allusion to Einstein's general theory of relativity. An important difference between physics and economics is that the field of practical application of Newtonian mechanics remains very wide, despite the discovery that it is a special case in the wider scheme of things. *The General Theory* is an unanswered response to the (continuing) perception that Classical theory does *not* explain the monetary production economy adequately and, despite the aspirations of its 19th century masters, has performed very poorly compared with Newton's theory in its field. Economic theory and methodology must sooner or later recognise the implications of time, if they are to be of scientific value. Setting the proper limits to the use of equilibrium analysis is as important in this respect as the development of such analysis within its legitimate domain, and opens the door to a richer, more pluralist, discipline for the 21st century.

NOTES

1. Contrast Mankiw (2003, p. 521).
2. It is common ground with orthodoxy that even the United States suffers from an inadequate capital stock, although the conclusion is reached by a full-employment argument (Mankiw, 2003, p. 212).
3. There are of course important differences between Keynes and Kalecki, see Kriesler (1997).
4. Contrast this with the suggestion that 'General Motors sells $10m in stock to the public and uses the proceeds to build a new car factory' (Mankiw, 2003, p. 25).
5. In similar vein, Chick and Caserta (1997) write: 'our agendum is to alter the perception that provisional equilibria are in some way imperfect, not really equilibria at all, and that only final equilibria should be taken seriously. Our view, per contra, is that finding final equilibria is a challenging but ultimately futile intellectual game and only provisional equilibria are suitable for use in economic models'.

Appendix to the Epilogue

AE.1   STAGFLATION

AE.1.1   Real wages and money-wages

In approaching the topic of stagflation it is vital, as in *G.T.* Chapter 2, to avoid the confusion of real with money-wages. The New Classical approach, through its denial of involuntary unemployment, implies that inflation in the money-wage reflects a condition of excess demand in the labour market. The rise in money-wages is taken to correspond to a rise in expected real wages necessary to draw extra labour into employment, a rise which cannot in fact be achieved, given the marginal product of labour. It is not important whether the money illusion is suffered by employers or workers. The NAIRU approach, by contrast, postulates a relationship between the rate of money-wage inflation and the level of unemployment, which (to the extent that this approach is separate from the New Classical) need not be based on formal equilibrium theory, but on historical and empirical generalisations about the response of wage-bargaining to the level of spare capacity or 'output gap'. Keynes himself distinguishes clearly between increases in the cost-unit that arise from changes in the level of employment (which he does not regard as inflation, *G.T.* 304), and those which arise from attempts to increase effective demand (measured in cost-units) above the level consistent with full employment. In the former case, increases in employment are associated with a *fall* in the aggregate real wage; while in the latter, he assumes that the factors of production by no means suffer money illusion, but respond to excess demand by raising the cost-unit to mop up the nominal excess, thereby maintaining their aggregate real reward. Only entrepreneurs are admitted to suffer money illusion, on occasion (*G.T.* 290).

AE.2   FULL EMPLOYMENT

AE.2.1   Liquidity risk and corporate finance

The theoretical argument for a relationship between investment and cashflow, in the case of large companies with ready access to capital markets, depends on a new equity issue discount driving a wedge between the marginal and average cost of capital. Modern Classical theory admits the possibility of such a discount as a second-order market imperfection, reflecting a temporary divergence of expectations between managers and investors (Modigliani and Miller, 1958). New Keynesian theory predicts a new issue discount arising from asymmetric information about the value of assets-in-place, and suggests this also may be intermittent (Myers and Majluf, 1984). Post Keynesian theory emphasises imperfect competition as the source of the new issue discount but relies mainly on the empirical evidence of a limited *net* inflow of external equity to the corporate sector (Kalecki, 1971; Wood, 1975). The demonstrable existence of a substantial *gross* flow of new issues of equity appears to undermine the premises of both New Keynesian and Post Keynesian theory, and to support the Classical assumption, shared by Keynes, that the supply of equity finance to large companies is elastic. However, this would not explain the established evidence that equity issues play an insignificant role in the finance of capital formation. The explanation of this phenomenon in terms of liquidity risk is based on two propositions:

A.   an adverse change in the state of long-term expectation is likely to impose a greater loss upon the reversal of investment in a new industrial asset than of an existing industrial asset;

B.   the new asset will accordingly be valued at a discount to the existing asset in proportion to the scale of the above effect and the strength of the preference of investors for the existing assets as a standard of value.

These propositions depend on the conventional valuation of industrial shares under fundamental uncertainty. In order to demonstrate them, we assume with Keynes that investors (here meaning outside financial investors) value the underlying assets and their prospective yields directly and that capital structure has no influence (no asymmetric information, no divergence of objectives between managers and investors). We also assume that investors expect the market to follow the convention that the value of a particular firm as a whole is a function of the current level and expected growth of its accounting earnings. Expected growth is heavily influenced by the trend of current earnings based on past performance. This relationship is usually expressed as the price-earnings or P/E ratio, and is perhaps the most widely accepted basis for comparing valuations of different companies. We assume investors apply the same P/E ratio to all sources of income owned by the same firm.

As before, it is helpful to discuss valuations in terms of q (now defined as the ratio of the value of an investment opportunity to its supply price), rather than in terms of marginal efficiency. The two measures are closely related, since q is the ratio of the present value of the prospective yield (discounted at an appropriate rate) to the supply price of an asset. For our purposes, we are interested in the relative valuation of new in terms of existing assets, corresponding to the wedge between the marginal and average cost of capital, so that it is appropriate to use, as the discount rate for the calculation of q, the implicit rate required by investors to hold the existing assets. This rate is Modigliani and Miller's 'cost of capital' (Keynes's rate of interest plus a premium both for 'risk proper' and the liquidity risk associated with the existing assets), so that in equilibrium at the margin $q = 1$. If q is calculated at the 'pure' rate of interest, q will exceed unity by an amount corresponding to the risk premium.

We assume that managers and investors hold the same best estimate of the prospective yield and we define this, following Keynes, as the 'actuarial' value of an asset in relation to its supply price, q_a. Let q_c be the 'conventional' value of the asset in relation to its supply price, which is a function of its current earnings and the P/E ratio. We assume the market value equals the conventional value, and is what the investor can obtain for the asset at short notice. The actuarial value can be realised only (a) if the investor holds the asset for its full life, or (b) when the prospective yield from the asset has been reflected in current earnings. Modigliani and Miller normally assume $q_a = q_c$, since they express the yield of an asset as a perpetual annuity (as does Keynes in *G.T.* Chapter 17), so that its prospective annual yield equals its current earnings and the P/E ratio is the inverse of the cost of capital. To do so assumes away the problem in hand.

The investor is concerned about the possibility of a change in the state of expectation during the period before the actuarial value is reflected in the conventional value. If $q_a > q_c$ and expectations change so that q_a falls to $q_a' \mid q_a > q_a' > q_c$ (where this expression means q_a' has the property that it falls between q_a and q_c), the investor cannot realise q_a' but only q_c. The anticipated cost of cutting losses and reversing the investment decision $(q_a - q_c)$ will be greater than the loss of actuarial value $(q_a - q_a')$. The investor will face an extra loss of the difference $(q_a' - q_c)$. If $q_a = q_c$ and expectations change so that q_a falls to q_a' and q_c falls to $q_c' \mid q_a' = q_c'$, the investor will suffer loss but only to the extent of the loss of actuarial value ($q_a - q_a' = q_c - q_c'$). There is no additional loss on account of a lack of liquidity ($q_a' - q_c' = 0$). This is Proposition A. It follows directly that given a choice between two assets $X \mid q_a = q_c$ and $Y \mid q_a > q_c$, with equal actuarial values but different conventional values, the investor will prefer X on grounds of liquidity. This preference will be reflected in a discount of Y relative to X, the size of the discount being a function of the size of the potential loss $(q_a' - q_c)$ and the 'moment' attributed to that potential loss by the investor. This is Proposition B. The discount is a direct corollary of Keynes's liquidity premium l (strictly, the difference between the two liquidity premia applicable to X and Y), although in this different formulation it is better expressed as a discount (say θ) to the actuarial value q_a. The discount θ is the difference between the increase in the market value of the firm at the time of an investment decision, and the increase in market value that managers believe will follow, once the benefit of the investment is reflected in current earnings. This discount may vary from asset to asset, from firm to firm, and from time to time.

It remains to be shown why X and Y should correspond to the existing and new industrial assets of Proposition A. Is there any systematic tendency for the actuarial and conventional valuations of new industrial assets to diverge more than do those of existing industrial assets? It is useful first to consider the main exceptions, the acquisition of another business and the purchase of premises. The acquisition of another business represents existing assets similar to the firm's own assets and, more importantly, the prospect of a stream of future revenue. The conventional valuation ratio placed on the target's revenue will either be the same as for the firm's existing revenue, or differ by a determinate multiple reflecting any differences in the nature of the business and sector ratings. Any changes in the conventional valuation will tend to affect equally the value of both the firm's existing and newly acquired assets.

The purchase of premises generates an immediate net income yield in the form of rental, whether by saving existing outlay or generating new revenue. The valuation of such property is conventional, usually expressed in terms of rental yield or years-purchase. There is no reason to expect major divergence between the effects of a change in the state of long-term expectation on the conventional valuations of an industrial property and of the firm's existing assets.

By contrast, an ordinary industrial asset does not directly generate a rental but represents simply a production cost (fixed assets differing only in being consumed over more than one accounting period) whose value is realised only through sales of finished goods or services. The realisation of this value depends on the asset being employed in combination with the other resources of a 'going concern'. A financial investor can place no conventional value on the asset in isolation. An industrial investment decision, whether or not it involves fixed assets, may involve greater uncertainty but otherwise is no different in kind, only in degree, from any other major production decision. It is of the same kind as the decisions to employ a new key person, to appoint a major new contractor, to adopt a new product design, or to organise production by a new method. It is hard to envisage the stock market placing a value on a training course for a human resources manager.

This analysis leads to an important distinction between cost-reducing and sales-generating investment. Much investment is made to reduce the costs associated with delivering an existing stream of sales. Such opportunities arise from the growth of demand and from technological change, and include bringing in-house work previously contracted out, or replacing existing technology. Alternatively, investment is also made in order to generate or capture sales, particularly although not exclusively relevant when product markets are not perfectly competitive. This includes product innovation, with its related direct and equipment costs, but also advertising and distribution costs, and investment in new inventories. The polar example is the start-up of a new business, where a period of trading losses may be a necessary investment before a profitable level of sales can be reached.

Fundamental uncertainty applies to both kinds of investment, but as a tentative generalisation it would appear that cost-reducing investment has the advantage of creating an immediately visible increase in the stream of net revenue of the business as a whole, provided the new technique itself is well-proven. Sales-generating investment is an altogether more doubtful proposition. Even in a perfectly competitive Marshallian product market there is scope for misjudgement of consumer preferences and the rate of matching innovation by competitors, and major innovations in product or process always have unpredictable results. This is a particular problem if there is any significant 'gestation' period between the investment and resulting sales revenue.

In terms of the earlier analysis, the actuarial and conventional valuations of cost-reducing investment will tend to be close together. As with property, the net revenue from such investments is quickly reflected in the conventional valuation of the firm's shares. In the case of sales-generating investment, a divergence between the two valuations is to be expected during the gestation period, which in some cases may be several years. This analysis suggests that the reference to new industrial assets in Proposition A must be construed as referring, in general, only to sales-generating investments.

It remains to be shown why such a 'new asset discount' would result in a new issue discount, since the investment decision should affect the value of the existing shares, however the new asset is financed. If new assets are valued at a discount to old assets, for the reasons set out in the previous paragraphs, this merely increases the 'actuarial' marginal efficiency required to induce investment in the new asset. In terms of market value, the value of the firm increases (or decreases) as q_c is greater or less than unity. This does not in itself create a new issue discount, or wedge between the average and marginal cost of capital. To make the link between the new asset and new issue discount requires us to drop Keynes's abstraction from the difference between managers and investors. Keynes clearly wished to conduct his argument at as high a level of abstraction as possible, but he was conscious of this distinction and indeed recognised it as the hallmark of the development of organised investment markets. Only if the difference is fully recognised can a distinction be made between the marginal and average cost of capital.

Unlike managerial theory and the agency model, which place their emphasis on a divergence of objectives between managers and investors, the point here is a difference in confidence, in the greater or lesser moment attributed to the potential loss arising from a change in the state of long-term expectation. In the terms used above, managers have a lower θ than external investors for a given potential loss $(q_c - q_a')$. This difference can be understood in terms of the defining characteristic of the entrepreneur:

> Enterprise only pretends to itself to be mainly actuated by the statements in its own prospectus, however candid and sincere. Only a little more than an expedition to the South Pole, is it based on an exact calculation of benefits to come. Thus if the animal spirits are dimmed and the spontaneous optimism falters, leaving us to depend on nothing but a mathematical expectation, enterprise will fade and die;— though fears of loss may have a basis no more reasonable than hopes of profit had before. (*G.T.* 162)

Schumpeter notes that the entrepreneur 'has no function of a special kind ... [and] simply does not exist' within the ergodic system of general equilibrium (Schumpeter, [1934] 1961, p. 76). The distinctive characteristic of the entrepreneurial decision is that:

everything depends upon intuition, the capacity of seeing things in a way which afterwards proves to be true, even though it cannot be established at the moment, and of grasping the essential fact, disregarding the inessential, even though one can give no account of the principles by which this is done. (ibid., 85)

The defining role of the entrepreneur is to create 'new combinations' (ibid., 65), to initiate a process of creative destruction (ibid., 252–5), making decisions which are crucial in the sense of Shackle (1974) and literally change the world. To adapt Keynes's phrase, the entrepreneur acts today to create the future. This difference in 'animal spirits' can explain a difference in confidence between managers and investors even on the strong assumption that both share the same actuarial valuation of the investment opportunity.

The argument for a new issue discount hinges on the *difference* in confidence between managers and investors: it does not require that managers ignore liquidity risk altogether. Indeed, this analysis formalises Kalecki's 'principle of increasing risk' and the liquidity element of Keynes's borrower's risk, as an explanation of a limit to gearing in terms of confidence in the current state of long-term expectation. It also makes clear that investment in financial (including property) assets and in cost-reducing assets will often be financed by debt, since managers perceive the liquidity risk as low in these cases.

Turning to equity, we can now explain a differential new issue discount, which applies to the finance of capital formation but not to the use of equity to acquire financial and property assets, and existing industrial assets. Nor indeed will such a discount apply to the refinance of existing debt with equity, given the assumption of no asymmetric information, so that the issue is not a signal of bad news.

The bulk of industrial capital formation is undertaken by large corporations, whose managers control the business and investment decisions and financial investors own most of the shares. Fundamental uncertainty, through conventional valuation and liquidity-preference, leads investors to discount the value of new assets that do not generate an immediate income yield, relative to the value of the existing assets represented by the value of the firm's shares. This discount is a function of the potential loss from a change in the state of expectation and the moment given to that loss. It corresponds directly to the liquidity element of the premium for lender's risk in *The General Theory*, subject that the premium is relative to the cost of capital (for existing assets) rather than the rate of interest. Managers and investors give different moments to this liquidity risk, managers usually a lower moment based on the optimistic spirit required of entrepreneurs. This difference does not reflect a divergence of objectives or asymmetric information: managers are assumed to act in the interests of existing investors, and both are assumed to share the same actuarial valuation of the new asset, given the current state of expectation.

In these circumstances, a decision by managers to invest in a new industrial asset is reflected in a fall in the share price, which may be a fall in absolute or relative terms. An absolute fall means an objective fall in the share price expressed in money terms. A relative fall means a fall relative to the management valuation, which cannot be observed directly. Faced with this potential fall in the share price, the managers' decision to invest will depend upon the availability of financial slack (money reserves and capacity to issue secure debt). The availability of internal finance allows managers to invest, confident that the share price will rebound, once the temporary discount is eliminated. Existing investors will eventually derive the full benefit of the new asset. On the other hand, if internal finance is not available, a new issue has to be made at the discounted share price, resulting in a permanent dilution, whether in absolute or relative terms. If managers act in the interests of existing investors, this will be avoided. Investment opportunities that would be profitable at the average cost of capital implicit in the market value of the company's existing assets (such that $q_a > 1$) may be passed up. Exceptionally profitable opportunities, that do not produce absolute dilution, face a wedge between the marginal and average cost of capital in the form of relative dilution, which rises with the profitability of the opportunity. This extra cost puts a premium on financial slack, and provides another reason for delaying investment where possible, in addition to the value of any 'real option'.

The full development of the thesis of this section, including a detailed investigation of the empirical evidence, can be found in Hayes (2003).

AE.2.2   The reform of company law

There is no simple blue-print for the reform of private corporations to be found in *The General Theory*, in Keynes's other writings or anywhere else, but a number of observations can be made upon the strength of this analysis. The challenge is to devise a set of institutions that not only allow freedom of enterprise but allow the entrepreneurs to pursue their craft to the limit, without the artificial constraint of an insufficient level of effective demand. Although radical proposals for corporate reform are often seen as anti-competitive, our analysis suggests that what is needed is more competition between entrepreneurs, not less. It is important to distinguish between enterprise itself and the corporate form that it takes. As Adam Smith suggests (in a different context, and for different reasons), if it can be demonstrated that the institution of incorporation does not always and necessarily operate in the public interest, the institution is not beyond challenge and scrutiny with a view to improvement. It is normal in a modern corporation for its marketing, production and technological skills, which create real income, to be subordinate to the purely financial goals of shareholders: for the entrepreneur to be more the servant of the rentier than the master of industry. When the entrepreneur is also the owner, enterprise is not constrained by the liquidity-preference of the rentier, beyond the rate of interest. So the challenge is to reform the corporation so as to remove this constraint.

First of all, the corporation's objectives need to become consistent with the full-employment, capital-saturated, steady state, permitting it to maximise profits on its existing assets without the perpetual drive to accumulate further. The measure of corporate success would include a return to shareholders no more than a 'margin to cover risk and the exercise of skill and judgement' (*G.T.* 375) over the minimum rate of interest consistent with price stability, and thus be compatible with a degree of competition of 100%, with temporary departures from 100% arising from changes in production in line with tastes, technology and natural resources. This almost certainly means that that corporation's legal object would need to give greater priority than at present to the interests of stakeholders such as consumers, employees, suppliers and the community, in relation to those of its shareholders. The object of the corporation as the carrying-on of an enterprise would need to be more fully distinguished from the pursuit of the financial interests of the shareholders.

Secondly, it is hard to avoid the conclusion that a modification of corporate objectives along these lines can only become effective through some limitation of the rights of the external shareholders in corporations, in other words, of the rights of the rentier over the entrepreneur. It is precisely for this reason that proposals to make corporations more accountable to stakeholders (as opposed to shareholders) have been fiercely resisted by those representing the rentier interest.[1] The precise shape of any such reform would be a matter for intense debate, but might include (for example) the limitation of the scope of the hostile takeover together with the removal of limited liability from listed shares, other than preference shares carrying a dividend fixed by some formula in relation either to nominal value or to an external index (such as consumer or property prices).

The purpose of limiting the hostile take-over would be to prevent the removal, by the shareholders, of a board of directors that was acting on a considered judgement of the correct balance (from the perspective of the enterprise) between the sometimes conflicting interests of stakeholders, which was not in the best interests of the shareholders taken in isolation. The removal of limited liability for listed equity shares would serve two purposes. On the one hand, open-ended equity returns and their associated capital gains would remain available to shareholders who accepted unlimited liability, but those who wished the protection of limited liability would have to settle for a fixed return (at a rate determined by the market). Assuming that most financial investors would need limited liability, the listed preference share market would thus become an only slightly more exciting version of the bond market, with the yield premium over bonds reflecting only 'the margin to cover risk', while the unlisted ordinary shareholders (including directors, private equity investors, and perhaps employees who were prepared to take the risk) could continue to earn open-ended returns by the exercise of their 'skill and judgement'. It is not self-evident that the preference dividend need be significantly less than the actual equity returns achieved by portfolio investors on average and over time, although the currently favourable tax treatment of capital gains would need to be reconsidered. Furthermore, this would not prevent the realisation of capital gains by successful entrepreneurs. On the other hand, the preference dividend would help to protect the rentier preference shareholders from oppression by the entrepreneurial equity shareholders, if in the event of default in the payment of the dividend, the preference shareholders had the power to compel a sale of all the shares in the corporation, listed and unlisted. Thus rentier shareholders could use the hostile take-over to protect themselves from abuse, but not to dominate the wider interests of the enterprise itself.

In the case of the UK, this would make companies, in this respect, more similar to associations incorporated with limited liability under co-operative law. Opposition to such proposals could not be based on the popular, but unwarranted, claim that the equity market is currently a significant source of investment for capital formation by large corporations, its primary role in the Classical parable. Indeed, reforms along these lines would encourage precisely such a role, since preference shares would not suffer dilution, and thus the issue of new shares to finance capital formation would not face the disincentive associated with ordinary shares. ▶ **AE.2.1** Furthermore, pension and other institutional funds would be encouraged naturally into the finance of new capital formation, and be less vulnerable to the boom and bust of the financial bubble, making equity investment a safer option for the prospective pensioner (Hayes, 2006c).

Another form of objection would be that such reforms would reduce enterprise and efficiency by entrenching incumbent corporate management: the principal–agent problem that occupies much of the finance literature. Part of the response to this objection is to accept, point-blank, that the interests of an enterprise and of its stakeholders taken as a whole may indeed conflict with those of the financial shareholders – but is this necessarily a bad thing? Corporate America has found many devices for keeping Wall Street at bay, and does not apologise for doing so. Enterprise is more than the rentier interest, and rentiers can be given a fair return on new share issues, determined by supply and demand, without wholly subordinating enterprise to their interests. Nevertheless, like all stewards, managers must be kept honest by an effective system of corporate governance. Effective stakeholder governance is likely to be more 'political' than purely shareholder governance, because of the greater scope for conflicts of interest between stakeholders, and may perhaps require two-tier boards and similar devices to ensure a separation between policy disputes and day-to-day management. Democracy is always messier than aristocracy, but is the price of freedom.

If the economic critique is accepted, time and experience will show the best way to bring the governance of private corporations more into line with the public interest in full employment.

AE.3 GROWTH AND INNOVATION

AE.3.1 Involuntary unemployment and global poverty

The scandal of our time is the poverty of two-thirds of the world's population amidst the unprecedented plenty of the West, no less urgent a problem for us than was the mass unemployment of the industrialised countries in the 1930s for Keynes. Neither global terrorism nor fascism can be blamed entirely on large-scale under-employment, but it would be foolhardy to deny any connection. Economists of all persuasions agree on the need for economic development in some form. In the steady state of the Classical parable, growth in employment, capital equipment and income through technical progress are facets of the same process, since by assumption all available useful factors of production are fully employed. Growth of income comes about through the shaking up of the allocation of resources, the development and strengthening of market institutions, the encouragement of enterprise and the removal of traditional obstacles to the movement of human and physical resources to their most profitable application: very much in the spirit of

Marshall and Pigou. What is missing from this analysis is Keynesian involuntary unemployment, made easier to dismiss by the absence of registered unemployment with its associated welfare benefits in most regions, where involuntary unemployment is 'disguised', to use Robinson's phrase (1936).

The Classical parable conjures up the image of an agrarian people, or their children, giving up a traditional, comfortable, but undemanding way of life for the opportunities and excitement of the bright lights of the global economy. There is a grain of truth in this, of course, but the grim Malthusian vision of the process is nearer the mark. People leave the land, not usually because they prefer less leisure time or have acquired the education and skills to command attractive jobs in the industrial or public sectors, but more often than not through pressure of population, expropriation by money-lenders and landlords, or to meet the demands of government for payment of tax in money. Capital-goods are heterogeneous, and there are physical and economic limits to how much labour can be employed with any given capital equipment. In the Malthusian case, the diminishing returns from the application of labour to the land create a limit to employment in agriculture, the level depending on the form of land tenure: in the case of the yeoman household working its own freehold land, the average product of labour must exceed the subsistence minimum, while the tenant farmer will not hire labour beyond the (lower) level of employment where the marginal product of labour on the marginal land equals its subsistence (Ricardo's basic insight). Population in excess of that requirement must depart this earth, or at least from agriculture. Employment opportunities outside subsistence agriculture (or in the domestic service of landowners, the military or the bureaucracy of state) require the technology to produce competitively with a vast variety of additional kinds of produced capital-good; the skill and judgement of the entrepreneur both in ensuring the efficient use of labour and in correctly judging the prospective yield from investment in the capital-goods themselves; and a level of effective demand to warrant the employment. There is nothing in a surplus of labour or any other factor of production, *per se*, that will automatically induce this complex *enterprise* to take place. Everything depends on the expectations (and effectiveness) of entrepreneurs.

Many, perhaps most, households in both the rural and urban regions of the developing world exhibit considerable enterprise, as they must if they are to survive. With wage-employment rationed, each household must employ itself with the human and physical capital resources at its disposal, to provide goods and services for its own needs and for exchange in the market. The alternative to market employment is not leisure, but a portfolio of different kinds of self-employment, ranging from subsistence agriculture or horticulture, through petty trade and manufacture, to purely domestic production in preparing food, making and mending clothes and basic utensils. The concept of leisure, beyond physiological and social requirements, is alien to most women in the developing world (and not only there). There is full employment, but not in the sense of the second Classical postulate, since the real wage exceeds the marginal disutility of labour, nor in Keynes's preferred sense, that output is inelastic to changes in effective demand.

The presence of under-employed labour cannot directly affect either the level of employment or the real wage, which are both determined by effective demand. Downward pressure on money-wages, through competition from under-employed workers, can only increase employment if the fall in money-wages leads to an increase in effective demand (see Section 5.2). Thus under-employed households are simply excluded from participation in the social production possibility set through the labour market and thrown back onto their own limited individual production possibilities to earn a marginal product, if any, less than the market real wage. In this context, the growth of effective demand is a potent source of increases in aggregate income, both in total and per capita, independent of changes in the quantity and technical efficiency of the aggregate capital equipment, as under-employed labour is drawn from the informal sector into employment at a higher real wage.

The self-sufficiency of the Jeffersonian homestead is not an option for the vast majority. Measures to encourage self-employment, although perhaps desirable on other grounds, can lead to an excessive degree of competition (over 100%) in markets with low barriers to entry (e.g. rickshaw services), and poor households are rightly cautious about making significant and uncertain investments using borrowed money. Higher incomes invariably require larger scale industry and more complex technology to produce them, as well as the money-capital to finance working and liquid capital-goods and to absorb the contingencies arising from liquidity risk, let alone to finance fixed equipment. In the agricultural sector, this investment may be achieved through co-operatives of self-employed farmers; in other sectors, investment may be undertaken and employment offered by firms motivated by the objective of maximising labour income, sometimes in the form of co-operatives, but also in one or another form of social or community enterprise (Hayes, 2006d). Such firms are sometimes supported by specialist financial institutions that allow 'labour to hire capital' and enable the firms to make decisions to produce and create income from employment and profits, that would otherwise be forgone for lack of effective demand (e.g. Shared Interest, 2006; Oikocredit, 2006). Keynes himself noted in 1909 that co-operative credit societies in India might 'prove to be a powerful agency for the emancipation of the peasant from the village moneylender and for the much-needed direction of new capital into agriculture' (*C.W.* XV, p. 35), even if subsequent history has shown the importance and difficulty of maintaining good governance in co-operatives, as in all associations. There is nothing, in principle, to prevent private industrial and financial entrepreneurs taking similar steps, instead or alongside such labour-driven firms, to expand production and employment, but equally there is nothing in the market mechanism to guarantee that they will do so, simply because under-employed labour is available (Studart, 2002). The character of the labour-driven enterprise that creates employment in areas of poverty and under-employment thus matches in many respects what will be required of large private corporations, if they are ever to achieve and maintain the Classical steady state of full employment and capital-saturation.

AE.4   CONCLUSION

AE.4.1   Keynes and Pigou

Perhaps the last word should go to Arthur Pigou, to whom *The General Theory* was, perhaps, principally addressed as the holder of Marshall's chair. From the initial hostility of his original review (1936), Pigou had moved by 1950 to the position where he could write, magnanimously:

> In my original review-article on the *General Theory* I failed to grasp its significance and did not assign to Keynes the credit due for it. Nobody before him, so far as I know, had brought all the relevant factors, real and monetary at once, together in a single formal scheme, through which their interplay could be coherently investigated. His doing this does *not*, to my mind, constitute a revolution. Only if we accepted the myth – as I regard it – that earlier economists ignored the part played by money, and, even when discussing fluctuations in employment, tacitly assumed that there weren't any, would that word be appropriate. I should say rather, that in setting out and developing his fundamental conception, Keynes made a very important, original and valuable addition to the armoury of economic analysis. (Pigou, 1950, pp. 65–6, original emphasis)

NOTE

1. See Chapter 2 of DTI (2000) and the quoted responses to the consultation on the reform of company law. The advocates of 'stakeholder' governance have lacked a convincing economic argument (i.e. a case in terms of competitiveness, employment and economic growth, the main objectives of the reform proposals) to counter the traditional view (supported by Classical economic theory) that corporations are run most efficiently and in the public interest when run primarily in the interests of shareholders, subject to the constraints imposed by law, custom and public opinion.

References

KEYNES

References are to pages in *The Collected Writings of John Maynard Keynes*, edited by D. E. Moggridge, London: Macmillan, 1971–89, denoted by *C.W.* and the volume number, except in the case of *The General Theory* (*G.T.*). The volumes cited, with original publication dates where appropriate, are as follows:

V	*A Treatise on Money: 1, The Pure Theory of Money*, 1930
VI	*A Treatise on Money: 2, The Applied Theory of Money*, 1930
VII	*The General Theory of Employment, Interest and Money*, 1936
VIII	*A Treatise on Probability*, 1921
IX	*Essays in Persuasion*, 1931 (including *How to Pay for the War*, 1940)
X	*Essays in Biography*, 1933
XIII	*The General Theory and After: Part I Preparation*
XIV	*The General Theory and After: Part II Defence and Development*
XV	*Activities 1906–1914: India and Cambridge*
XXIX	*The General Theory and After: A Supplement*

OTHER AUTHORS

Amadeo, E. J. (1989), *Keynes's principle of effective demand*, Aldershot UK and Brookfield US: Edward Elgar.

Ambrosi, G. M. (2003), *Keynes, Pigou and Cambridge Keynesians*, Basingstoke: Palgrave Macmillan.

Arestis, P. and Sawyer, M. C. (2004), 'On the effectiveness of monetary policy and of fiscal policy', *Review of Social Economy*, **62** (4), pp. 441–63.

Arrow, K. J. and Hahn, F. H. (1971), *General Competitive Analysis*, San Francisco: Holden-Day.

Asimakopulos, A. (1984), 'Long-period employment in *The General Theory*', *Journal of Post Keynesian Economics*, **7** (2), pp. 207–13.

Asimakopulos, A. (1989), 'The nature and role of equilibrium in Keynes's *General Theory*', *Australian Economic Papers*, **28**, pp. 16–28.

Backhouse, R. E. (2004), 'History and equilibrium: a partial defense of equilibrium economics', *Journal of Economic Methodology*, **11**, pp. 291–305.

Barens, I. and Caspari, V. (1997) 'Own-rates of interest and their relevance for the existence of underemployment equilibrium positions', in Harcourt and Riach (eds), vol. 1, pp. 283–303.

Bibow, J. (2000), 'The loanable funds fallacy in retrospect', *History of Political Economy*, **32** (4), pp. 789–831.

Brown, A. (1992), 'Keynes and the quantity theory of money', in B. Gerrard and J. Hillard (eds), pp. 167–92.

Bunting, D. (2001), 'Keynes's Law and its critics', *Journal of Post Keynesian Economics*, **24** (1), pp. 149–63.

Carvalho, F. J. C. (1990), 'Keynes and the long period', *Cambridge Journal of Economics*, **14**, pp. 277–90.

Casarosa, C. (1981), 'The microfoundations of Keynes's aggregate supply and expected demand analysis', *Economic Journal*, **91**, pp. 188–94.

Casarosa, C. (1984), 'The microfoundations of Keynes's aggregate supply and expected demand analysis: a reply', *Economic Journal*, **94**, pp. 941–5.

Chamberlin, E. H. (1933), *The theory of monopolistic competition*, Cambridge MA: Harvard University Press.

Chick, V. (1983), *Macroeconomics after Keynes*, Oxford: Philip Allan.

Chick, V. (1992a), 'A comment on John Nevile's notes on aggregate supply', *Journal of Post Keynesian Economics*, **15** (2), pp. 261–2.

Chick, V. (1992b), 'The small firm under uncertainty: a puzzle of *The General Theory*', in B. Gerrard and J. Hillard (eds), pp. 149–64.

Chick, V. (1997), 'The multiplier and finance', in Harcourt and Riach (eds), vol. 1, pp. 164–82.

Chick, V. (1998), 'A struggle to escape: equilibrium in *The General Theory*', in S. Sharma (ed.), pp. 40–50.

Chick, V. and Caserta, M. (1997), 'Provisional equilibrium and macroeconomic theory', in P. Arestis, G. Palma and M. C. Sawyer (eds) *Markets, Employment and Economic Policy: Essays in honour of G. C. Harcourt*, London: Routledge, vol. 2, pp. 223–37.

Chick, V. and Dow, S. C. (2001), 'Formalism, logic and reality: a Keynesian analysis', *Cambridge Journal of Economics*, **23** (6), pp. 705–21.

Cohen, A. J. and Harcourt, G. C. (2003), 'Retrospectives: whatever happened to the Cambridge capital theory controversies?', *Journal of Economic Perspectives*, **17** (1), pp. 199–214.

Colander, D. (2001), 'Effective supply and effective demand', *Journal of Post Keynesian Economics*, **23** (3), pp. 375–81.

Crotty, J. R. (1996), 'Is New Keynesian investment theory really "Keynesian"? Reflections on Fazzari & Variato', *Journal of Post Keynesian Economics*, **18** (3), pp. 333–57.

Darity, W. and Young, W. (1997), 'On rewriting Chapter 2 of *The General Theory*', in Harcourt and Riach (eds), vol. 1, pp. 20–27.

Davidson, P. (1962), 'More on the aggregate supply function', *Economic Journal*, **72** (286), pp. 452–7.

Davidson, P. (1965), 'Keynes's finance motive', *Oxford Economic Papers*, **17**, pp. 47–65.

Davidson, P. (1972), *Money and the real world*, London: Macmillan.

Davidson, P. (1986), 'Finance, funding, saving and investment', *Journal of Post Keynesian Economics*, **9** (1), pp. 101–10.

Davidson, P. (1996), 'Reality and economic theory', *Journal of Post Keynesian Economics*, **18** (4), pp. 477–508.

Davidson, P. (2002), *Financial markets, money and the real world*, Cheltenham UK and Northampton MA: Edward Elgar.

Davidson, P. (2006), 'The declining dollar, global economic growth and macro stability', *Journal of Post Keynesian Economics*, **28** (3), pp. 473–93.

Davidson, P. and Smolensky, E. (1964), *Aggregate Supply and Demand Analysis*, New York: Harper and Row.

Dequech, D. (1999), 'Expectations and confidence under uncertainty', *Journal of Post Keynesian Economics*, **21** (3), pp. 415–30.

Dequech, D. (2003), 'Conventional and unconventional behavior under uncertainty', *Journal of Post Keynesian Economics*, **26** (1), pp. 145–68.

De Vroey, M. (2004), 'The history of macroeconomics viewed against the background of the Marshall–Walras divide', *History of Political Economy*, **36** (supplement), pp. 57–91.

Dixit, A. K. and Pindyck, R. S. (1994), *Investment under uncertainty*, Princeton: Princeton University Press.

Dow, A. C. and Dow, S. C. (1985), 'Animal spirits and rationality', in T. Lawson and H. Pesaran (eds) *Keynes's economics: methodological issues*, London and Sydney: Croom Helm, pp. 46–65.

Dow, S. C. (1997), 'Endogenous money', in Harcourt and Riach (eds), vol. 2, pp. 61–78.

DTI (2000), *Modern company law for a competitive economy: developing the framework*, London: Department of Trade and Industry, URN 00/656.

Dutt, A. K. (1987), 'Keynes with a perfectly competitive goods market', *Australian Economic Papers*, **26**, pp. 275–93.

Eatwell, J. (1983), 'The long-period theory of employment', *Cambridge Journal of Economics*, **7** (3–4), pp. 269–85.

Eichner, A. S. (ed.) (1979), *A Guide to Post Keynesian Economics*, London: Macmillan.

Fama, E. F. (1970), 'Efficient capital markets: a review of theoretical and empirical work', *Journal of Finance*, **25** (2), pp. 383–417.

Fishburn, G. (2005), 'Natura non facit saltum in Alfred Marshall (and Charles Darwin)', *History of Economics Review*, **40**, pp. 59–68.

Fisher, I. (1930), *The Theory of Interest*, New York: Macmillan.

Fontana, G. (2004), 'Rethinking endogenous money: a constructive interpretation of the debate between horizontalists and structuralists', *Metroeconomica*, **55** (4), pp. 367–85.

Gerrard, B. and Hillard, J. (eds) (1992), *The Philosophy and Economics of J M Keynes*, Aldershot: Edward Elgar.

Glahe, F. R. (1991), *Keynes's The General Theory of Employment, Interest and Money: A Concordance*, Savage, MD: Rowman and Littlefield.

Glickman, M. L. (1994), 'The concept of information, intractable uncertainty, and the current state of the "efficient markets" theory: a Post Keynesian view', *Journal of Post Keynesian Economics*, **16** (3), 325–49.

Hahn, F. H. (1973), *On the notion of equilibrium in economics*, London: Cambridge University Press.

Hahn, F. H. (1977), 'Keynesian economics and general equilibrium theory: reflections on some current debates', in G. C. Harcourt (ed.), *The microeconomic foundations of macroeconomics*, London: Macmillan, pp. 25–40.

Hansen, A. H. (1953), *A Guide to Keynes*, New York: McGraw-Hill.

Hansson, B. (1985), 'Keynes's notion of equilibrium in *The General Theory*', *Journal of Post Keynesian Economics*, **7**, pp. 332–41.

Harcourt, G. C. (1995), 'The structure of Tom Asimakopulos's later writings', in G. C. Harcourt, A. Roncaglia, and R. Rowley (eds) *Income and employment in theory and practice: essays in memory of Athanasios Asimakopulos*, Basingstoke and London: Macmillan, pp. 1–16.

Harcourt, G. C. and Riach, P. A. (eds) (1997), *A 'Second Edition' of The General Theory*, London: Routledge.

Harrod, R. F. (1937), 'Mr Keynes and traditional theory', *Econometrica*, **5** (1), pp. 74–86.

Hayes, M. G. (2003), *Investment and finance under fundamental uncertainty*, unpublished PhD dissertation, University of Sunderland.

Hayes, M. G. (2006a), 'Comment: Lucas on involuntary unemployment', *Cambridge Journal of Economics*, **30** (3), pp. 473–7.

Hayes, M. G. (2006b), 'Value and probability', *Journal of Post Keynesian Economics*, **28** (3), pp. 527–38.

Hayes, M. G. (2006c), 'Financial bubbles', in P. Arestis and M. C. Sawyer (eds), *A Handbook of Alternative Monetary Economics*, Cheltenham UK and Northampton MA: Edward Elgar.

Hayes, M. G. (2006d), 'On the efficiency of Fair Trade', *Review of Social Economy*, forthcoming.

Hayes, M. G. (2007), 'The point of effective demand', *Review of Political Economy*, forthcoming.

Hicks, J. R. (1937), 'Mr Keynes and the "Classics": a suggested interpretation', *Econometrica*, **5** (2), pp. 147–59.

Hicks, J. R. (1939), *Value and Capital*, Oxford: Clarendon Press.

Hicks, J. R. (1972), 'Liquidity', *Economic Journal*, **72** (288), pp. 787–802.

Hicks, J. R. (1980), 'IS-LM: an explanation', *Journal of Post Keynesian Economics*, **3** (2), pp. 19–54.

Holt, R. P. F. and Pressman, S. (2001), *A New Guide to Post Keynesian Economics*, London and New York: Routledge.

Hoover, K. D. (1997), 'Is there a place for rational expectations in Keynes's General Theory?' in Harcourt and Riach (eds), vol. 1, pp. 219–37.

Howitt, P. (1997), 'Expectations and uncertainty in contemporary Keynesian models', in Harcourt and Riach (eds), vol. 1, pp. 238–60.

Kahn, R. F. (1989), *The Economics of the Short Period*, Basingstoke: Macmillan.

Kaldor, N. (1939), 'Speculation and economic stability', *Review of Economic Studies*, **7** (1), pp. 1–27.

Kalecki, M. (1971), *Selected essays on the dynamics of the capitalist economy 1933–1970*, Cambridge UK: Cambridge University Press.

King, J. E. (2002), *A history of Post Keynesian economics since 1936*, Cheltenham UK and Northampton MA: Edward Elgar.

Knight, F. H. (1921), *Risk, uncertainty and profit*, Chicago: Chicago University Press.

Kornai, J. (1971), *Anti-equilibrium*, Amsterdam: North-Holland.

Kregel, J. A. (1976), 'Economic methodology in the face of uncertainty: the modelling methods of Keynes and the Post-Keynesians', *Economic Journal*, **86** (342), 209–25.

Kregel, J. A. (1987), 'Keynes's given degree of competition: comment on McKenna and Zannoni', *Journal of Post Keynesian Economics*, **9** (4), pp. 490–95.

Kregel, J. A. (1997), 'The theory of value, expectations and Chapter 17 of *The General Theory*', in Harcourt and Riach (eds), vol. 1, pp. 261–82.

Kregel, J. A. (1998), 'Aspects of a Post Keynesian theory of finance', *Journal of Post Keynesian Economics*, **21** (1), pp. 111–33.

Kriesler, P. (1997), 'Keynes, Kalecki and *The General Theory*', in Harcourt and Riach (eds), vol. 2, pp. 300–322.

Lawson, T. (1997), *Economics and Reality*, London: Routledge.

Lawson, T. (2003), *Re-orienting Economics*, London: Routledge.

Leijonhufvud, A. (1968), *On Keynesian economics and the economics of Keynes*, New York: Oxford University Press.

Lerner, A. P. (1934), 'The concept of monopoly and the measurement of monopoly power', *Review of Economic Studies*, **1** (3), pp. 157–75.

Lerner, A. P. (1952), 'The essential properties of interest and money', *Quarterly Journal of Economics*, **66** (2), pp. 172–93.

Lucas, R. E. (1978), 'Unemployment policy', *American Economic Review*, **68** (2), *Papers and Proceedings*, pp. 353–57.

Lucas, R. E. (1981), *Studies in business-cycle theory*, Oxford: Basil Blackwell

Mankiw, N. G. (2003), *Macroeconomics* (5th edition), New York: Worth Publishers.

Marcuzzo, M. C. (1994), 'R F Kahn and imperfect competition', *Cambridge Journal of Economics*, **18** (1), pp. 25–40.

Marris, R. (1997), 'Yes, Mrs Robinson!', in Harcourt and Riach (eds), vol. 1, pp. 52–82.

Marshall, A. (1920), *Principles of Economics* (8th edition, 1949 reprint), London: Macmillan.

Marshall, A. (1923), *Industry and Trade* (4th edition), London: Macmillan.

Marshall, A. (1926), J. M. Keynes (ed.) *Official Papers by Alfred Marshall*, London: Macmillan.

McCombie, J. S. L. (2001a), 'The Solow residual, technical change, and aggregate production functions', *Journal of Post Keynesian Economics*, **23** (2), pp. 267–97.

McCombie, J. S. L. (2001b), 'What does the aggregate production function show? Further thoughts on Solow's "Second thoughts on growth theory"', *Journal of Post Keynesian Economics*, **23** (4), pp. 589–615.

McCombie, J. S. L. and Thirlwall, A. P. (2004), *Essays on Balance of Payments Constrained Growth: Theory and Evidence*, London: Routledge.

McCracken, P. et al (1977), *Towards Full Employment and Price Stability*, Paris: OECD.

Minsky, H. P. (1975), *John Maynard Keynes*, New York: Columbia University Press.

Minsky, H. P. (1983) [1977], 'The financial instability hypothesis', in J. C. Wood (ed.) *John Maynard Keynes – Critical Assessments*, London: Croom Helm, vol. 4, pp. 282–92.

Modigliani, F. (1944), 'Liquidity-preference and the theory of interest and money', *Econometrica*, **12** (1), pp. 45–88.

Modigliani, F. and Miller, M. H. (1958), 'The cost of capital, corporate finance and the theory of investment', *American Economic Review*, **48** (3), pp. 261–97.

Myers, S. C. and Majluf, N. S. (1984), 'Corporate financing and investment decisions when firms have information that investors do not have', *Journal of Financial Economics*, **13**, pp. 187–221.

Naylor, T. H. (1968), 'A note on Keynesian mathematics', *Economic Journal*, **78**, pp. 172–3.

Nevile, J. W. (1992), 'Notes on Keynes' aggregate supply curve', *Journal of Post Keynesian Economics*, **15** (2), pp. 255–60.

O'Donnell, R. M. (1997), 'Keynes and formalism', in Harcourt and Riach (eds), vol. 2, pp. 131–65.

O'Donnell, R. M. (1999), 'The genesis of the only diagram in the general theory', *Journal of the History of Economic Thought*, **21** (1), pp. 21–37.

Oikocredit (2006), *Financial Statements 2005*, Amersfoort, The Netherlands: Oikocredit Ecumenical Development Co-operative Society ua.

Pasinetti, L. L. (1997), 'The principle of effective demand', in Harcourt and Riach (eds), vol. 1, pp. 93–104.

Pasinetti, L. L. (2001), 'The principle of effective demand and its relevance in the long run', *Journal of Post Keynesian Economics*, **23** (3), pp. 383–90.

Patinkin, D. (1976), *Keynes' monetary thought*, Durham, NC: Duke University Press.

Patinkin, D. (1978), 'Keynes' aggregate supply function: a plea for common sense', *History of Political Economy*, **10** (4), pp. 577–96.

Pigou, A. C. (1932), *The Economics of Welfare*, 4th edition, London: Macmillan.

Pigou, A. C. (1933), *The Theory of Unemployment*, London: Macmillan.

Pigou, A. C. (1936), 'Mr J. M. Keynes' *General Theory of Employment, Interest and Money*', *Economica*, **3**, pp. 115–32.

Pigou, A. C. (1943), 'The Classical stationary state', *Economic Journal*, **53** (212), pp. 343–51.

Pigou, A. C. (1950), *Keynes's General Theory: a retrospective view*, London: Macmillan.

Reisman, D. (1986), *The economics of Alfred Marshall*, Basingstoke: Macmillan.

Robertson, D. H. (1926), *Banking Policy and the Price Level*, London: P. S. King.

Robinson, J. (1933), *The economics of imperfect competition*, London: Macmillan.

Robinson, J. (1934), 'What is perfect competition?', *Quarterly Journal of Economics*, **49** (1), pp. 104–20.

Robinson, J. (1936), 'Disguised unemployment', *Economic Journal*, **46** (182), pp. 225–37.

Robinson, J. (1977), 'What are the questions?', *Journal of Economic Literature*, **15** (4), pp. 1318–39.

Rogers, C. (1997), '*The General Theory*: existence of a monetary long-period unemployment equilibrium', in Harcourt and Riach (eds), vol. 1, pp. 324–42.

Rogers, C. (2006), 'Doing without money: a critical assessment of Woodford's analysis', *Cambridge Journal of Economics*, **30** (2), pp. 293–306.

Runde, J. H. (1998), 'Assessing causal explanations', *Oxford Economic Papers*, **50**, pp. 151–72.

Samuelson, P. A. (1947), *Foundations of Economic Analysis*, Cambridge MA and London: Harvard University Press.

Sardoni, C. (2002), 'On the microeconomic foundations of macroeconomics', in P. Arestis, M. Desai and S. Dow (eds), *Methodology, Microeconomics and Keynes: Essays in honour of Victoria Chick, Volume 2*, London and New York: Routledge, pp. 4–14.

Sawyer, M. C. (ed.) (1988), *Post Keynesian Economics*, Aldershot UK and Brookfield US: Edward Elgar.

Sawyer, M. C. (1992), 'The relationship between Keynes's macroeconomic analysis and theories of imperfect competition', in B. Gerrard and J. Hillard (eds), pp. 107–28.

Sawyer, M. C. (1998), 'Financial constraints on Keynesian macroeconomic policies', in S. Sharma (ed.), pp. 240–49.

Schumpeter, J. A. [1934] (1961), *The theory of economic development*, Oxford: Oxford University Press.

Shackle, G. L. S. (1974), *Keynesian Kaleidics*, Edinburgh: Edinburgh University Press.

Shared Interest (2006), *Annual review 2005*, Newcastle upon Tyne: Shared Interest Society Ltd.

Sharma, S. (ed.) (1998), *John Maynard Keynes: Keynesianism into the Twenty-first Century*, Cheltenham UK and Northampton MA: Edward Elgar.

Sraffa, P. (1926), 'The laws of returns under competitive conditions', *Economic Journal*, **36** (144), pp. 535–50.

Sraffa, P. (1960), *Production of commodities by means of commodities*, Cambridge UK: Cambridge University Press.

Studart, R. (2002), '"The Stages" of financial development, financial liberalization and growth in developing economies: in tribute to Victoria Chick', in P. Arestis, M. Desai and S. Dow (eds), *Money, Macroeconomics and Keynes: Essays in honour of Victoria Chick, Volume 1*, London and New York: Routledge, pp. 68–78.

Tarshis, L. (1939), *The determinants of labour income*, unpublished PhD dissertation, University of Cambridge.

Tarshis, L. (1947), *The Elements of Economics*, Boston: Houghton Mifflin.

Tobin, J. (1958), 'Liquidity-preference as behavior towards risk', *Review of Economic Studies*, **25** (2), pp. 65–86.

Tobin, J. (1980), *Asset accumulation and economic activity*, Oxford: Blackwell.

Torr, C. S. W. (1988), *Equilibrium, Expectations and Information*, Cambridge UK: Polity Press/Basil Blackwell.

Toye, J. (1998), '"In the long run, we are all dead": time in Keynes's early economics', in S. Sharma (ed.), pp. 30–39.

Trevithick, J. A. (1992), *Involuntary unemployment*, Hemel Hempstead: Simon & Schuster.

Walras, L. [1926] (1954), (translated by W. Jaffé), *Elements of Pure Economics*, London: George Allen and Unwin.

Weintraub, E. R. (2002), *How Economics became a Mathematical Science*, Durham NC: Duke University Press.

Weintraub, S. (1957), 'The micro-foundations of aggregate demand and supply', *Economic Journal*, **67** (267), pp. 455–70.

Weitzman, M. L. (1982), 'Increasing returns and the foundations of unemployment theory', *Economic Journal*, **92** (368), pp. 787–804.

Wood, A. J. B. (1975), *A Theory of Profits*, Cambridge UK: Cambridge University Press.

Wray, L. R. (1990), 'Boulding's balloons: a contribution to monetary theory', *Journal of Economic Issues*, **24** (4), pp. 1–20.

Index

accounting, 36–7, 80–82, 108–12
accumulation, 213–21
AD/AS diagram, 122, 175, 177,
    185–86
agency theory, 53, 173, 183, 217,
    228, 236
agents, 10, 13–14, 26, 28–31, 44,
    161
aggregate demand, 46, 49–50, 53,
    55, 58–61, 70–71, 74, 77, 98,
    100–102, 105, 107, 119, 130,
    131, 138, 173, 180, 185, 191–3,
    201, 208, 210, 214
    dealers and expectations, 59,
        102–4, 148
    function, 55, 71, 74, 98, 100,
        119, 130
aggregate production function,
    70, 85, 128, 140
aggregate supply, 22, 50, 60, 65,
    71–2, 126, 189, 191–4, 207,
    212
    function, 28, 34, 55–6, 71, 74,
        84, 91–3, 98, 100, 107, 119–
        20, 179–80, 188, 192–3, 207
    function and ordinary supply
        curve, 86–8
    price, 65, 71, 180–81, 189,
        191–3
    Z diagram, 66, 107, 185
    Z function, 91, 94
Amadeo, E. J., 22, 85
Ambrosi, G. M., 22

animal spirits, 150, 153, 155, 173,
    218, 228, 229
Aquinas, St Thomas, 142
Arestis, P., 213
Aristotle, 142
Arrow, K. J., 14, 27, 63, 65, 68
Asimakopulos, A., 61
assets see capital-goods; debt
asymmetric information, 14, 29,
    53, 155, 173, 215, 217, 224,
    229, 230
atomism see price-taking;
    competition, perfect

Backhouse, R. E., 22
Barens, I., 22
Bibow, J., 85
bonds see debt
borrowing see debt
Brown, A., 211
Bunting, D., 128
business cycles, 14, 22, 60
    'real', 22, 186, 198, 199

Cambridge controversies see
    capital, homogeneous;
    aggregate production function
capital, homogeneous, 30, 72
    see also heterogeneity
capital, marginal efficiency of,
    18, 32, 56, 138–9, 143–8,
    153–9, 170, 172–3, 176, 184,

187, 197–9, 202, 215–18, 225,
228
see also prospective yield
capital-goods
    finished, 5, 11, 17, 56–8, 89,
        105, 116, 198, 227
    liquid, 32, 89–90, 156, 211
    scarcity of, 97, 137, 142, 215,
        217
    working, 7, 57–8, 75, 89, 105,
        108, 116, 131, 133, 137,
        156–7
capital-saturation, 197, 199, 202,
    213–19, 231, 236
Carvalho, F. J. C., 61
Casarosa, C., 22, 61
Caserta, M., 222
cashflow, 217–8, 224
    see also finance, of investment
Caspari, V., 22
Chamberlin, E. H., 26–7, 35–6
Chick, V., 22, 28, 61, 79, 109,
    167–8, 181, 183, 194, 222
circular flow, 37, 108
Classical axioms
    ergodicity, 44, 162–3, 172, 228
    gross substitution, 139–40, 144,
        155
Classical dichotomy, 14
Classical postulates, 28, 35, 88,
    235
closed shops, 13, 35, 192, 216
    see also competition, degree of
Cobb-Douglas production
    function *see* aggregate
    production function
Cohen, A. J., 70
Colander, D., 79
company law, 230, 237
    see also ownership, reform

competition, 9–13
    as motive force, 9, 25, 142,
        154, 203
    degree of, xiv, 1, 11, 13, 26, 30,
        34–5, 39, 87, 170, 192, 194,
        216–8, 221, 231, 235
    degree of monopoly, 1, 11, 26,
        28, 35, 194
    imperfect, 26–8, 33, 140, 217,
        224
    monopolistic, 26, 36, 86, 194
    perfect, 11, 12, 14, 17, 20,
        25–7, 31–4, 36, 39, 47, 53,
        55, 59, 81, 89–90, 92, 108,
        116, 139–41, 146, 152, 171,
        180, 186, 188, 193, 195, 218,
        235
    polypolistic, 28
confidence, 21, 38, 77, 153, 155,
    172, 198
consumption, 6, 11, 16, 21, 29,
    36, 46, 48–50, 57–8, 60, 64–5,
    72–3, 76–80, 83–5, 88, 90,
    105–10, 113–42, 147, 157, 176,
    178–9, 186, 197, 201–3, 209,
    220
    subjective influences, 123, 141,
        179
convertibility, xiv, 1, 11, 20–21,
    31–2, 151–2, 165, 168
co-operatives, 235–6
corporate finance, xiv, 173, 208,
    217–18, 224–30
corporations, 29, 38, 78, 120, 127,
    208, 215–20, 229–33, 236–7
cost
    factor, 1, 15, 28, 71, 73, 79, 88,
        91–2, 107–8, 156, 158, 189
    labour, 51, 54
    long-period, 216

prime, 28, 73, 79, 90, 94, 156, 189, 192
supplementary, 72, 79–80, 88, 90, 109, 158
user, xiii–xiv, 13, 28–9, 56–7, 65, 70–73, 78–81, 84, 88–91, 96–7, 100, 107–8, 124, 126, 138, 156–58, 173, 181, 185, 189, 191, 207, 211–12
cost-unit, 15, 94, 177, 200–201, 204, 208–11, 223
see also wage-unit
Crotty, J. R., 155

Darity, W., 48
Darwin, Charles, 9
Davidson, P., 26, 31, 44, 63, 107, 109–10, 166, 185, 194, 214
De Vroey, M., 45, 68
debt, 30, 49, 81–3, 109–10, 122, 159, 173, 178, 216–18, 220, 229–30
debt deflation, 49, 178
demand, aggregate *see* aggregate demand
depreciation *see* cost, supplementary; cost, user; windfall gains and losses
Dequech, D., 23, 45
diminishing returns, 10, 26, 31, 33, 60, 86–8, 90–91, 97, 100, 135, 145–6, 155, 188, 191, 195, 234
discount
equity issue, 224–30
new asset, 224–30
see also interest, rate of
disequilibrium, 2–5, 8–11, 22, 44, 48–9, 51–4, 60, 74, 76, 96,

99–100, 113, 117, 179, 191, 199
Dixit, A. K., 155
Dow, S. C., 23, 45, 183
Dutt, A. K., 45, 69

Eatwell, J., 144, 221
econometrics, 207
economics
Classical, xiv, 2, 8–10, 13–19, 24, 27–8, 33, 36, 43, 46–51, 53, 59–60, 62–3, 72, 83, 94, 123, 125, 138, 140, 142, 144, 155, 159, 175, 177–8, 180–81, 192, 194, 200–202, 204, 206, 220–21, 224
heterodox, 2, 3, 25, 197, 200, 208
medieval scholastic, 202
mercantilist, 201–2
neo-classical, xi–xii, 80, 117, 126, 144, 147
neo-Ricardian, 221
New Classical, 22, 186, 191, 211, 223
New Keynesian, xi, 2, 22, 48, 186, 215, 224
Old Keynesian, xii, 2, 4, 15, 42, 55, 58, 69–70, 74–5, 78, 80, 105–6, 108, 114, 120, 126, 141, 147, 174–5, 178, 204, 208–209
Post Keynesian, xi, xiii, xvi, 2, 3, 26, 31, 37, 55, 65, 74–5, 150, 178, 185, 195, 209, 214–15, 224
schools of thought, 2, 200–203
effective demand, 54–9, 125–7, 130–31

point, xiii, 1, 19, 54–5, 59–61,
    63, 74, 98–9, 104, 114, 117,
    125, 136, 193, 196
  principle, 14, 16, 34, 47, 54,
    56, 60, 63–7, 69, 73, 78,
    84–5, 104, 107, 116–17, 119,
    121, 158, 174, 177–9, 185,
    190, 195, 207, 218, 221
efficient markets hypothesis,
    148–9, 161
Einstein, Albert, 221
employment, 46–60, 177–81
  full, xiv, 2, 8, 9, 11–12, 15,
    34–5, 48–50, 60, 114, 117,
    123, 135, 142, 144–6, 154–5,
    178–80, 186, 188, 191–2,
    195, 197–200, 202–205,
    208–19, 223, 233, 235, 236
  function, 34, 56, 67, 87, 130,
    176, 179–80, 188, 192–5
  long-period, 22, 61, 76,
    95–100, 102, 136, 179, 193
equilibrium, 3–9, 175–6
  criteria, 3, 113–17
  daily, 59, 73, 147
  dynamic, 22, 24, 199
  fulfilment of expectations, 9,
    61, 73–5, 113–14, 117, 208
  general, xv, 4, 7, 22–3, 26, 43,
    48, 54, 67, 75, 162, 180, 193,
    228
  inter-temporal, 34, 68, 85, 156,
    181, 207, 219
  long-period, xiv, 2, 6–10,
    12–13, 19–20, 22–3, 28, 31,
    35, 54, 56, 61, 69, 76, 85,
    95–105, 124, 127, 136,
    145–6, 158, 170, 178, 190,
    193, 199, 204, 206–7, 216,
    219, 220–21

market clearing, 3, 7, 10, 14,
    16, 51, 114
  market-period, 5, 7, 10, 12, 13,
    34, 78, 81, 85, 114–16,
    120–21, 132–5, 140
  mechanical, 4, 9–11, 24, 55,
    73–6, 113–17, 120, 147, 175,
    182, 198
  monopolistic, 35, 194
  over time, 83, 106, 114, 117,
    127, 149, 207
  partial and general, 7–8
  preferred allocation, 14, 79,
    117
  shifting, 43–4, 61
  short-period, xiii, 6–9, 12–13,
    19, 22, 26, 28, 31, 35, 39, 49,
    54, 56, 59, 63, 71, 76, 84–5,
    87, 90, 96–7, 99, 103, 113,
    115, 144–7, 151, 157–8,
    178–9, 193, 195
  state of rest, 3
  static, 4, 37, 59, 95, 133, 176,
    207
  stationary, 43, 61, 181
  system, 8, 9, 14, 34, 54–5, 60,
    70, 84, 175, 195, 207
  temporary, 5, 49, 65, 68,
    115–16, 125, 137
  see also disequilibrium
euthanasia of the rentier, 31, 146,
    198, 219
ex ante/ex post analysis, 73,
    113–17, 135–7
exogenous and endogenous, 8–9,
    14–16
expectation, 16–20, 39–42
  long-term, xiv, 1, 7, 18–19, 39,
    65, 68, 77, 94, 98, 104–5,
    119–20, 136, 138–9, 142–55,

159, 165, 169, 175, 178, 198,
207, 217, 224, 226, 228, 229
short-term, xiii, 7, 18–19, 39,
55, 59, 73, 76–7, 85, 89, 94,
97, 99, 101, 104–5, 121, 130,
147, 149, 155, 190, 194
see also rational expectations
expectation, state of, xiii, 1, 7,
18–19, 21–2, 39–40, 59, 61,
67–9, 73, 75–8, 83–5, 87, 90,
95–8, 101–6, 113, 115, 117,
119–20, 131, 136–7, 145–7,
154, 158, 164, 171–2, 176,
179–81, 190, 193, 195, 203,
206–9, 211–12, 220–21, 225,
229

factor markets, 3, 4, 11, 14–15,
33, 54, 83, 116, 147, 177, 207
Fama, E. F., 161
finance, vii, 32, 36–7, 80–82,
84–5, 90, 108–10, 112, 207,
211, 213, 215–16, 224, 229,
230, 232, 233, 235, 239–41,
243
and banks, 37–8, 139, 212–13
motive, 37, 110
of investment, 215–19, 224–33,
235
financial structure, 31, 38, 45, 218
see also corporate finance
fiscal policy, 22, 121, 124, 204,
213, 214,
Fishburn, G., 22
Fisher, I., 49, 72, 128, 140, 167,
173, 179
Fontana, G., 45
foreign
balance, 187, 201, 209, 213,
214, 220

investment, 140, 187, 201
trade, 120, 124

game theory, 4
Glickman, M. L., 155
growth, economic 6, 7, 22, 24, 46,
70, 85, 181, 197–8, 201, 213,
219–20, 224, 233, 235, 237

Hahn, F. H., 14, 22, 27, 63, 65, 68
Hansen, A. H., 78, 91, 106–7,
113–14, 116, 130, 135–7, 143,
147, 185
Hansson, B., 61
Harcourt, G. C., 7, 70
Harrod, R. F., 22, 184, 198
Hayes, M. G., 68, 155, 230, 232,
235
heterogeneity, 15, 63–5, 69–70,
84, 86, 105, 114, 155, 168, 171,
180, 185, 189, 210, 220, 234
Hicks, J. R., 14, 20, 22, 26–7, 49,
65, 68, 74, 80, 83, 97, 106,
113–14, 116–18, 140, 147, 175,
178, 184–5
Hoover, K. D., 23
Howitt, P., 23

income, xiii, 6–7, 29–31, 36–9,
49, 55, 57–8, 60–61, 69–92,
101–16, 119–38, 140, 171, 175,
179–80, 184–5, 190–95, 203,
210, 212–13, 220, 225–6, 229,
233, 235
aggregate, 32, 65, 75, 78–9, 84,
108–9, 124–5, 133–5, 140,
165, 235
and effective demand, 6, 57–8,
74–6, 115, 126, 130–31, 180
and employment, 71, 130

and market prices, 125–7,
    132–5
and user cost, 57–8, 70–73
as value of output, 57, 72, 79,
    84, 107–8, 115, 141
distribution, 2, 11, 28, 31, 46,
    121, 235
entrepreneurial, 29, 71
factor, 78, 108, 119, 121,
    130–31, 208
gross and net, 79–80
gross domestic product, 108
real, 79, 106, 122–3, 127, 231
see also proceeds
industry
    as a whole, 8, 55–6, 69, 71,
        87–8, 91–3, 105, 180, 188,
        190, 192–4, 213
    structure, 11, 28, 30, 72, 194,
        215, 221
inflation, xiii, 167, 174, 179–80,
    188, 191–92, 199–200,
    208–14, 223
    see also stagflation; price-level
interest, rate of, 7, 24, 32, 37, 45,
    49, 80, 82–5, 111, 117, 121,
    123–5, 138–47, 151–7, 160,
    167, 172, 175, 182, 184,
    190–91, 199, 201–2, 212, 225,
    229, 231
    liquidity-preference theory of,
        153–4
    long- and short-term, 37–8
    real, 167, 173
    see also loanable funds
international financial system,
    214–15
investment, 78–83, 138–74,
    215–21, 224–32
    current, 79

over-investment, 197, 199
    see also capital-saturation
investment-demand schedule,
    139, 144–6, 155, 172
investment-saving identity, 69,
    80, 84, 113, 108–17, 124,
    141–2, 144, 147, 155
IS-LM, 106, 175, 184–5, 196

Kahn, R. F., 29, 45
Kaldor, N., 20
Kalecki, M., 26, 29, 128, 194,
    215–18, 222, 224, 229
Keynes effect, 177
Keynesian cross, 57, 74, 91, 106,
    114
Knight, F. H., 26–7, 42
Kornai, J., 22
Kregel, J. A., 22, 61, 89, 158,
    173, 194
Kriesler, P., 222

labour, xv, 6–8, 12–15, 17, 25,
    28–30, 35, 46–53, 55, 58–68,
    70, 75, 84, 86–9, 91–8, 107,
    117, 124–5, 139, 140, 144, 146,
    156–7, 177, 180–82, 186,
    188–9, 192, 200, 203–204,
    209–14, 223, 234–5
    disutility, 125, 188, 235
    marginal product, 28, 35, 47,
        53, 70, 88, 91–4, 107, 125,
        213, 223, 234–5
    market flexibility, 51, 53, 186,
        210, 212, 214
    supply, 1, 25, 33, 46–7, 51–2,
        56, 124–5, 186, 192
    unit, 63, 86, 98, 189

land, xi, 6–7, 21, 30, 48, 86–8,
91–2, 142, 151–2, 202, 212,
219, 234
Lawson, T., 22, 183
Leijonhufvud, A., 14
lending *see* debt
Lerner, A. P., 26, 35, 145
limited liability, 231–2
liquidity, xiii–xiv, 3, 8, 12, 16,
19–21, 42–3, 110, 138, 143,
151–5, 164–72, 175, 202, 207,
211–12, 216, 218–19, 224–6,
229, 235
compartments, 139–41, 144,
153, 155
investment markets, 164–5
preference, xiv, 18, 32, 37–39,
42, 45, 49, 56, 68, 77, 98,
120, 139–44, 147, 151–4,
176, 181, 184, 197, 202, 208,
211–13, 229, 231
premium, 151, 167–9, 211, 226
risk, 224–30
loanable funds, 37, 45, 80–81, 83,
85, 108–17, 144, 147, 173,
184–5, 196, 213
Lucas, R. E., 5, 62–3, 68, 186,
214

Majluf, N. S., 224
Malthus, Robert, 202
Mankiw, N. G., 22, 45, 68, 85,
106, 118, 137, 173, 196, 222
Marcuzzo, M. C., 45
marginal productivity theory, 33,
53, 88, 91–3, 138, 141–2, 144,
156, 186, 211
marketability *see* convertibility
Marris, R., 45

Marshall, Alfred, 2–13, 17–19,
22–5, 33–5, 45, 48–9, 54–6, 58,
60, 62, 67, 69, 70–71, 84, 90,
95, 106, 115–16, 134, 139, 142,
175, 181, 204, 206–7, 211, 234,
236
McCombie, J.S.L., 85, 128, 214
McCracken, P., 211
microfoundations and
macrofoundations, 87, 180
Miller, M. H., 224–5
Minsky, H. P., 31, 140, 198, 217
Modigliani, F., 224–5
monetary economy, 8, 14–15, 17,
36, 60, 79, 117, 142, 195,
203–4
monetary policy, xiv, 37, 53, 174,
178, 191, 197, 199, 208–10,
213–14
monetary production economy,
47–8, 50, 54, 69–70, 83, 124–5,
180–81, 206, 222
co-operative economy, 53, 59
entrepreneur economy, 60
neutral economy, 60
money, xiv, 1, 3, 11, 14–17,
20–21, 29–32, 36–8, 43, 45–7,
49–50, 53–4, 59–60, 66, 68, 70,
73, 80–82, 85, 92, 94, 107,
109–11, 122, 138–43, 147–8,
152–4, 155–160, 164–72,
174–93, 200, 202–4, 208–12,
221, 223, 230, 234–6
and debt, 139–44, 153–4
and payments, 36–7
and rate of interest, 138, 153–4
demand for, 37, 45, 59, 110,
179, 187
endogenous, 37–8, 178

essential properties, 143, 148,
    155, 202
neutrality, 14, 21, 53
quantity of, 15–16, 37–8, 53,
    56, 80, 141, 143, 174–5,
    177–8, 181–2, 184, 189, 191,
    197, 201, 210, 212–13
real balances, 16, 49, 122, 175,
    177–8, 182, 184–5
supply *see* quantity of
money illusion, 191, 223
multiplier, 125–7, 132–5
employment, 100
investment, 125
logical, 116, 127, 135–7
Myers, S. C., 217, 224

NAIRU, 200, 223
national accounts, 80, 108
natural rate
of interest, 118, 211
of unemployment, 54, 186, 200
Naylor, T. H., 196
Nevile, J. W., 91
Newton, Isaac, 154, 222

Oikocredit, 236
output
and income, 70–73
heterogeneity, 65, 189
of industry as a whole, 56, 69,
    70, 87–8, 192
ownership
and control, 29, 164–5, 224–33
hostile takeover, 231
reform, 219, 230–33
stakeholders, 231–3

Pasinetti, L. L., 60
Patinkin, D., 22, 91, 93, 129–30

perfect foresight, 26–7, 40, 96,
    149, 159, 162
period, 5–7
long, xiii, 7, 12–13, 18, 22, 25,
    35, 55, 61, 76, 90, 94–8,
    100–104, 120–21, 126,
    145–7, 166, 178–9, 190, 193
market, 6–7, 10, 12, 16–17,
    33–4, 56, 89, 115, 126, 132,
    135
secular, 6, 95
short, xiii, 6–9, 12–13, 18–19,
    30, 33–5, 59, 61–2, 69, 76,
    92, 115–16, 119, 121, 145–6,
    152, 156, 158, 178
permanent income hypothesis,
    128
Phillips curve, 182, 191
Pigou effect, 49, 60, 127–8,
    178–9, 186
Pigou, A. C., 22, 25, 27–8, 32, 34,
    48–9, 53, 56, 60, 62–3, 79, 85,
    122, 127–8, 140, 142, 156,
    178–9, 186, 190, 207, 221, 234,
    236
Pindyck, R. S., 155
plan and outcome *see* ex ante/ex
    post analysis
population, 6–7, 40, 43, 95, 125,
    163, 170, 198, 213, 215, 219,
    233, 234
poverty, 204, 233–6
price
as monetary concept, 37, 70
expectations, 17, 39, 57, 59, 71,
    73, 101–6, 208
factor, 14–16, 92, 94
market, 10–13
normal, 10–13, 18, 34

price-level, xiv, 15, 28, 37, 49,
    53, 56, 122, 126, 128, 166, 168,
    174, 178, 181–2, 185, 188–9,
    195–6, 200, 202, 208, 210–12
    and user cost, 189, 211–12
price-taking, 13, 25–8, 33, 35
    see also competition, perfect
principle of increasing risk, 229
probability, 25, 39–43, 45, 148,
    153, 159, 162–4, 169–73
proceeds, 28, 39, 58, 61, 71, 91,
    102, 107, 119–20, 130, 152,
    189
production possibility set, 192–5,
    235
    social and domestic, 234–5
production time, 76, 84, 96–101,
    156–9, 179, 190, 193
profit *see* income, entrepreneurial
propensity to consume, 119–27
    average and marginal, 120–23
    marginal, 10, 120–23, 126–7,
        129, 132, 135–6, 140
    as stability condition, 10, 120,
        123, 126–7, 132, 135, 140,
        228
prospective yield, 32, 39–40, 44,
    72, 87, 108, 143, 145–6, 148–9,
    151–8, 161, 165, 171–2, 224–5,
    234
psychological factors, 8, 56,
    175–6

quantity theory of money, 15, 37,
    60, 94, 182, 193, 202, 208, 211

random walk *see* efficient markets
    hypothesis
rational expectations, 19, 22–3,
    43–4, 76, 96, 147, 149, 161

see also expectation; price,
    expectations
raw materials *see* capital-goods,
    liquid
Reisman, D., 45
research and development, 220
    see also technology
retained earnings *see* cashflow
Ricardo, David, 2, 48, 91, 203,
    206, 234
risk
    actuarial, 42, 153, 169–73
    borrower's, 172
    lender's, 172
    liquidity, 21, 42–3, 152, 154–5,
        169–73, 218–19, 224–5, 229,
        235
Robertson, D. H., 37, 73, 80–81,
    90, 108–10, 114, 199, 200
Robinson, Joan, 7, 26–8, 31, 34,
    36, 47, 168, 216, 234
Rogers, C., 45
Runde, J. H., 22

Samuelson, P. A., 44, 135
Sardoni, C., 45
saving, 48–9, 69, 78–85, 104,
    109–10, 113–17, 123–5, 132,
    141–2, 147, 184, 203, 215–16,
    226
Sawyer, M. C., 34, 213
Schumpeter, J. A., 228
Shackle, G. L. S., 23, 229
Shared Interest, 236
Smith, Adam, 2–3, 5, 10, 202,
    231
Smolensky, E., 63, 107
Solow growth model *see*
    aggregate production function
Sraffa, P., 86–8, 155, 221

stability
  of prices, 176, 200
  of value, 166–9
stagflation, xiv, 174, 180, 200,
  208, 211, 223
stationary state, 7, 18–19, 24, 34,
  43–4, 95, 106, 128, 149, 181
steady state, 4, 7, 18, 34, 43, 95,
  106, 136, 149, 170, 172, 181,
  199, 207, 215–17, 219, 231,
  233, 236
stickiness, 13–16, 50, 54, 60, 69,
  117, 169, 175, 177–8, 185–6
stock exchange, 11, 164–5
  bubble, 232
Studart, R., 236
supply, aggregate *see* aggregate
  supply
supply price, industry, 55, 70–73,
  192–5
systems, open and closed, 8–9,
  16, 176, 183

Tarshis, L., 26, 45, 158
technology, 8, 12–13, 16, 24–5,
  29, 34, 39, 44, 46, 123, 157,
  162, 175, 180, 182, 215–16,
  219–21, 227, 231, 234–5
Thirlwall, A.P., 214
time, 17–20, 73, 221–2
  and capital-goods, 73, 84, 156
  and uncertainty, 138–55
  calendar *see* time, historical
  day, 6
  historical, xiii, 6–9, 13, 16, 18,
    20–22, 29, 76, 121, 149, 154,
    162, 218, 221
  lag, 127
  long run, 14, 22, 45, 173

long term, 9, 15, 19, 22, 24, 49,
  60, 80, 95, 121, 123, 141,
  145, 155, 178
period of production, 6–7,
  18–19, 22, 73, 85, 94, 97,
  101, 115, 119, 146, 190, 212
preference, 37, 141, 220
production period, 7, 22, 32,
  56, 58–9, 64–5, 73, 75,
  89–90, 96–7, 101, 105, 115,
  130, 148–9, 158–9, 181, 190,
  211
short run, 14, 22, 186
short term, 1, 8, 18, 24–5, 71,
  95, 98, 120–21, 126, 141,
  145–6, 149, 162, 175, 179,
  190, 221
Tobin, J., 42, 128
Torr, C. S. W., 60
Toye, J., 45
trade cycle *see* business cycle
Treatise on Money, 8, 12, 20–21,
  37, 80, 85, 122, 152
Treatise on Probability, 40, 45,
  207
Trevithick, J. A., 45

uncertainty, 42–3, 45, 102, 138,
  140, 144, 148, 150–51, 155,
  161, 163, 167–9, 171, 211–12,
  224, 227, 229, 239, 240–42,
  255–6
  and liquidity, 166–9
  and long-term expectation,
    43-5
  and probability, 39–42, 149–50
  and risk, 43–5, 169–73
  and time, 138–55
under-consumption, 197, 201–203

under-employment, 9, 48, 60,
144, 197, 201–203, 212–13,
216, 218, 233, 236
unemployment
frictional, 25, 27, 35, 46, 62–3,
68, 186, 200, 203, 212, 214
involuntary, 11, 14–15, 35–6,
46, 48, 50–53, 59–60, 62–3,
67, 186, 193, 200, 208, 211,
213–15, 223, 234
search, 35, 62–3
voluntary, 62–3
units of measure, 36, 69, 70–73
user cost, xiii, xiv, 13, 28–9,
56–7, 65, 70–73, 78–81, 84,
88–91, 96–7, 100, 107–108,
124, 126, 138, 156–59, 173,
181, 185, 189, 191, 207, 211,
212
usury laws, 202

value
conventional, 148, 150, 153–4,
159–65, 171, 207, 224–7,
229
fundamental, 148, 150, 155,
159–64, 170–72, 207
theory of, 1–2, 10, 15–17, 31,
34, 56, 69, 72, 84, 86, 88,
181, 195, 206, 221
variables and parameters, 8–9, 13,
103, 175, 182
variance, statistical, 41–2, 161
see also risk, actuarial

wages
money-wage, 24, 31, 46, 50,
53, 59, 91, 93, 121, 174, 177,
182, 186–7, 200, 223
money-wage and employment,
177–81
money-wage and price-level,
181–82
real wage, 31, 46–7, 50–53, 55,
60, 93–4, 117, 177, 180,
186–8, 223, 235
wage-unit, 56, 79, 86, 91, 148,
166, 169, 182, 185, 189, 209,
210, 212
Walras, Leon, 3, 9, 11, 13, 24, 45,
62, 67, 144, 175
wealth, 8, 16, 25, 43, 45–6,
49–50, 83, 95, 122, 127, 129,
140–41, 151–2, 178, 182,
202–203
Weintraub, E. R., 22
Weintraub, S., 107, 185
Weitzman, M. L., 60
Wicksell, Knut, 118, 155
windfall gains and losses, 61, 72,
75, 90, 101, 108, 121–2,
130–31, 180
Wittgenstein, Ludwig, 207
Wood, A. J. B., 224
working capital *see* capital-goods,
working
Wray, L. R., 85

Young, W., 48

NEW DIRECTIONS IN MODERN ECONOMICS

Post-Keynesian Monetary Economics
New Approaches to Financial Modelling
Edited by Philip Arestis

Keynes's Principle of Effective Demand
Edward J. Amadeo

New Directions in Post-Keynesian Economics
Edited by John Pheby

Theory and Policy in Political Economy
Essays in Pricing, Distribution and Growth
Edited by Philip Arestis and Yiannis Kitromilides

Keynes's Third Alternative?
The Neo-Ricardian Keynesians and the Post Keynesians
Amitava Krishna Dutt and Edward J. Amadeo

Wages and Profits in the Capitalist Economy
The Impact of Monopolistic Power on Macroeconomic Performance
in the USA and UK
Andrew Henley

Prices, Profits and Financial Structures
A Post-Keynesian Approach to Competition
Gokhan Capoglu

International Perspectives on Profitability and Accumulation
Edited by Fred Moseley and Edward N. Wolff

Mr Keynes and the Post Keynesians
Principles of Macroeconomics for a Monetary Production Economy
Fernando J. Cardim de Carvalho

The Economic Surplus in Advanced Economies
Edited by John B. Davis

Foundations of Post-Keynesian Economic Analysis
Marc Lavoie

The Post-Keynesian Approach to Economics
An Alternative Analysis of Economic Theory and Policy
Philip Arestis

Income Distribution in a Corporate Economy
Russell Rimmer

The Economics of the Profit Rate
Competition, Crises and Historical Tendencies in Capitalism
Gérard Duménil and Dominique Lévy

Corporatism and Economic Performance
A Comparative Analysis of Market Economies
Andrew Henley and Euclid Tsakalotos

Competition, Technology and Money
Classical and Post-Keynesian Perspectives
Edited by Mark A. Glick

Investment Cycles in Capitalist Economies
A Kaleckian Behavioural Contribution
Jerry Courvisanos

Does Financial Deregulation Work?
A Critique of Free Market Approaches
Bruce Coggins

Pricing Theory in Post Keynesian Economics
A Realist Approach
Paul Downward

The Economics of Intangible Investment
Elizabeth Webster

Globalization and the Erosion of National Financial Systems
Is Declining Autonomy Inevitable?
Marc Schaberg

Explaining Prices in the Global Economy
A Post-Keynesian Model
Henk-Jan Brinkman

Capitalism, Socialism, and Radical Political Economy
Essays in Honor of Howard J. Sherman
Edited by Robert Pollin

Financial Liberalisation and Intervention
A New Analysis of Credit Rationing
Santonu Basu

Why the Bubble Burst
US Stock Market Performance since 1982
Lawrance Lee Evans, Jr.

Sustainable Fiscal Policy and Economic Stability
Theory and Practice
Philippe Burger

The Rise of Unemployment in Europe
A Keynesian Approach
Engelbert Stockhammer

General Equilibrium, Capital, and Macroeconomics
A Key to Recent Controversies in Equilibrium Theory
Fabio Petri

Post-Keynesian Principles of Economic Policy
Claude Gnos and Louis-Philippe Rochon

Innovation, Evolution and Economic Change
New Ideas in the Tradition of Galbraith
Blandine Laperche, James K. Galbraith and Dimitri Uzunidis

The Economics of Keynes
A New Guide to *The General Theory*
Mark Hayes

Money, Distribution and Economic Policy
Alternatives to Orthodox Macroeconomics
Edited by Eckhard Hein and Achim Truger

Modern State Intervention in the Era of Globalisation
Nikolaos Karagiannis and Zagros Madjd-Sadjadi